The Great Sioux War 1876-77

The Best from
Montana The Magazine of Western History

The Great Sioux War 1876–77

The Best from
Montana The Magazine of Western History

Edited by
Paul L. Hedren

Montana Historical Society Press, Helena
1991
Distributed by the University of Nebraska Press

The articles in this anthology are from:
Montana The Magazine of Western History
Montana Historical Society
225 N. Roberts St.
Helena, Montana 59620

The Montana Historical Society Press

Cover art by Paul Dyck, Rimrock, Arizona
Cover design by Finstad Visual Design, Helena, Montana
Typeset in Baskerville by Arrow Graphics & Typography, Missoula, Montana.
Printed by Thomson-Shore, Inc., Dexter, Michigan.

Library of Congress Cataloging-in-Publication Data
The Great Sioux War: the best from Montana the magazine of western history/edited
by Paul L. Hedren.
     p.   cm.
     Includes bibliographical references and index.
     ISBN 0-917298-23-3:   ISBN 0-917298-24-1 (pbk.)
     1. Dakota Indians—Wars, 1876. I. Hedren, Paul L. II. Montana
E83.876.G738   1991   90-46450
973.8′2 — dc20   CIP

For Mother

Contents

Illustrations

Maps

Preface

In its four decades of publication, *Montana The Magazine of Western History* has emerged as the leading scholarly publisher of articles on the Great Sioux War of 1876-1877. *Montana* also has been a major contributor of articles on the life, accomplishments, and controversies of George Armstrong Custer, the mercurial lieutenant colonel of the Seventh Regiment of the United States Cavalry who was such a central figure in that war. Certainly the envied quality of the journal partly explains this preeminence, but geography encourages the journal's leading role on the topic as well because so much of the conflict originally played across the eastern Montana landscape.

With dozens of essays published over the years, it has long been my desire to compile an anthology of the "best" Sioux War articles from *Montana*. The values of such a publication are several. A Sioux War anthology might reinvigorate spirited discussions of the causes, successes, and tragedies of this greatest of American Indian wars. Moreover, some of the journal's earliest issues are becoming difficult to obtain, yet they offer vital scholarship and deserve continuing circulation. Such a volume, too, would provide a compendium of delightful reading material.

Charles E. Rankin, editor of the magazine and of the Montana Historical Society Press, concurred with the merits of such an anthology and encouraged the project. I wanted to assemble a "Sioux War" anthology, not simply a "Custer" reader. While these stories can obviously intertwine, I tried to maintain distinctions in assembling the collection. I attempted, as well, to appreciate broad historical aspects of the war. One reads in this collection, for instance, about the transcontinental railroads and about territorial politics because these stories, in their own way, are features of the Sioux conflict. Obviously there is still much on combat and Custer. I considered the scholarly merits of every essay. While each of the original authors would welcome the chance to change a word here or there, I believe that each essay is a significant contribution to the story of the war. These are personal value judgments, of course, and I will forever welcome debate on the selections.

Several precepts guided me in the preparation of this anthology. A certain ethnocentricity is apparent in several of the articles. At first I considered eliminating this, but instead came to view it as a reflection of time. I urge modern readers to look beyond it. As well, *Montana* has matured stylistically through the years. One reads somewhat interchangeably, for instance, of Little Big Horn and Little Bighorn. Today geographers and editors prefer the latter but this, too, was left as originally presented. I certainly do hope that the obvious typographical errors are corrected. Finally, with such rich photographic collections held by the Montana Historical Society, Chuck Rankin and I chose to reillustrate the work using these holdings almost exclusively. The Huffman and Haynes collections at the Montana Historical Society are remarkable, and they remain largely untapped Sioux War resources!

A number of individuals graciously helped me shape this anthology. The surviving original authors were generous with their encouragement, and I appreciate their many fine letters of support. Chuck Rankin is both an unselfish friend and a talented editor, and this work is much improved by his involvement. Glenda C. Bradshaw, MHS editorial assistant, kept the project on track. Delores Morrow and Rebecca Kohl of the Montana Historical Society photograph archives helped me through their collections. Douglas C. McChristian, historian at the Custer Battlefield National Monument, was prompt with answers to the oddest questions. I carry on a seemingly endless debate about the Sioux War with Paul Andrew Hutton and Jerome A. Greene, and they never seem to tire of my single-mindedness. As well, together or paired, the three of us have personally explored most of the War's forts and battle sites, and we forever look forward to the next "Sioux War expedition." Jerry, too, read the introduction and offered many helpful suggestions for improvement. And my wife Janeen and my daughters Ethne and Whitney allowed me to again sit at the keyboard when I probably should have been throwing a baseball or riding a bike. Thanks everyone!

Paul L. Hedren
Williston, North Dakota
Autumn 1990

O. D. Wheeler (right) interviewed several Cheyennes, including White Bull (left), about the battle of the Little Bighorn in June 1901. Interpreter William Rowland sits in center. (L. A. Huffman, photographer, Montana Historical Society Photograph Archives)

The Great Sioux War:
An Introduction

Wherever we went, the soldiers came to kill us, and it was all our own country. It was ours already when the Wasichus made the treaty with Red Cloud, that said it would be ours as long as grass should grow and water flow. That was only eight winters before, and they were chasing us now because we remembered and they forgot.

Black Elk
(1863–1950)[1]

Black Elk's memory of the tragic Great Sioux War of 1876–1877 rings horribly true. At once, this prolonged conflict was an unprecedented military saga dominated by nationalistic impulses, great personalities, and unparalleled armed clashes. So too was it a regrettably repetitive American story of unsuccessful Indian treaties, of an Indian people wishing to live in the manner of their ancestors, and of the eventual domination and thorough destruction of a flowered culture. Our interpretations of this war have matured in the many years since Sitting Bull surrendered at Fort Buford in 1881. No longer do we solely remorse the killing of George Armstrong Custer at the Little Bighorn, or Crazy Horse at Camp Robinson. Instead, we want to know and understand the protagonists and appreciate their motives. Perhaps most importantly, we seek balance.

Several vital elements underlie the seeming inevitability of this remarkable conflict. By the 1850s the Teton or Western Sioux Indians dominated the prairies of Nebraska, Dakota, Wyoming, and Montana. Numbering some thirty-five thousand people—far more than any other Plains tribe—the seven principal bands of the Western Sioux had evolved a flourishing culture dependent upon the great buffalo herds that roamed the northern grasslands. Sioux art forms

---

1. John G. Neihardt, *Black Elk Speaks, Being the Life Story of a Holy Man of the Oglala Sioux* (New York: William Morrow & Company, 1932; reprint, Lincoln: University of Nebraska Press, 1988), 134. Wasichu is a Sioux term for white man, having no reference to skin color.

were extraordinarily advanced, and distinct spiritual and societal rules fixed a natural order in their world.[2]

The Sioux deservedly claimed many cultural distinctions. Among them, their prowess at war became a renowned and much feared attainment. Honed at a tender age, manly skills with weaponry and horses were immediately useful in annual hunting cycles and in the predatory capture of enemy property. Warfare also fitted larger societal needs, insuring independence and security through aggression. The Sioux had not simply inherited the plains; they had methodically conquered competitive tribes and territory in a quest for economic and social benefit. By the time white men arrived on the prairies, these cultural values had been instilled for generations.[3]

In addition, the Sioux were a shrewdly adaptive people. Their acquisition of horses in the mid-eighteenth century spurred their rapid conquest of the buffalo prairies. From Euro-American fur traders the Sioux also acquired firearms, powder, knives, cloth, and other trade goods that facilitated their domination of neighboring tribes. By the mid-nineteenth century, the Tetons lived an advanced, self-sustaining existence that in its own way was as dominant as that of the invading whites. But, as one ethnohistorian observes, the powers of ritual and trade that allowed Sioux cultural fluorescence "also carried the seeds of its destruction."[4]

The first Anglo-American movements west to Oregon, Utah, and California skirted the northern plains lands of the Sioux, and the Fort Laramie Treaty of 1851 was a genuine attempt to establish harmony between red and white cultures. But the treaty brought no peace, and with increasing contact came bloodshed. The 1854 clash in Wyoming between Brevet Second Lieutenant John L. Grattan's small Sixth Infantry command and Minneconjou and Brulé Sioux, and the retaliatory Blue Water Creek fight in Nebraska the next year between Colonel William S. Harney's troops and Brulé Sioux led by

---

2. The number is Robert M. Utley's in *Frontier Regulars: The United States Army and the Indian, 1866-1890* (New York: Macmillan Publishing Co., 1973), 239. For a superior examination of Sioux culture and society, see Royal B. Hassrick, *The Sioux, Life and Customs of a Warrior Society* (Norman: University of Oklahoma Press, 1962).

3. On the social and economic values of war, see Hassrick, *The Sioux, Life and Customs,* 57-71. On the importance of territorial domination, see John C. Ewers, "Intertribal Warfare as the Precursor of Indian-White Warfare on the Northern Great Plains," *Western Historical Quarterly,* 6 (October 1975), 387-410; and Richard White, "The Winning of the West: The Expansion of the Western Sioux in the Eighteenth and Nineteenth Centuries," *Journal of American History,* 65 (September 1978), 319-43.

4. Raymond J. DeMallie, "The Sioux in Dakota and Montana Territories: Cultural and Historical Background of the Ogden B. Read Collection," in *Vestiges of a Proud Nation, The Ogden B. Read Northern Plains Indian Collection,* ed. Glenn E. Markoe (Burlington, Vt.: Robert Hull Fleming Museum, 1986), 22.

Little Thunder and Spotted Tail only portended a disastrous future for the Indians.[5]

When harassed on their perimeters, the Sioux at first simply withdrew to the vast northern buffalo ranges where their traditional lifeways were little affected by the vices of the invading culture. White incursions into Sioux country remained rare, even into the early years of the Civil War. The discovery of gold in western Montana in 1862 and 1863, however, constituted the first dramatic step toward war.

Miners bound for Montana took several different routes to the gold fields. Some came up the Missouri River on shallow-draft steamboats to Fort Benton, an American Fur Company trading post located just below the Great Falls of the Missouri in central Montana. Others traveled overland from Minnesota across northern Dakota Territory to Fort Union, another American Fur Company outpost, and then trailed west to Fort Benton. The most popular routes, however, radiated north from the old Oregon Trail. Of these, the Sioux particularly objected to the newly blazed Bozeman Trail, which angled through central Wyoming along the eastern face of the Bighorn Mountains and into Montana. For the Sioux, the Bozeman Trail sliced straight through their traditional buffalo hunting country.[6]

Predictably, the tribesmen lashed out violently at incursions through their land, and troops at Fort Laramie and lesser outposts along the Oregon Trail and Missouri River were powerless to react. Tension on the northern plains intensified in the wake of the successive retaliatory campaigns waged against the Sioux during the years after the Minnesota Uprising of 1862, and after Colonel John M. Chivington attacked Cheyenne and Arapahoe Indians at Sand Creek, Colorado, in 1864. General Patrick E. Conner's campaign up the Bozeman Trail in 1865 and his fight with Arapahoes on the Tongue River in August further steeled Indian resistance to an invasion of the northern plains.[7]

Although commissioners parleyed with the Sioux and other plains tribes in 1865 and 1866 in an attempt to stem the bloodshed, the

5. For more on these 1850s episodes, see LeRoy R. Hafen and Francis Marion Young, *Fort Laramie and the Pageant of the West, 1834-1890* (Glendale, Calif.: Arthur H. Clark Company, 1938; reprint, Lincoln: University of Nebraska Press, 1984); and David Lavender, *Fort Laramie and the Changing Frontier* (Washington, D.C.: U.S. Department of the Interior, 1983).

6. For detail on these routes, see William S. Greever, *The Bonanza West: The Story of the Western Mining Rushes, 1848-1900* (Norman: University of Oklahoma Press, 1963), 215-37; and Dorothy M. Johnson, *The Bloody Bozeman* (New York: McGraw-Hill Book Company, 1971).

7. Kenneth Carley, *The Sioux Uprising of 1862* (St. Paul: Minnesota Historical Society, 1961); Robert H. Jones, *The Civil War in the Northwest* (Norman: University of Oklahoma Press, 1960); and Robert M. Utley, *Frontiersmen in Blue: The United States Army and the Indian, 1848-1865* (New York: Macmillan Company, 1967), 261-340.

army's calculated defense of the Bozeman Trail in the summer of 1866 betrayed the government's true intention. The establishment of forts Reno, Phil Kearny, C. F. Smith, and Fetterman in 1866 and 1867 became, in effect, a declaration of war, and the enraged Sioux contested everything.

Indian resistance to the Bozeman Trail was marshaled by the Oglala chief Red Cloud. With allied Sioux, Northern Cheyenne, and Northern Arapahoe warriors Red Cloud virtually halted movement on the trail. In December 1866 Red Cloud and the young Oglala warrior Crazy Horse decoyed Captain William J. Fetterman and eighty men to a barbarous death in the hills above Piney Creek in northern Wyoming. Twice in August 1867 in episodes known as the Hayfield fight, near Fort C. F. Smith, and the Wagon Box fight, near Fort Phil Kearny, vastly outnumbered troops fought off determined Sioux attackers. Only the recent receipt of new breechloading Springfield rifles and timely howitzer fire saved these episodes from Fetterman-like consequences.[8]

In effect, the Sioux shut down the Bozeman Trail to all but military traffic. Red Cloud demanded the closure of the trail and the abandonment of the forts. Fortuitously for the Sioux, the government was finding the maintenance of its military presence on the Bozeman Trail increasingly hard to justify. No one conceded the Montana gold fields, but the steady advance of the transcontinental railroad across southern Wyoming soon offered an alternative for reaching them. In 1868 peace commissioners at Fort Laramie negotiated a new treaty with the northern Indians. At face value, the pressing issues of the war, the trail, and the forts were settled, with the Sioux demands prevailing. Less understood was the government's interest in transforming these Sioux into agriculturalists, which was addressed in a number of treaty articles. Perhaps most significant of the new treaty's terms were stipulations concerning a Great Sioux Reservation and designating unceded hunting lands — matters which became the basis of the Great Sioux War.[9]

An amicable relationship, however, seemed to have been established initially. The new reservation, which included the Black Hills, was carved directly from the heart of traditional Sioux territory. At new agencies located along the Missouri River, the Indians received seeds and agricultural tools, along with food, clothing, and other bounty

---

8. Utley, *Frontier Regulars*, 93-129.

9. For comprehensive discussions of the 1868 treaty see Utley, ibid., 130-41, 236-66; Paul Andrew Hutton, *Phil Sheridan and His Army* (Lincoln: University of Nebraska Press, 1985), 282-301; and Paul L. Hedren, *Fort Laramie in 1876: Chronicle of a Frontier Post at War* (Lincoln: University of Nebraska Press, 1988), 1-18.

from white society. The Sioux were free to live anywhere on the vast reservation and they could roam at will into the unceded buffalo hunting country, which extended west of the reservation to the Bighorn Mountains. The government conceded this tract as a game preserve but not as land for settlement by Indians or whites. Most Sioux ignored the distinction and continued their traditional nomadic ways.

Two final episodes in the 1870s hastened the specter of a major Sioux war. Encouraged by the government, surveyors staked out a route for a northern transcontinental railroad across Dakota Territory and into Montana. While the actual advance of iron rails beyond Bismarck was stymied by the nation's economic problems in 1873, the Sioux vigorously challenged the presence of surveyors and army columns in the Yellowstone River valley.

The Sioux were angered even more when an 1874 exploring expedition led by Lieutenant Colonel George Armstrong Custer, Seventh Cavalry, penetrated the Black Hills. Custer's official mission was to site a new military post; unofficially, but equally clear was his intention to report on the presence of gold. Confirmation of gold in the Black Hills in mid-1874 brought a rush of miners into the district and ultimately triggered the Great Sioux War.[10]

Despite mounting pressures, the Grant administration attempted to avert war with the Sioux. Bound legally and morally by treaty obligations that forbade white settlement of Sioux land, the army spent the winter of 1874–1875 removing miners from the Black Hills. But this was a futile exercise as thousands found their way to the new El Dorado. In 1875 a presidential commission headed by Senator William B. Allison of Iowa attempted to purchase the Black Hills from the Sioux but his efforts were thwarted at every turn. Calls for a military solution to the mounting "Sioux problem" grew increasingly sharper, meanwhile, and President Ulysses S. Grant finally prescribed such an answer at a White House meeting on November 3, 1875. Among others in attendance were the secretaries of Interior, Zachariah Chandler, and War, William W. Belknap, as well as Lieutenant General Philip H. Sheridan, and Brigadier General George Crook. Brushing aside obligations to the Sioux, Grant decreed that the Black Hills would be opened. Moreover, tolerance for those Indians living in the unceded hunting country evaporated; they would be forced back to the reservation.[11]

---

10.   On Custer, gold, and the Black Hills, see Donald Jackson, *Custer's Gold: The United States Cavalry Expedition of 1874* (New Haven: Yale University Press, 1966); and Watson Parker, *Gold in the Black Hills* (Norman: University of Oklahoma Press, 1966).

11.   Hedren, *Fort Laramie in 1876*, 13-18; Watson Parker, "The Majors and the Miners: The Role of the U.S. Army in the Black Hills Gold Rush," *Journal of the West*, 11 (January 1972), 99-113; Hutton, *Phil Sheridan and His Army*, 291-99; John S. Gray, *Centennial Campaign: The Sioux War of 1876* (Fort Collins: Old Army Press, 1976), 9-34; and Albert

In the midst of winter, runners carried the government's ultimatum to the scattered northern bands but none of these people returned to the Sioux agencies. On February 1, 1876, secretary Chandler officially certified to Belknap that the Sioux problem was the war secretary's to solve. Two of the army's affected generals, Sheridan and Crook, had already commenced campaign preparations quietly, and were awaiting this formal cue. With Brigadier General Alfred H. Terry in St. Paul, these commanders duly appreciated the desirability of tracking the Sioux to their winter camps. "Sitting Bull's War," as it became known, was finally at hand.

The non-reservation Sioux were camped throughout the Yellowstone, Powder, and Tongue River country, living comfortably and unthreatened, as they had for generations. Many of these bands were known at the agencies, where they appeared occasionally to collect supplies and annuities, but they rebelled at the notion of settling at the agencies permanently. Small bands of Cheyennes, traditional allies of the Sioux, also were scattered through the Powder River country. Estimates suggested that as many as three thousand Sioux and four hundred Cheyennes occupied the unceded country in early 1876. Called northern Indians or northern roamers, some had, indeed, received but ignored the government's mid-winter order to come in.[12]

Remarkably, in early 1876 military commanders and Indian agents alike took little heed of the predictable springtime agency defections. Each April and May bands of agency Sioux tracked to the buffalo country just as quickly as the grass greened. Soon ten thousand to fifteen thousand Indians filled the lower Yellowstone basin. Represented were the seven divisions of the Teton Sioux under such headmen as Black Moon, Gall, Big Road, Crow King, Lame Deer, and Spotted Eagle. Cheyenne bands under Two Moon, Lame White Man, and Dirty Moccasins swelled their numbers. Even Inkpaduta, survivor of the 1862 Minnesota Uprising, joined with a handful of Eastern Sioux followers.[13]

Of the dozens of Sioux and Cheyenne leaders prominent in the war, four individuals stood out: Sitting Bull and Crazy Horse on the war front; and Red Cloud and Spotted Tail at the agencies. To the whites, Sitting Bull was the ultimate embodiment of Sioux hostility. Unyielding in his hatred of white people and their continued encroachment on Indian lands, Sitting Bull exerted broad influence and leadership as a war and political chief, and as a visionary. He

---

L. Hurtado, "Public History and the Native American: Issues in the American West," *Montana The Magazine of Western History*, 49 (Spring 1990), 58-62.

12.   Gray, *Centennial Campaign*, 321-34.

13.   Gray, ibid.; Utley, *Frontier Regulars*, 254; and Neihardt, *Black Elk Speaks*, 95.

had taken no role in Red Cloud's Bozeman Trail conflict or in the Fort Laramie Treaty council of 1868, and he was widely known across the Upper Missouri country as the archetype non-reservation Sioux Indian.[14]

Crazy Horse, thirty-six years old and nine years younger than Sitting Bull, was equally lordly and intractable. He possessed remarkable abilities as a warrior, and his influence grew invincible after the initial clashes of the war. Both Sitting Bull and Crazy Horse, of course, had such visible and antagonistic postures that the Sioux War soon became synonymous with their names. Lesser camp circles rallied to them for nearly two years, and in this unique cohesion came awesome strength. In the wake of early campaign failures, army commanders trembled at the thought of pitching into such a coalition, and it became a field objective eventually to separate and defeat the Sitting Bull and Crazy Horse camps individually.[15]

The Oglala Chief Red Cloud and the Brulé Chief Spotted Tail, on the other hand, took no fighting roles in 1876. Their influence was potent, however. Soldiers and agents feared them, and their respective agencies in Nebraska tallied thousands of Tetons. Whites well remembered how Red Cloud had master-minded war on the Bozeman Trail. Yet, a decade later, Red Cloud now counseled moderation among his followers. He had visited Washington, D.C., and understood the tragic futility of the war. He did not support the fighting, and he ultimately had a hand in its end. Spotted Tail also argued restraint. He, too, had war-time memories dating to Harney's attack in 1855. Neither Red Cloud nor Spotted Tail capitulated values. Rather, both men exhibited a wisdom that made the best of this culturally shocking time. They knew that gains were but temporary, and that the old world would never be restored.[16]

The military commanders who opposed the Sioux and Cheyennes were equally forceful individuals. The Sioux War fell within the jur-

---

14.   Utley, *Frontier Regulars*, 236-37. For a useful biography of this great leader, see Stanley Vestal, *Sitting Bull, Champion of the Sioux* (Norman: University of Oklahoma Press, 1957).

15.   The best biography of this unique warrior is Mari Sandoz, *Crazy Horse: The Strange Man of the Oglalas* (N.Y.: Alfred A. Knopf, 1942), but see also Richard G. Hardorff, *The Oglala Lakota Crazy Horse: A Preliminary Genealogical Study and An Annotated Listing of Primary Sources* (Mattituck, New York: J. M. Carroll & Company, 1985); and Eleanor H. Hinman, "Oglala Sources on the Life of Crazy Horse" in *The Eleanor H. Hinman Interviews on the Life and Death of Crazy Horse*, ed. John M. Carroll (N.p.: Garry Owen Press, 1976) reprinted from *Nebraska History*, 57 (Spring 1976), 1-51.

16.   For vital works on Red Cloud and Spotted Tail, see George E. Hyde, *Red Cloud's Folk: A History of the Oglala Sioux Indians* (Norman: University of Oklahoma Press, 1957); James C. Olson, *Red Cloud and the Sioux Problem* (Lincoln: University of Nebraska Press, 1965); and George E. Hyde, *Spotted Tail's Folk: A History of the Brulé Sioux* (Norman: University of Oklahoma Press, 1974).

isdiction of the army's Military Division of the Missouri, headquartered in Chicago and commanded by Lieutenant General Philip
H. Sheridan. Sheridan, one of the Union's greatest commanders, dictated the strategy of the 1876 war and skillfully manipulated his
players to insure success. Sheridan's chief lieutenants were Brigadier
General Alfred H. Terry, who commanded the Department of Dakota
from St. Paul, and Brigadier General George Crook, commanding
the Department of the Platte, headquartered in Omaha. Subordinate
to Terry and Crook were officers like Colonels John Gibbon and
Joseph J. Reynolds, Lieutenant Colonels George A. Custer, Eugene
A. Carr, and William B. Royall, and later, colonels Wesley Merritt,
Nelson A. Miles, and Ranald Mackenzie. Each of these field-grade
officers had substantial command and combat experience gained during the Civil War and afterward on the frontier.[17]

The anticipated wintertime strike against the non-reservation Sioux
was thwarted early in 1876 by the weather. The northern plains could
be blasted by arctic chills one week, blanketed by a foot of snow in
another, swept by blizzards the next day, then warmed by chinooks
that melted it all away half a week later. Weather on the northern
plains could never be predicted, and people and planning invariably
suffered from it.

Of the several dozen military posts that ringed the vast Upper
Missouri and Yellowstone country, Sioux War geography dictated
several logical staging areas, including Fort Ellis, near Bozeman in
western Montana, Fort Abraham Lincoln, on the Missouri River near
Bismarck, and Fort Fetterman, in east-central Wyoming. From these
locations Sheridan expected that troops would strike into the unceded hunting country, harass the nomadic Sioux, and force their
return to the Dakota agencies.[18]

General Crook was first into the field. Near February's end he had
organized the Bighorn Expedition, embracing twelve companies of
soldiers drawn from the Second and Third Cavalry and Fourth Infan-

---

17. Recommended biographies of these 1876 Indian fighters include Hutton, *Phil
Sheridan and His Army;* John W. Bailey, *Pacifying the Plains: General Alfred Terry and the
Decline of the Sioux, 1866-1890* (Westport, Conn.: Greenwood Press, 1979); Jerome A.
Greene, "George Crook," in *Soldiers West: Biographies from the Military Frontier,* ed. Paul
Andrew Hutton (Lincoln: University of Nebraska Press, 1987), 115-36; Robert M. Utley,
Cavalier in Buckskin: George Armstrong Custer and the Western Military Frontier (Norman:
University of Oklahoma Press, 1988); James T. King, *War Eagle: A Life of General Eugene
A. Carr* (Lincoln: University of Nebraska Press, 1963); Don E. Alberts, *Brandy Station
to Manila Bay: A Biography of General Wesley Merritt* (Austin: Presidial Press, 1980); Virginia
W. Johnson, *The Unregimented General: A Biography of Nelson A. Miles* (Boston: Houghton
Mifflin Company, 1962); and J'Nell L. Pate, "Ranald S. Mackenzie," in Hutton, ed.
Soldiers West, 177-92.
18. On Sioux War geography, see Hedren, *Fort Laramie in 1876,* 19-47.

try regiments, numbering some nine hundred men. Colonel Joseph Reynolds, Third Cavalry, commanded the expedition, but Crook accompanied the expedition as an adviser. Harsh winter weather pummeled the soldiers, yet the column snaked northward across the Powder River country toward the Tongue River. On March 16 Crook cut Reynolds loose with half the command to close on a suspected Sioux camp. At dawn on March 17 the troops charged into one hundred Indian lodges clustered along the Powder River. The troops scattered the Indian inhabitants, destroyed tepees and their contents, gathered up some seven hundred to eight hundred Indian ponies, and withdrew toward Crook and the remainder of the command.[19]

Reynolds's soldiers might have found merit in their attack had they withdrawn from the village with any dignity. In fact, the camp was altogether hastily abandoned under sharp Indian fire. Four dead soldiers were left on the field, and that night the Indians retrieved their ponies. Crook was outraged at Reynolds for mismanaging the engagement, particularly for losing the horses, and brought court-martial charges against the colonel and several subordinates. At first Crook and Reynolds believed they had attacked Crazy Horse's camp, but they learned it had been a band of Cheyennes under Old Bear. Not previously active figures in the conflict, the Northern Cheyennes thereafter fought prominently beside the Sioux. For the United States Army, the St. Patrick's Day clash was a portentous opening encounter.

While Crook reorganized his command, Colonel John Gibbon moved eastward from Fort Ellis on March 30. The likelihood of wintertime success was eluding the troops quickly, and they faced the grim prospect of a summer campaign. Gibbon and his second officer, Major James S. Brisbin, led some 450 men drawn from the Seventh Infantry and Second Cavalry. His orders were stated simply: to scout the north bank of the Yellowstone River.[20]

Terry, meanwhile, was personally overseeing final assembly of the Dakota Column at Fort Abraham Lincoln. The entire Seventh Cavalry, plus elements of the Seventeenth, Sixth, and Twentieth Infantry regiments, about 925 men, comprised Terry's command, which also featured the mercurial George Armstrong Custer and three Gatling guns. Neither

19. On the Powder River fight, see John G. Bourke, *On the Border With Crook* (New York: Charles Scribner's Sons, 1891), 256-82; and J. W. Vaughn, *The Reynolds Campaign on Powder River* (Norman: University of Oklahoma Press, 1961).

20. For primary accounts on Gibbon's operation see, John Gibbon, *Gibbon on the Sioux Campaign of 1876* (Bellevue, Neb.: Old Army Press, 1969); James H. Bradley, *The March of the Montana Column: A Prelude to the Custer Disaster* (Norman: University of Oklahoma Press, 1961); and Edward J. McClernand, *On Time for Disaster: The Rescue of Custer's Command* (Glendale, Calif.: Arthur H. Clark Company, 1969; reprint, Lincoln: University of Nebraska Press, 1989).

Custer nor the Gatling guns would serve Terry or the army particularly well in 1876. The Dakota column marched west on May 17, thinking the Sioux were still south of the Yellowstone. As their Indian opposition swelled with agency defectors, the field commanders continued to believe their greatest challenge simply would be to trap the Indians and force a fight.

In Wyoming, Crook fielded an even larger expedition in late May. Most of his Powder River veterans returned to their originating stations, and Crook pulled together twenty fresh companies of soldiers from the Second and Third Cavalry, and Fourth and Ninth Infantry regiments—nearly eleven hundred men. Dubbed the Bighorn and Yellowstone Expedition, Crook exhibited renewed confidence in the prospects of a successful campaign. He had received reports from the Red Cloud and Spotted Tail agencies that fighting men were headed to the northern camps in unprecedented numbers, but he shared Sheridan's and Terry's belief that they would never stand and fight. Fielding twenty-five hundred men in the different commands was deemed amply adequate for the mission.

For all their showy conviction, among the three commanders only Crook demonstrated any initial campaign zeal. Gibbon moved cautiously, avoiding Indian contact while guarding the Yellowstone. Terry, too, could have sought his quarry more aggressively. The Indian camps were predictably in any of the successive river drainages flowing into the Yellowstone, but Terry wanted to join with Gibbon before scouting for Sioux systematically. Unlike Gibbon and Terry, Crook thrust straight into hostile country, effectively employing Indian scouts. After establishing a base camp in the northern Bighorn Mountains where Sheridan, Wyoming, is located today, he crossed the Tongue River and marched toward Rosebud Creek. As his soldiers prepared morning coffee there early on June 17, it was the Sioux who became the aggressors.

For six hours Sioux and Cheyenne warriors parried with Crook's troops in the battle of Rosebud Creek. From a high ridge, the general tried to direct an action that spread for miles around. Since the Sioux had precipitated the fight, Crook believed their village lay nearby. Despite pressure from the warriors, Crook ordered a squadron of Third cavalrymen under Captain Anson Mills to advance down the Rosebud to find and attack that supposed camp. Crook planned to support this sortie just as quickly as he could disengage his troops, but the fighting boiled fiercely and he was forced to recall his horsemen. To Crook's good fortune, Mills returned to the battlefield promptly, putting himself opportunely behind the Sioux and Cheyennes. When attacked from the rear, the warriors quit the fight.[21]

---

21.   On the Rosebud Creek fight see Bourke, *On the Border with Crook*, 452-79; John F. Finerty, *War-Path and Bivouac, or The Conquest of the Sioux* (Norman: University of

Crook momentarily held the field, having sustained casualties of ten killed and twenty-one wounded. Crazy Horse later estimated Indian casualties at thirty-nine killed and sixty-three wounded. As the general walked the battlefield that evening replaying the day's action in his mind, he had to have felt confused by his foe. Plains Indians were supposed to be impossible to trap, and it certainly was not their style to initiate a major encounter. Yet they fought tenaciously at the Rosebud, bringing a thousand or more warriors to a field of their choosing. One senses that the more Crook thought about this day, the more tentative he became. Crook labeled the battle of the Rosebud a victory, and it might have been had he pursued the Indians to their base. Instead, however, he evacuated his entire command to Goose Creek and spent the next six weeks "reinforcing" his expedition.[22]

On the Yellowstone, meanwhile, Terry and Gibbon united the Dakota and Montana columns and plotted their own advance. While Crook parried with the Sioux on June 17, Major Marcus A. Reno and a scouting column of Seventh cavalrymen found abundant Indian signs on the Tongue and lower Rosebud drainages. Armed with this intelligence, Terry, Gibbon, Custer, and Brisbin conceived a pincer movement against a village believed, correctly as it turned out, to be on the Little Bighorn River. Custer's Seventh Cavalry would move swiftly up the Rosebud, cross to the Little Bighorn, and prevent an Indian escape to the south. With the slower moving infantry, Terry and Gibbon would block retreat from the north. Somewhere between them, together or not, Custer or Terry would fight the Sioux. Apologists evermore have overblown this "plan." In truth it was appropriate and simple. It had to be.[23]

Custer relished the prospect of charging with his regiment. He was in deep trouble with the Grant administration because of certain indiscreet political accusations, and the President had personally stripped him from command of the Dakota Column. Here, finally, was Custer's opportunity to redeem himself by doing a soldier's duty. With characteristic gusto he marched up the Rosebud, saw where a major Indian trail crossed the divide west to the Little Bighorn and followed it. From a ridge on the divide at dawn on June 25, Custer's scouts observed evidence of a village on the Little Bighorn. The scouts

of Oklahoma Press, 1961), 64-98; J. W. Vaughn, *With Crook at the Rosebud* (Harrisburg, Penn.: Stackpole Company, 1956); and Neil C. Mangum, *Battle of the Rosebud: Prelude to the Little Bighorn* (El Segundo, Calif.: Upton & Sons, 1987).

22. James T. King, "General Crook at Camp Cloud Peak: 'I am at a loss What to Do,'" *Journal of the West*, 11 (January 1972), 114-27.

23. Gray, *Centennial Campaign*, 125-50; and Edgar I. Stewart, *Custer's Luck* (Norman: University of Oklahoma Press, 1955), 233-57.

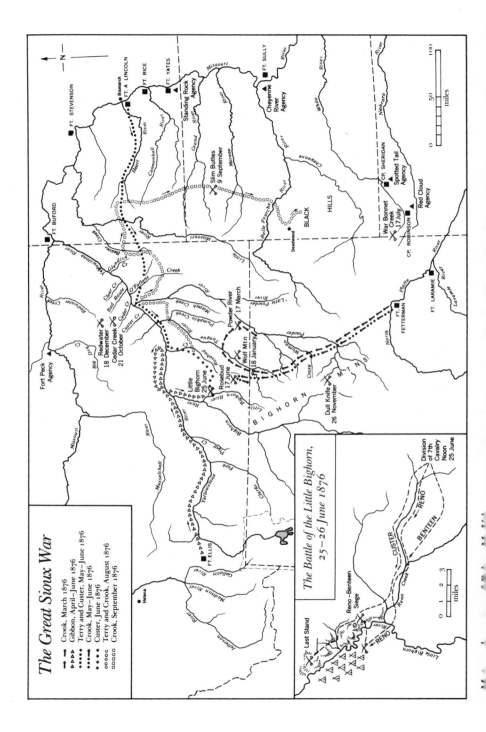

The Great Sioux War

Crook, March 1876
Gibbon, April–June 1876
Terry and Custer, May–June 1876
Crook, May–June 1876
Custer, June 1876
Terry and Crook, August 1876
Crook, September 1876

*The Battle of the Little Bighorn,
25–26 June 1876*

could not determine its size, but it was occupied by Sioux. The Seventh Cavalry crossed the divide about noon. At Custer's front the troops chanced upon the rear guard of a small Indian camp ambling toward the larger village. Custer learned, too, that another small party of Indians had been seen on his back trail and that shots had been exchanged. Conventional wisdom held that the large encampment, once discovered, would scatter, and he was sure that these two unrelated encounters would trigger such flight.

Custer was confident of his regiment's ability to handle the Sioux. Oblivious to Crook's shock at the Rosebud, he advanced hurriedly to the Little Bighorn, dividing the Seventh into three battalions, plus a packtrain guard enroute. Troopers led by Major Reno were first to reach the river at mid-afternoon. To their amazement, before them lay the largest Indian village ever seen on the plains. The winter roamers had indeed been reinforced, and here were some ten thousand Sioux and Cheyennes, including fifteen hundred to two thousand warriors. In fact, the village was still growing when Custer found it on June 25. The simple demands for grass and game would prevent it from remaining together very long, but at this single moment in time, the Sioux were massed for one of the greatest victories in Indian history.

As Custer positioned for a blow from the east, Reno's battalion struck the village from the south. Unfortunately for the Seventh Cavalry, the battle never unfolded conventionally. Reno's troopers were overwhelmed by Sioux defenders who, in turn, lashed at Custer before he could seize any offensive advantage. Custer beckoned his third battalion and pack train forward, but the commander and his five companies were killed before the regiment could regroup. Survivors of Custer's command entrenched themselves on a hilltop southeast of the village and fought desperately for another day and a half before the Sioux and Cheyennes departed. The army would anguish over this defeat for years and blame would be thrown everywhere. Cut to its simplest analysis, everything that could have gone wrong for Custer and his soldiers did go wrong.[24]

Terry and Gibbon advanced according to plan up the Little Bighorn on the morning of June 27. The Indian village scattered

---

24. For the most vital primary and secondary sources on the battle of the Little Bighorn, see comprehensive bibliographies in Gray, *Centennial Campaign;* Stewart, *Custer's Luck;* Jerome A. Greene, *Evidence and the Custer Enigma: A Reconstruction of Indian-White History* (Golden, Colo.: Outbooks, 1986); W. A. Graham, *The Custer Myth: A Source Book of Custeriana* (Harrisburg: Stackpole Company, 1953); Kenneth Hammer, ed., *Custer in '76: Walter Camp's Notes on the Custer Fight* (Provo: Brigham Young University Press, 1976); and Robert M. Utley, *Custer Battlefield, A History and Guide to the Battle of the Little Bighorn* (Washington, D.C.: U.S. Department of the Interior, 1988).

before them, and soon Custer's dead were discovered on the eastern banks of the river. The field was a grisly sight. The soldiers spent several days burying 265 casualties and evacuating another fifty-three wounded. From a mooring at the mouth of the Little Bighorn River the steamboat *Far West* took the injured to Fort Abraham Lincoln in a record-setting river trip. Terry and Gibbon, meanwhile, parked themselves on the Yellowstone and reevaluated the Sioux War.[25]

At his headquarters in Chicago, General Sheridan was as stunned by these events as his field generals. As a means of forcing governmental control, Sheridan had long advocated establishing strong military posts in the very heart of Sioux country. Knowing that Congress would surely relent in the aftermath of Custer's defeat, he pressed again for construction of such posts. At the same time his commanders pleaded for reinforcements. Sheridan insured that many new regiments were transferred to the war zone. Eventually almost forty percent of the entire U.S. Army would be deployed against the Sioux.

First among the outside troops to arrive in the Sioux country was the Fifth Cavalry commanded by Colonel Wesley Merritt. Initially deployed along the road from Cheyenne, Wyoming, to the Black Hills to protect stagecoaches and gold seekers, the Fifth Cavalry also watched the Red Cloud and Spotted Tail agencies in Nebraska. When army commanders learned of the proposed flight of some eight hundred Cheyennes from Red Cloud, they threw a block across Warbonnet Creek, Nebraska, on July 17, and prevented these Indians from rallying with the northern camps. Warbonnet was a quick clash and almost bloodless, but for the first time Sheridan received a positive report from the field.[26] His troops had finally prevailed in a critical encounter.

Sheridan soon ordered the Fifth Cavalry north to join General Crook's command and replaced them with the Fourth Cavalry under Colonel Ranald Mackenzie, plus a battalion from the Fourth Artillery. Mackenzie was generally regarded as the finest cavalry officer in the army, and his troops eventually played a major role in the war. Terry, meanwhile, was reinforced by a battalion of the Twenty-second Infantry commanded by Lieutenant Colonel Elwell S. Otis, along with most of the Fifth Infantry regiment commanded by Colonel Nelson A. Miles. As Crook and Terry awaited these troops, they scouted the sur-

---

25. Richard G. Hardorff, *The Custer Battle Casualties: Burials, Exhumations and Reinterments* (El Segundo, Calif.: Upton & Sons, 1989); Joseph Mills Hanson, *The Conquest of the Missouri: Being the Story of the Life and Exploits of Captain Grant Marsh* (New York: Murray Hills Books, 1946).

26. Charles King, *Campaigning With Crook and Stories of Army Life* (New York: Harper & Brothers, 1890), 13-52; and Paul L. Hedren, *First Scalp For Custer: The Skirmish at Warbonnet Creek, Nebraska, July 17, 1876* (Glendale, Calif.: Arthur H. Clark Company, 1980).

rounding countryside cautiously and finally opened direct com-munications with each other. The Indians still controlled the Powder and Tongue River country. They never again massed in the numbers seen at the Little Bighorn, but they continually threatened the army's isolated supply bases, preyed on travelers bound for the Black Hills, and repeatedly harassed the large army camps.[27]

While the troops muddled in the field, a presidential commission headed by George W. Manypenny assembled at the Red Cloud Agency to deliver a final ultimatum to the Sioux. In the "Agreement of August 15, 1876," the Sioux learned that they must give up the Black Hills and all rights to the unceded hunting lands to the west. Moreover, henceforth they must reside on the reservation and "live like white men," or they would have other privileges terminated. Red Cloud and the agency chiefs agonized over these harsh terms for weeks, but the ultimatum left nothing to debate. With no choice, the Sioux relented. On paper and among the agency people, the Black Hills question was finally settled.[28]

Terry and Crook combined their forces on August 10 and moved slowly down the Yellowstone valley. After the Little Bighorn, Terry's fighting resolve was spent, and in early September he disbanded his expedition. Thus far, the army was bested on nearly all fronts while the northern roamers were, if anything, strengthened and demon-strated no willingness to submit. With the war proceeding aimlessly, the fresh infantry troops of Miles and Otis received orders to establish a cantonment at the mouth of Tongue River. This continuing field pres-ence was of some comfort to Terry as he departed for St. Paul. Crook, on the other hand, elected to follow the fading Indian trails, despite being exhausted and short of supplies. These trails led Crook eastward into the Dakota Territory and then south toward the Black Hills.

The travails of the Bighorn and Yellowstone Expedition and its march to Deadwood have legendary qualities still widely remembered in American military annals. Cool fall rains turned the prairie into a soggy wasteland. Crook's troops consumed the last of their regular field rations about September 7 and thereafter ate horses and mules. The campaign soon became known as the "Starvation March."[29]

But fate had turned against the Sioux. The first indication of declining fortunes came when an advance party from Crook's col-

---

27. Hedren, *Fort Laramie in 1876*, 146-53; and Utley, *Frontier Regulars*, 268-69.

28. Hedren, *Fort Laramie in 1876*, 155-58; and Olson, *Red Cloud and the Sioux Problem*, 224-30.

29. King, *Campaigning With Crook*, 90-123; Finerty, *War-Path and Bivouac*, 171-85; and Paul L. Hedren, *With Crook in the Black Hills: Stanley J. Morrow's 1876 Photographic Legacy* (Boulder, Colo.: Pruett Publishing, 1985).

umn charged into one of their villages on September 9 at Slim Buttes, in present-day northwestern South Dakota, and precipitated two days of scattered fighting. Crook now campaigned on reservation land where, at least in theory, the Sioux were safe residents. Yet in the aftermath of the Rosebud and Little Bighorn battles the army felt no sympathy for these tribesmen. That the camp contained Seventh Cavalry relics only served to reinforce the army's self-righteous defense of the attack.

The Slim Buttes Sioux were mostly Minneconjou led by American Horse. Crook did not know of a larger camp nearby containing Crazy Horse's people. Warriors from that camp rushed to the aid of their kin. At Slim Buttes, the fighting was often heated and Crook's thrusts and parries lent a Rosebud-like quality to the engagement. The general prevailed on the field where he destroyed the village and took captives, and he finally offered Sheridan the first significant army victory in 1876. Casualties totaled three soldiers killed and twelve wounded, with estimates varying between seven and eighteen Indians killed.[30]

Crook disbanded the Bighorn and Yellowstone Expedition at Camp Robinson in late October. Before departing for their winter stations, these troops supported Ranald Mackenzie in unhorsing and disarming the Red Cloud Agency Sioux. The actions at Red Cloud, repeated at the other Sioux agencies, were borne of frustration. The army intended that all Indians returning from the north surrender their weapons and horses, and they initiated this measure among the agency people first. It mattered little to the army that few of these agency dwellers supported the summer's hostilities, and it comforted the agency Indians even less to be told that their surrendered ponies would be sold and the value returned in the form of live cattle. Few cattle ever appeared.[31]

Despite a momentary lull in field movements, the army made numerous inroads during the fall that helped the government effect its preferred solution to the Sioux War. Miles' infantry entrenched itself firmly at the confluence of the Tongue and Yellowstone rivers in a post known as Cantonment Tongue River. The post became the first of Sheridan's long-desired permanent garrisons in the Yellowstone country. Far up the Powder River in north-central Wyoming, other soldiers under the command of Captain Edwin Pollock,

---

30. King, *Campaigning With Crook*, 116-33; Finerty, *War-Path and Bivouac*, 186-205; Bourke, *On the Border With Crook*, 362-80; and Jerome A. Greene, *Slim Buttes, 1876: An Episode of the Great Sioux War* (Norman: University of Oklahoma Press, 1982).

31. Hedren, *Fort Laramie in 1876*, 184-87; Richmond L. Clow, "General Philip H. Sheridan's Legacy: The Sioux Pony Campaign of 1876," *Nebraska History*, 57 (Winter 1976), 461-77; and Forrest W. Daniel, "Dismounting the Sioux," *North Dakota History*, 41 (Summer 1974), 8-13.

Ninth Infantry, established Cantonment Reno. Sheridan had argued for two posts in the heart of Sioux country, and Congress eventually authorized seven to guard the Great Sioux Reservation, its perimeters, and the unceded lands.[32]

Small but heated Indian fighting continued across the war zone. Few northern Indians came to the agencies, and although they were not massed as in summer, travel for whites remained dangerous. A sharp clash occurred on Richard Creek southwest of Fort Laramie on October 14. That same month Sitting Bull's warriors repeatedly harassed army supply activities along the Yellowstone, often halting movement entirely. Twice that month Sitting Bull conferred with Otis and Miles, but his strident talk of the army vacating Indian country only prompted Miles to conclude "that something more than talk would be required."[33]

Miles seized an opportunity to close against Sitting Bull on October 21 at Cedar Creek, Montana. In a running fight his infantrymen captured great quantities of winter food, equipage, and tepees. Two infantrymen were wounded and five Indians killed in the engagement. Sitting Bull and Crazy Horse did not yet understand that Miles' aggressiveness at Cedar Creek and elsewhere would doom Indian chances in the war. Righteousness was not debated; the government intended to prevail.[34]

General Crook amassed another huge force, meanwhile, at Fort Fetterman, this one twenty-six companies strong, with cavalry under the immediate command of Colonel Mackenzie, Fourth Cavalry, and infantry and artillery components in the charge of Lieutenant Colonel Richard I. Dodge, Twenty-third Infantry. Counting civilians and Indian scouts — including Sioux and Cheyennes who had recently surrendered at the Nebraska agencies — some twenty-two hundred men marched north November 14 in search of the northern Indians. After passing the new Cantonment Reno, Crook's scouts learned of a large Cheyenne village in the southern Bighorn Mountains. Crook ordered Mackenzie forward with the cavalry units, and in a particularly decisive engagement on November 25 and 26 on the Red Fork of the Powder River, Dull Knife's Cheyenne village was leveled. Casualties were heavy on both sides, with some twenty-five Cheyennes

32. Hedren, *Fort Laramie in 1876*, 202-5; Robert A. Murray, *Military Posts in the Powder River Country of Wyoming, 1865-1894* (Lincoln: University of Nebraska Press, 1968), 110-18; Utley, *Frontier Regulars*, 290-91.

33. Hedren, *Fort Laramie in 1876*, 183; John S. Gray, "Sitting Bull Strikes the Glendive Supply Trains," *Chicago Westerners Brand Book*, 28 (June 1971), 25-27, 31-32; and Utley, *Frontier Regulars*, 273.

34. Jerome A. Greene, *Yellowstone Command: Colonel Nelson A. Miles and the Great Sioux War, 1876-1877* (Lincoln: University of Nebraska Press, forthcoming), chap. 4.

and six soldiers killed. Without food and shelter the Cheyennes suffered greatly and many withdrew to the agencies.[35]

A lack of forage and harsh December weather forced Crook's retirement from the field, but his Powder River Expedition crippled the Cheyennes. Farther north, Miles received a number of Sioux and Cheyenne who talked surrender. At the same time he deployed his Fifth Infantry aggressively. Twice in December in engagements on Bark Creek and Ash Creek, in northeastern Montana, detachments under First Lieutenant Frank Baldwin clashed with and scattered Sitting Bull's followers. These episodes demonstrated unwavering soldier determination and threatened the Sioux in their homes during winter, the most vulnerable season.[36]

As yet, however, such thrusts by field commanders generally represented reactions to Indian movements rather than attempts to direct it. After disbanding his third expedition, Crook's troops played no further role on the campaign front. The Sioux were largely along the Yellowstone anyway, within striking distance of Miles' infantrymen. Ever quick to respond to opportunity, Miles moved up the Tongue River at year's end with seven companies of Fifth and Twenty-second infantrymen, and on January 8 encountered some five hundred Sioux and Cheyenne warriors under Crazy Horse in the battle of Wolf Mountain. Miles deployed his troops brilliantly and might have crushed the warriors had a blizzard not set in to halt the battle. Evermore, however, Crazy Horse was contained on the south side of the Yellowstone, apart from Sitting Bull's followers. Moderates in the northern camps pointed to the Red Fork and Wolf Mountain sufferings as the inevitable consequences of prolonging the war. The Indian alliance was disintegrating.[37]

Frustrated by Miles' resolve, Sitting Bull led many of his followers north into Canada in January. Other small bands surrendered at the agencies. Crook orchestrated a peace mission at the Spotted Tail Agency, meanwhile, sending Spotted Tail himself north to Crazy Horse's camp to promote surrender. Many bands came in with Spotted Tail when he returned two months later, but Crazy Horse's people

35. John G. Bourke, *Mackenzie's Last Fight with the Cheyennes* (Governor's Island, New York: Military Service Institution, 1890; reprint, Bellevue, Neb.: Old Army Press, 1970); John D. McDermott, ed., *The Dull Knife Symposium* ([Sheridan, Wyo.]: Fort Phil Kearny/Bozeman Trail Association, [1990]); and Sherry L. Smith, *Sagebrush Soldier: Private William Earl Smith's View of the Sioux War of 1876* (Norman: University of Oklahoma Press, 1989).

36. Green, *Yellowstone Command*, chap. 5; and Robert H. Steinbach, *A Long March, The Lives of Frank and Alice Baldwin* (Austin: University of Texas Press, 1989), 110-15.

37. Greene, *Yellowstone Command*, chap. 6; and Don Rickey, Jr., "The Battle of Wolf Mountain," *Montana The Magazine of Western History,* 13 (April 1963), 44-54.

were not among them. With Crook's endorsement, Red Cloud went north in April to talk again with Crazy Horse. He returned several weeks later bearing encouraging news that the Oglala chief would come to the Red Cloud Agency. Both Spotted Tail and Red Cloud reported that the northern Indians had suffered terribly during the winter and that they were starving.[38]

The surrender of Crazy Horse at Camp Robinson, Nebraska, on May 6, 1877, marked the beginning of the end of the Great Sioux War. His camp tallied 899 people, 146 lodges, and some twenty-two hundred ponies and mules, and his influence still ranked with the greatest of Indian leaders. Ironically, while Crazy Horse's surrender at Camp Robinson constituted a final proud processional that awed Indian and white spectators alike, it also marked the close of the Oglalas' centuries-old life style and the dawn of a new age.

Mass surrenders at all of the Sioux agencies in the spring of 1877 spelled the virtual end of the war. By First Lieutenant John G. Bourke's estimate, forty-five hundred Indians had surrendered at the Nebraska agencies since January. Miles contended with small fugitive bands in the Yellowstone country, but even they realized they would never be left alone. On May 7 at Muddy Creek, a small tributary to Rosebud Creek, Miles charged into fifty-one lodges of Minneconjou Sioux under Lame Deer, who had vowed never to surrender. Lame Deer and thirteen others were killed in the fight, as were four soldiers. Lame Deer's son, Fast Bull, and 225 others escaped, however, and eluded Miles' troops all summer, only to give up finally at Camp Sheridan that fall.[39]

By summer, another of Sheridan's new military posts was rising on a bluff overlooking the confluence of the Little Bighorn and Bighorn rivers, barely fifteen miles from the Custer Battlefield. Soon to be called Fort Custer, the post was further indication that the Yellowstone Basin would never again belong to the Sioux. On January 29, 1879, when Custer Battlefield was proclaimed a National Cemetery, it was already well designated as the military's shrine to the Great Sioux War.[40]

If the events of June 1876 at Rosebud Creek and Little Bighorn River represented high water marks for Sioux resistance to white settlement, the slaying of Crazy Horse at Camp Robinson on September

---

38. Oliver Knight, "War or Peace: The Anxious Wait for Crazy Horse," *Nebraska History*, 54 (Winter 1973), 521-44; and Harry H. Anderson, "Indian Peace-Talkers and the Conclusion of the Sioux War of 1876," *Nebraska History*, 44 (December 1963), 233-55.

39. Jerome A. Greene, "The Lame Deer Fight," *By Valor & Arms*, 3 (Number 3, 1978), 11-21.

40. Richard Upton, ed., *Fort Custer on the Big Horn, 1877-1898* (Glendale, Calif.: Arthur H. Clark Company, 1973); and Don Rickey, Jr., *History of Custer Battlefield* (N.p.: Custer Battlefield Historical & Museum Association, 1967).

5, 1877, certainly was among the lowest. Crazy Horse did not fare well after his surrender because military and Indian authorities feared his momentary flight to the Powder River country or to Sitting Bull. Crook, usually a sympathetic officer in such matters, ordered Crazy Horse's arrest and removal to a prison in Florida. The chief resisted and was bayoneted by a private of the Fourteenth Infantry. Crazy Horse died about midnight on September 5, 1877.[41]

For five years Sitting Bull remained the unfinished business of the Sioux War. During the winter of 1877–1878 some four thousand Indians, representing all bands of the Teton Sioux, rallied with him on the Canadian prairies between the North-West Mounted Police posts at Wood Mountain and Fort Walsh. Faced with limited food and tense relations with the Canadian Indians, theirs was a difficult life. The Mounted Police treated Sitting Bull and his followers fairly but laid down rules and enforced them strictly. The land was not yet pressed by Canadian settlers, but neither did residence there pose a solution for the Sioux. Occasionally small bands crossed back into Montana to hunt buffalo in the Big Open country or along the Missouri River. News of their presence invariably reached Miles at Fort Keogh, and he rushed troops to the field, closing with the hunters on several occasions, including one protracted encounter on the Milk River in July 1879.[42]

Terry led a peace mission to Sitting Bull's Canadian camp in October 1877 in an unsuccessful attempt to induce that chief's surrender. Ultimately it was the diminishing buffalo herds on both sides of the international boundary that decided the Indians' fate. In the late 1870s a succession of small bands surrendered, mostly at the Fort Peck Agency in northeastern Montana. Sitting Bull and 187 followers were the last holdouts, and their surrender at Fort Buford on July 19, 1881, symbolically closed the pages of the Great Sioux War. A great tribe was finally under government control.[43]

While the Great Sioux War successfully opened the Black Hills and the northern plains to white settlement, the Sioux experienced a succession of tormenting episodes as the new world crashed upon them.

---

41.   E.A. Brininstool, *Crazy Horse, the Invincable Ogalalla Sioux Chief* (Los Angeles: Wetzel Publishing Co., 1949); Robert A. Clark, ed., *The Killing of Chief Crazy Horse* (Lincoln: University of Nebraska Press, 1988); John M. Carroll, "Foreword," to *The Oglala Lakota Crazy Horse*, by Richard G. Hardoff, 9-17.

42.   DeMallie, "The Sioux in Dakota and Montana Territories," 42-54; Fraser J. Pakes, "Sitting Bull in Canada, 1877-81," *English Westerners' Brand Book*, 20 (October 1977–January 1978); Finerty, *War-Path and Bivouac*, 236-58.

43.   Christopher C. Joyner, "The Hegira of Sitting Bull to Canada: Diplomatic Realpolitik, 1876-1881," *Journal of the West*, (January 1974), 6-18; Utley, *Frontier Regulars*, 284-88.

Establishment of the Pine Ridge and Rosebud agencies in south-western Dakota Territory in 1878 finally removed the Oglala and Brulé Sioux from their revered Nebraska homeland. Spotted Tail's murder in mid-1881 at the hand of a fellow Brulé eliminated his name from the roster of prominent Sioux War survivors. Removal of some nine million acres from the Sioux Reservation by the Sioux Land Commission of 1889 and the murder that year of Sitting Bull himself were relic gasps of the 1876 War, as was the Ghost Dance-related anni-hilation of another 150 Sioux men, women, and children at Wounded Knee Creek in South Dakota in 1890. Red Cloud, forever in the midst of Sioux affairs, survived the Ghost Dance troubles and lived until December 10, 1909, to see the new day.[44]

---

44. On these tragic transitional years see George E. Hyde, *A Sioux Chronicle* (Norman: University of Oklahoma Press, 1956); Jerome A. Greene, "The Sioux Land Commission of 1889: Prelude to Wounded Knee," *South Dakota History*, 1 (Winter 1970), 41-72; Robert M. Utley, *The Last Days of the Sioux Nation* (New Haven: Yale University Press, 1963); and Olson, *Red Cloud and the Sioux Problem*.

HARPER'S WEEKLY.

A JOURNAL OF CIVILIZATION.

Vol. XX.—No. 1024.]   NEW YORK, SATURDAY, AUGUST 12, 1876.   [WITH A SUPPLEMENT. PRICE TEN CENTS.

Entered according to Act of Congress, in the Year 1876, by Harper & Brothers, in the Office of the Librarian of Congress, at Washington.

"STRUCK IT RICH!"—PROSPECTING IN THE BLACK HILLS.—Drawn by John A. Randolph.—[See Page 655.]

PART ONE
Sioux War Prelude

Of the wonderful and diverse intrigue marking the Great Sioux War of 1876–1877, the conflict's numerous causes have sparked a remarkably spirited debate since the day fighting commenced on the Montana prairies more than a century ago. The essays of Part I, which consider what was at stake in the war from both white and Indian perspectives, are proof enough of the historical controversies surrounding the conflict.

Mark H. Brown, a premier Montana historian, urges careful examination of the relationships in the vast Yellowstone basin between the Sioux Indians and land-coveting cattlemen in his "New Focus on the Sioux War," published in *Montana* in late 1961. Brown bases his argument on an interpretation of Sioux War geography, particularly on a unique definition of the upper limits of the unceded lands granted by the Fort Laramie Treaty of 1868. Maintaining that the treaty did not give the Sioux the right to hunt buffalo in the lower Yellowstone region, he contends that Indians and bison were distinct barriers to white settlement. No one quibbles with Brown's contention that Sioux Indians and buffalo herds were barriers to cattlemen, but others have argued that the Sioux had a complete right to hunt in eastern Montana until the "Agreement of August 15, 1876," which among other things, abrogated the hunting provision of the 1868 treaty.

In the next selection, Harry H. Anderson, affiliated with the South Dakota State Historical Society when his essay appeared in *Montana* in 1962, challenges Brown's interpretation of the war's origins. Anderson argues convincingly that the 1868 treaty did include the lower Yellowstone region as rightful Sioux hunting territory. More importantly, Anderson contends that the Black Hills were of greater significance in the dispute than expansion of the cattle frontier. Ultimately, of course, the great bison herds, disputed hunting rights, the Black Hills gold fields, and possession of the Yellowstone country were all underlying issues of the Sioux War of 1876–1877.

Our third essay unveils the plight of Montana's Indians in 1876. Michael P. Malone and Richard B. Roeder find a litany of shrinking homelands and corrupt agency administrations. One by one the mountain and plains tribes lost land to advancing stockmen. As the Indians became increasingly dependent upon the agencies for their welfare, these tribesmen faced an oft-suspected but rarely proved case of short measure and shoddy material. Despite the Indians' treaty-granted right to hunt in the Yellowstone country in the 1870s, most Montanans regarded the Sioux as interlopers. Moreover, although white citizens were shocked by Custer's defeat at the Little Bighorn, they generally ignored the Indians' unheeded degredation and despair on the reservations.

Of the many agents at work on behalf of the white man's advance across the trans-Mississippi West, none had greater impact than the transcontinental railroads. In a 1970 *Montana* essay, Robert G. Athearn chronicles the army's close relationship to these railways. He notes how advance of the first transcontinental line across Wyoming brought quick abandonment of the Bozeman Trail garrisons. He also describes how two of the earliest western land-grant railroads — the Union Pacific and the Kansas Pacific — forced a corridor through traditional Indian lands and provided white settlers a means for pouring into previously remote and dangerous areas. In addition, Athearn assesses the transcontinental lines' economic impact on the West, especially their providing cheap long-haul rates, as well as their influence on formulation of new military strategies for protecting the frontier. By 1876 two lines served Sioux War country — the Northern Pacific Railroad, which had advanced as far as Bismarck, and the Union Pacific Railroad, which crossed from Omaha, Nebraska, to Ogden, Utah, to link with the Central Pacific and on to California. In 1877 General Crook was particularly pleased by the prospect of a Union Pacific branch line running through Wyoming into Montana, and agreed with the company's directors that wherever the railroads went "the Indian question is practically settled."

A New Focus
On The Sioux War

by Mark H. Brown

This distillation of source material researched by Mark Brown for his new book "The Plainsmen of the Yellowstone" is not as far out of context in this issue as may first appear. Wallis Huidekoper, noted Montana cowman, once said that there were three basic barriers to the range cattle industry on the frontier: The Indian, the buffalo, and lack of transportation to market. Mr. Brown's thesis clearly relates to the breaking of the first—and probably the greatest of these barriers—the Sioux Nation.

After the coming of the railroad and subjugation of the Indian, the Yellowstone drainage became one of the great cattle regions of the West, which it has continued to be to this day. Granville Stuart, Montana's most articulate early Cattle King, gave the Big Horn drainage of the Yellowstone first priority of all available range when he made his historic survey before establishment of the great DHS Ranch, initially capitalized at $150,000, in the Spring of 1880. (But it was not located there because of respect for the Crow Indian Reservation, and so DHS located instead on Flatwillow, east of the Judith Basin and south of the Missouri.)

Certainly the Yellowstone country's part in the Sioux War was significant, and in this re-analysis, Mark Brown sets the stage for the day of the cattlemen which inevitably followed the final taming of the terrible Sioux.

"Figures don't lie, but liars can figure." So went a little jingle a half century ago that could be backed up with convincing algebraic equations which proved that, "Therefore, one equals two." Many who have made an effort to delve into the subject of history know that the field of mathematics is not the only one where formulae can be marshalled which supposedly prove something which cannot be substantiated by facts. Curiously, most studies of what was undoubtedly the most

*Mark H. Brown, "A New Focus on the Sioux War," *Montana The Magazine of Western History*, 11 (October 1961), 76-85.

Cattle herds, such as this one seen along the Powder River in Montana, quickly displaced buffalo as the prime grazers of the prairies. (L. A. Huffman, photographer, Montana Historical Society Photograph Archives)

spectacular Indian war of the West—the Sioux War of 1876, sometimes called Sitting Bull's War—are rather thoroughly permeated with serious garbling and wild distortion. The story of the military campaigns has been badly beclouded by undue attention given to the sensational death of a flamboyant officer (Custer) and a large part of his command.

However, by far the most serious errors are those which have been made in connection with the causes of this war. These shortcomings hinge around two things. One is that it has been fashionable to make the U.S. Government the whipping boy for what occurred. The other is that many who have written so glibly are obviously poor students of both background data *and geography*—two extremely important fields in any study dealing with military history.

Although there may be some justification for overlooking a few of the causes of this conflict, there can be no excuse for ignoring one military document, dated September 23, 1876, in which some of the causes are listed—particularly when it contains this thought-provoking statement: *"The occupation by the settlers of the Black Hills country had nothing to do with the hostilities which have been in progress."* This sentence may be found in the annual report of the Commanding General of the Department of the Platte. The author was General

George Crook, and it was written immediately following his return to Fort Omaha after leading two expeditions against Sitting Bull and his followers. If the unsavory rape of the Black Hills had "nothing to do" with the war which was then in full swing, just what did bring this struggle about?

To properly understand what happened, it is necessary to leaf back through the pages of history to the year of 1727. This is the date when the French, who were then starting to probe the western wilderness for a route to the *Mer de 'l Ouest* (the Pacific Ocean), began to realize that the Sioux were a proud, arrogant, warlike people. Eleven years later, la Verendrye lost to them a party containing his favorite son, a priest, and nineteen men.

Pressured by the Chippewas, who had acquired firearms from the traders, the Sioux slowly withdrew from the Great Lakes region and moved westward. Lewis and Clark found some of these people along the Missouri in 1805 and, probably, the founding of Fort Laramie in 1834 provided an excuse to roam still farther to the west. And when emigrants began to travel the Oregon Trail in great numbers these Indians were not long in discovering that this was a fertile field for scalps and plunder.

All of this may be likened to the prologue of a play. To continue the comparison, Act I begins in the summer of 1851. Thomas Fitzpatrick, Indian Agent for the Upper Platte and Arkansas Agency, had prevailed upon the Government to hold a grand council with all the tribes of the northern part of the high plains for the purpose of working out a treaty which would stabilize relations between the Indians and the travelers going westward. Such a treaty was drawn up and approved by the Indian leaders, later—with some changes—by Congress, but it came to naught because it was never officially promulgated by the President.

Although "The Treaty of 1851" never really became a treaty, one very noteworthy precedent was set. When the general areas were outlined which were considered to be the domain of each tribe, all agreed that the region belonging to the Crows consisted of almost the entire Yellowstone *Basin*—except for the country east of the channel of the Powder River, and that part of the Yellowstone *valley* between the mouth of the Powder and the Missouri. Fifteen years later, the same bands of Teton Sioux who approved this division of territory were insisting fiercely that a very considerable part of this area belonged to *them*.

These squatters' rights of the Crows extended back a good many years before 1851. When the Northwest Company's trader, François Antoine Larocque, traveled with the Crows over a considerable part of the Yellowstone Basin in 1805—the year before William Clark and his party floated down the Yellowstone—they obviously considered this area their hunting grounds. And if the *Gens des Chevaux* (Horse Indians) with whom la Verendrye's two sons and their two companions hoped to travel westward from the village of the "Mantannes" (Mandans?) were actually the Crows, then the Absaroka were in this area well before 1742.

Indian depredations along the Oregon trail brought a series of developments in the years following this first "treaty" meeting. Public clamor finally forced the Government to dispatch a military expedition into the Powder River country in 1865, but this was a futile effort—for a number of reasons: Even as the soldiers hunted for Sioux marauders, pacifists argued in Washington that kind words and not bullets held the solution to the problem. And in the end they prevailed, leaving the Teton Sioux in possession of a considerable portion of what, in 1851, had been firmly agreed was Crow Country.

Having now demonstrated that it was unwilling to back its military forces with effective support, the Government tried to do two things which were dramatically opposed: It tried to make a treaty with the hostile Sioux who believed that they had won a decisive victory, while on the other hand it agreed with the now clamoring settlements in western Montana that they should have a road—*with military protection*—through the very area where the military expedition against the Sioux had fizzled. When troops passed through Fort Laramie in 1866 on their way to fortify what was then commonly known as the Montana Road (alias the Bozeman Trail), the Sioux left the "treaty" proceedings in a rage and began a determined offensive against the soldiers and all who tried to use the road.

If the Government was being illogical, the hostiles were acting with even less reason. Colonel Carrington's wife, in her exposé of official muddling during 1866–1868, recorded the proceedings of a council held at Fort Phil Kearney in July 1866 with certain Cheyenne chiefs. When the question was asked why the Sioux and Cheyennes claimed land which belonged to the Crows, three of them answered promptly, "The Sioux helped us. We stole the hunting grounds of the Crows because they were the best. . . . We fight the Crows because they will not take half and give us peace with the other half." It is small wonder that discerning Army officers and others regarded with scorn the "treaty" which was finally negotiated.

Whatever claims the Crows may have had to this country were abrogated by the Treaty of 1868. This gave to the Sioux as a reservation what is, roughly, that part of South Dakota lying west of the Missouri River. But far more important were the provisions contained in Article XVI:

> The United States hereby agrees and stipulates that the country north of the North Platte River and east of the summits of the Big Horn Mountains, shall be held and conceded Indian territory, and also stipulates and agrees that no white person or persons shall be permitted to settle upon or occupy any portion of the same; or without the consent of the Indians, first had and obtained, to pass through the same; and it is further agreed by the United States, that within ninety days after the conclusion of peace with all the bands of the Sioux nation, the military posts now established in the territory, in this article named, shall be abandoned, and that the road leading to them, and by them to the settlements of Montana, shall be closed.

Some confusion exists as to the extent of these Unceded Hunting Grounds, which included part of northwestern Nebraska, the northeastern quarter of what is now Wyoming, and the *extreme* southeastern corner of Montana. For all practical purposes, the northern boundary, as defined when the Sioux ceded this area on September 26, 1876, coincides with the present Wyoming-Montana state line except for a small area east of the channel of the Powder River, a matter about which it cannot be presumed that the renegade Sioux were ignorant. Nor can it be presumed that they did not know that Articles III, IV, and V specifically prohibited them from committing depredations on the whites!

The commissioners who negotiated with the Sioux at Fort Laramie in 1868 also negotiated a treaty with the Crows at the same time. This set aside as a reservation for the Absaroka that part of Montana lying west of the 107th Meridian (near Sheridan, Wyoming) between the Wyoming-Montana state line and the channel of the Yellowstone river. Those who would understand why the Government had to chastise the Sioux in 1876 must keep clearly in mind the geographical boundaries of both the Unceded Hunting Grounds and the Crow Reservation.

In the years following 1868 it was common practice to divide the Sioux into two general groups—those who made a pretense of living on the reservation, and those who did not. The latter, a small group, were generally referred to as renegades and their guiding spirit was the medicine man, Sitting Bull. It was this fraction which comprised the hard core of the hostiles and it varied in size from season to season. During the summer months, many left the reservation and joined these people in their wanderings, and when winter came they went back to the agency. It was this fraction which floated back and forth that accounted for a large part of the formidable force which assembled in the valley of the Little Big Horn in June 1876. Sitting

Bull's followers did not attend the negotiations held at Fort Laramie in 1868 — nor did any of the commissioners dare go out and try to persuade them to come in. This task was performed single-handed by Father DeSmet who, with an escort of friendly Sioux, found these people along the Powder River (a few miles above its mouth) and was successful in getting representatives to accompany him to Fort Rice, on the Missouri, where the treaty was finally concluded.

Thus, in the summer of 1868, this group was apparently not living on what became either the Unceded Hunting Grounds or the Sioux Reservation. Furthermore, evidence indicates that they were not interested in living within the confines of either of these areas, or submitting to any regulations. Only the year before this treaty was signed, Sitting Bull told trader Charles Larpenteur at Fort Union:

> I have killed, robbed, and injured too many white men to believe in a good peace. They are medicine, and I would eventually die a lingering death. I had rather die on the field of battle. . . . [The other Sioux and Assiniboines had better] do as he did — go to the buffalo country, eat plenty of meat, and when they wanted a good horse, go to some fort and steal one. Look at me. . . . See if I am poor, or my people either. The whites may get me at last, as you say, but I will have good times until then.

The finding of gold in the Black Hills by a government-sponsored expedition in the summer of 1874 and the rush of greedy prospectors into what the press heralded as "The Land of Promise" is a well known part of the Sioux story. Equally well known are the incidents which followed — the objections of the "reservation" Sioux, the feeble and ineffective effort of the Government to eject the trespassers, the stormy session at Fort Robinson on September 20, 1875 when the bitter Sioux refused to sell the Black Hills, and, finally, the much criticized ultimatum was sent out in the early winter to the roving bands ordering them to come in and settle on the reservation *at once*.

The picture presented by these facts is a most deceptive one. Obviously, the Government was responsible for an unsavory situation. And, unfortunately, the fact that an estimated 1,500 warriors left the reservation the following summer and joined the hostiles has served to further screen the true causes of this Indian war. Those who have assumed that this situation was to blame for the war have failed to appreciate the background which Crook summarized in the one pregnant sentence previously quoted.

It is doubtful if General Crook, who had been transferred from Arizona in the Spring of 1875, was familiar with all the ramifications of the Sioux problem. However, the previously noted annual report for 1876 shows clearly that he was familiar with both the stipulations contained in the Treaty of 1868 and what had been happening within the confines of the Department of the Platte. His report begins as follows:

> At the date of my annual report for 1875, September 15, the settlers along the line of the Pacific Railroad in Wyoming, Nebraska and Colorado, were very much excited and exasperated by the repeated incursions made upon them by Indians coming from the north, and although many of the trails of stolen stock ran directly upon the Sioux Reservation, the Agency Indians always asserted that the depredations were committed by certain hostile bands under Crazy Horse, Sitting Bull and other outlaw chiefs.
>
> These bands roamed over a vast extent of country, making the Agencies their base of supplies, their recruiting and ordnance depots, and were so closely connected by intermarriage, interest and common cause with the Agency Indians, that it was difficult to determine where the line of peaceably disposed ceased and the hostile commenced. In fact it was well known that the treaty of 1868 has been regarded by the Indians as an instrument binding upon us but not binding upon them. . . .

After quoting Articles III, IV, and V in which the Sioux agreed not to commit depredations on the whites, Crook stated:

> It is notorious that, from the date of this treaty to the present, there has been no time that the settlers were free from the very offenses laid down in the sentences quoted.

While this guerrilla warfare was a constant irritation, what happened in the Yellowstone valley—often far removed from the nearest point of the Unceded Hunting Grounds—was much worse.

To properly understand the incidents which happened in the Department of the Dakota (which included most of what is now North Dakota and Montana), some knowledge of the history of this area is necessary. Prospectors and settlers of various kinds flocked to the gold fields in southwestern Montana in the early 1860s, and soon the fertile valley of the Gallatin River became an important agricultural area for the gold camps. The treaty of 1868 closed the most direct land route to "America" — or "the States" as it was more commonly called. In the same year, Fort Ellis was established to guard the western ends of the Bozeman and Bridger Passes, which led directly from the upper end of the Gallatin valley to the "Big Bend" of the Yellowstone. Bozeman sprang up near the post; and the Government established the Crow Agency about fifteen miles below the site of the present town of Livingston, on the Yellowstone. As the settlements increased in size, so did their insistent clamor for a satisfactory road to the east. Stimulated by this, and the railway surveys of 1853, the Northern Pacific Railroad was pushed westward from Minnesota. In 1871, surveying parties were poised at Bozeman and at Fort Rice ready to survey the route between the Bozeman Pass and Bismarck. This, then, was the background for the Sioux troubles in Montana Territory in an area in which the Treaty of 1868 gave them no treaty rights whatever—except for one very small area which is of practically no importance.

Father DeSmet found the camp of the renegades, which he estimated at 4–5,000 souls—"big and little," near the mouth of the Powder. Old newspaper files are mute proof that these Indians continued to roam over much of southeastern Montana, hunting, stealing, fighting the Crows, and murdering whites in the years following the signing of the treaty:

(August 8, 1870) ". . . The Crows . . . were out on their buffalo hunts but were attacked by the Sioux, and compelled to abandon the hunting ground . . . . Some seventy lodges of the Sioux are on the [Yellowstone River], about seventy miles from the Agency and one thousand lodges at old Fort C. F. Smith. . . ."

(October 27, 1870) ". . . a party of 25 men . . . were cutting lumber at the mouth of the Yellowstone river, six miles from Fort Buford when they were suddenly attacked by a party of Sioux, led by 'Sitting Bull'. . . . Chas Teck, . . . some 500 yards from the party . . . was suddenly surrounded, killed and scalped, being completely riddled with arrows . . . ."

(July 26, 1871) [A traveler from Bozeman reported in Helena] ". . . . About 10 o'clock on Monday morning a band of Indians, supposed to have been Sioux or Crows, were seen . . . four miles below Hamilton . . . running off stock . . . two men were shot and killed [in cold blood] . . . ."

(July 27, 1874) "Indians, supposed to be Sioux and the same party that lingered in the vicinity of the [Crow] Agency two or three weeks recently . . . again appeared in the Yellowstone valley Sunday. Parties coming in from that vicinity to Bozeman were fired upon along the road and kept in the rear, while the Indians came to within a mile of Bozeman and run off several large herds of horses, and even cut the picket ropes of horses around Fort Ellis and run them off . . . ."

(July 24, 1875) ". . . . On the 16th instant a war party of Sioux visited [Carroll, the "low-water" port on the Missouri] and succeeded in stampeding a herd of horses. Not content with this herd, in which there were twelve splendid animals, the gentle wards [of the Government] paid us another visit the following day . . . ."

Although some settlers disliked all Indians and hence the Crows, all hated the Sioux in no uncertain fashion. In 1872, when some

This "Snug Little Home Among the Big Cottonwoods," so titled by Montana photographer L. A. Huffman, shows clearly the type of cattle ranches that filled the unceded hunting lands in the wake of the Great Sioux War. (Montana Historical Society Photograph Archives)

consideration was being given the idea of moving the Crows to the Judith Basin, south of the Missouri, the editor of the *Bozeman Avant Courier* stated in an editorial:

It is a well known fact, notwithstanding assertion to the contrary, that the Crow Indians, so far from exhibiting, as a tribe, hostility to the whites, have looked upon them as their friends and protectors, and instead of being a source of perpetual menace to our people, they have been an aid to the military posts established on the frontier, as, by their well-known animosity to the various bands of the Sioux nation, they have assisted in keeping that warlike tribe away from our settlements, and past experience has demonstrated that a raid by the Sioux in force would bring with it an attendant train of horror before which our trouble with the red devils, bad as they have been, would pale into the veriest insignificance.

In April and May of 1874, Governor B. F. Potts (a rather scatterbrained individual) deluged the Secretary of Interior with letters urging that the Crows be issued a supply of first-class arms, and that they, together with a force of frontiersmen, be encouraged to initiate a determined offensive against the Sioux. Secretary Delano's answer dated May 22nd is particularly interesting because it admits— officially—that the Sioux were a source of serious trouble *before* Custer found gold in the Black Hills. The Secretary wrote:

> The solution to the "Sioux Question" cannot be reached by the method indicated. Its settlement would be, by such means, greatly retarded, and . . . can only result in exciting the Sioux to greater hostility to the whites; and endanger the success of efforts now being made to bring the disaffected tribes upon Reservations and prevent the peaceful progress of the various wagon trains through the country from Judith Basin to Carroll. . . ."

As noted, the Northern Pacific Railroad surveyors began to work out a line between Bismarck and Bozeman in 1871. In this year the party from the east lost two men to unidentified hostile Indians on the prairies of Dakota. When the western party returned to Bozeman the *Avant Courier* noted:

> The party saw no hostile Indians on the trip, although fresh signs were visible every day . . . About one hundred and fifty lodges of Sioux were ascertained as being camped on the Big Horn. The Crows were with the surveying party a portion of the time, making several sorties, capturing stock from the Sioux, which showed them in close proximity to the party.

The next year the military escort with the eastern party had two brushes with the Sioux in the eastern part of the Yellowstone valley and one surveyor and some scouts had narrow escapes. The western party was heavily escorted by Major E. M. Baker and 420 soldiers and civilians. When this force was camped along the Yellowstone a few miles east of where Billings is now located, a large force of Sioux— probably Hunkpapa under Black Moon and with Sitting Bull present—attempted a surprise attack before dawn. After several hours of skirmishing the Indians withdrew having killed two soldiers and wounding two others. For reasons which are no longer clear, the survey party turned back a few days later.

In 1873 the eastern party came back to complete the survey between the mouth of the Powder and the vicinity of Pompeys Pillar. This was an unwieldy body numbering 1,531 soldiers and scouts, and 375 civilians—exclusive of the surveyors. The Sioux dogged their steps from a point opposite the mouth of the Tongue until the work was completed, picking off stragglers and fighting two engagements with the cavalry portion of the escort. One of these was an attempted ambush and the other a pitched battle just below the mouth of the Big Horn in which an estimated 800–1,000 warriors took part.

Since gold fever continued in Montana Territory for years after the first rich finds, early in 1874 the Yellowstone Wagon Road and Prospecting Expedition left Bozeman for the Yellowstone valley. Ostensibly, the primary purpose of this group was to work out a road from Bozeman to the supposed head of navigation on the Yellowstone River but the 147 men who made up this group were actually interested in but one thing—gold! This well organized party was composed of experienced frontiersmen and Civil War veterans. Before they returned they had whipped the Sioux in three fights: One of these took place just outside the eastern boundary of the Crow Reservation; the other two in the valley of the Little Big Horn—well inside the boundary. One participant estimated the force opposing them in the last fight at "not . . . less than one thousand," and Lieutenant James Bradley wrote a year or so later:

> The number of Indians who participated in the battle was variously estimated at 1000 to 1500. They afterwards admitted at Fort Peck that it was the combined force of three large camps under the leadership of the famous Sitting Bull.

In a letter dated March 7, 1875, the commanding officer of Fort Ellis made this summary of the situation for General Terry who commanded the Department of Dakota:

> These Indians controlled by Sitting Bull are the head and font of all the difficulties with the Indians belonging north of the Platte . . . They are mostly Uncpapas, with bands of Broken Arrows, Blackfoot Sioux and Yanctonians and usually about thirty lodges of Northern Cheyennes . . . .
>
> Sitting Bull's bands are the ones who fought General Stanley, Col. Baker [who escorted the N.P.R.R. Surveyors], and the Citizens expedition last spring, that went down the Yellowstone and who raided in the Yellow Stone Valley and stole horses last Summer from the head of Gallatin Valley. They are openly and defiantly hostile and occupy-

ing a section of country centrally located to the different Indian Agencies excite these Indians more or less to hostilities to the whites and commit depredations about the different agencies to involve the Agency Indians in trouble.

These Indians keep the road from Montana to the east completely shut up and are of great injury to the development of Montana. . . .

These Indians hold complete control of the Yellow Stone and Powder River Country and fight any party of citizens who go into it and are looked upon by a great many Indians at the agencies as being able to defy the power of the Government, the effect of which is discontent and mutinous Condition among the agency Indians hard to control by the Government Officials and Chiefs disposed to be peaceful.

Although the Sioux renegades had precipitated a never-ending string of complaints, trouble became inevitable late in 1874, when the newly-appointed Crow Agent, ex-Confederate general Dexter E. Clapp, requested permission to move the Crow Agency to Rosebud Creek. It was one thing for the Secretary of Interior or the Commissioner of Indian Affairs to cold-shoulder complaints from settlers and Army officers, but it was quite another matter to resolve complaints which arose within their own official "family."

Clapp's reasons for wishing to move were sound. His request was approved even though it raised a storm of protests from nervous citizens of Bozeman and the commanding officers of both Forts Ellis and Shaw. Although the reasoning of the civilians and the military were selfish, those of the latter group did have some logic behind them — the new location was 73 miles farther away from Fort Ellis and squarely on one of the routes used by Sioux war parties going to and from the upper Yellowstone. Clapp started to build the new agency in June 1875, and trouble was not long in coming. On the 5th of the following month he began a letter to the Commissioner of Indian Affairs with, "I am unfortunately obliged to report depredations and a murder committed at or near the New Crow Agency by Sioux Indians." Other letters which followed at more or less regular intervals related similar troubles — employees killed and wounded, cattle-horses-mules stolen, and so much danger that a large part of his labor force was tied up with guard duties. And he begged that pressure be put on the Army to furnish protection — which the commanding officers at Forts Shaw and Ellis flatly refused to provide.

There were no uncertainties in identifying the hostiles as Sioux and at times they left behind telltale articles which had been issued at agencies. In his annual report dated March 4, 1876, Clapp detailed troubles which had occurred in the Yellowstone valley during the past year — 17 attacks made on whites (as well as a number on Crow camps), 9 men killed and 10 wounded, 86 horses and mules stolen, 52 oxen killed or stolen, and delays caused in his construction work which cost an estimated $4,500–6,000. Clapp also pointed out that the Crows continually complained that the Sioux were better armed and better mounted than they, "that the larger and most fertile portion of their reservation is permanently occupied by their enemies," and that the impression was being created that the whites could not protect themselves, much less the Crows.

> And, I respectfully urge, that such action shall be taken as shall effectively quiet the hostile Indians in the Yellowstone country, and give to the whites peace, and to the Crows opportunity for the progress of civilization.

These incidents, added to the complaints of civilians on the frontier and the pointed criticism of Army officers, finally drove home the fact that the olive branch which certain misguided individuals had persisted in waving for the past decade was definitely *not* the answer to how to handle the Sioux renegades. It was one thing to shrug off Colonel Stanley's Fort Peck a "den of iniquity" and Crook's saying that the Red Cloud Agency "deliberately harbored thieves," but it was quite another matter to meet Clapp's blunt statements that the Sioux were raising hell on the Crow Reservation and that it was high time that someone put an end to it. It was only a question of time until the Secretary of Interior had to admit that his employees were not capable of handling the situation. Finally, in 1875, the General of the Army was given the task of doing what discerning officers had always been certain they would eventually have to do — *whip the Sioux into submission.*

This is why Crook was correct when he wrote, *"The occupation by the settlers of the Black Hills had nothing to do with the hostilities which have been in progress."* Likewise, this is why it is irrelevant to argue that the order requiring the hostiles to come on the reservation in mid-winter was unreasonable and inhumane. There is not the slightest evidence to indicate they would have complied had the weather been perfect.

When these incidents are placed in their proper geographical relation, the campaigns of this war take on a new appearance. Only one fight of note, the Battle of Slim Buttes, took place on either the Unceded Hunting Grounds or the Sioux Reservation. And, of course, the famous battle of the Little Big Horn which cost the lives of 265 soldiers and scouts was fought — *on the Crow Reservation!*

Tents and wagons of the Custer expedition dotted the Black Hills landscape in 1874. (William Illingworth, photographer, South Dakota State Historical Society)

A Challenge To Brown's Sioux Indian Wars Thesis

by Harry H. Anderson

In the previous issue of this magazine, Colonel Mark H. Brown presented a reinterpretation of the causes of the Sioux War of 1876. He focused attention upon certain heretofore largely ignored geographic factors, and gave emphasis to the hostile actions by groups of non-agency Sioux, or "renegades" as he chooses to name them. This approach is certainly an interesting one, and its author is to be complimented for departing from the greatly overplayed military narrative in an attempt to get at some of the more basic issues. Less commendable, however, is the cavalier manner in which he tossed off, as poor students of geography and what he calls "background data," those who have maintained in earlier writings that a definite connection exists between the causes of the Sioux War of 1876 and the opening to white settlers of the Black Hills gold fields.

In reality, blaming the Sioux for the war is not a new approach. Both the military authorities and certain Indian service officials did so at the time of the hostilities.

But this view, despite the refinements made in it by Colonel Brown, are subject to serious question. Dispelling the air of authority implied by Colonel Brown's criticism of others, one finds important errors of both fact and interpretation in his argument. Through the use of broader evidence (which Brown was either unaware of or chose to ignore) it is possible to show a relationship between the Black Hills gold rush and the 1876 hostilities. To begin with, there are contradictions in Colonel Brown's discussion of the tribal boundaries provided for in the Fort Laramie treaty of 1851. On one hand he bases the rights of the Crows to certain areas in the Yellowstone basin upon the provisions of this treaty; but then states that the agreement "never really

*Harry H. Anderson, "A Challenge to Brown's Sioux Indian Wars Thesis," *Montana The Magazine of Western History*, 12 (January 1962), 40-49.

became a treaty" because it was not proclaimed by the President. It hardly seems consistent to argue possession rights on the basis of a document which, technically at least, may be regarded as unofficial. Taking a more practical view of the 1851 treaty, it should be noted that after the Senate altered the length of time it was to remain in force (and this change was agreed to by *all* the tribes party to the agreement), the document was then considered to be a lawful treaty. Money was appropriated by Congress from 1852 through 1866 to supply the tribes with annuity goods called for by it. Furthermore, in realistically examining the land claims of one tribe against another, it should be kept in mind that the argument which held the most importance among the Indians themselves was their ability to hold by force of arms the territory they claimed. While the several treaties of 1868 may have abrogated the claims of the Crows to certain lands in the Yellowstone valley (in terms of their ability to occupy and hold these lands) the Crows had actually lost their rights nearly a decade earlier. In 1867 a member of the commission investigating the Fetterman "massacre" reported from Fort Phil Kearny:

> the country from the Powder River to the Yellowstone was their [Crow] country until 1859, when they were driven from it by the Sioux.

This statement was based upon information obtained from both the military officers at Phil Kearny and the Crows themselves. Thus, with the expiration of the Fort Laramie treaty in 1866, the Crows indeed had lost their claims to these lands both in a technical and a practical sense.

After extended negotiations, treaty relations were resumed by the United States with the Crows and Sioux at Fort Laramie in 1868. Colonel Brown's presentation of the circumstances connected with the Sioux agreement and several of its important provisions requires clarification on several points. The first concerns the identity of the Indians with whom the treaty was negotiated. The emphasis on the name of Sitting Bull conveys the strong implication that this individual was the all-powerful ruler of the hunting bands which inhabited the country north of the Black Hills and west to the Big Horn Mountains. Sitting Bull may have been the leader of a considerable portion of the Hunkpapa and Blackfeet tribes (and even this is open to dispute by some), but there were very large camps of other Sioux— the Miniconjous, Oglalas, and Sans Arcs—who in no way acknowledged any authority of Sitting Bull over them. The very fact that the hostilities which the 1868 treaty brought to a close were called "Red Cloud's War" indicates that Sitting Bull did not play a dominant role in it. All reliable evidence concerning the Fetterman fight discloses that the Hunkpapas of Sitting Bull were not present in significant strength.

One must merely examine the names of the chiefs who signed the treaty at Fort Laramie to find such leaders of the hunting bands as the Miniconjou's Lone Horn, Elk-that-Bellows-Walking, and eventually, Red Cloud himself. The second named could, in some respects, be considered the peer of even Sitting Bull as a non-reservation Indian. During the closing days of the Sioux War of 1876, after the other hostiles had either gone in to surrender or followed Sitting Bull into exile in Canada, this chief still attempted to continue the old hunting existence of the Sioux. He was finally hunted down by Colonel Nelson A. Miles, and his camp destroyed on a tributary of the Rosebud. In the official records of that engagement of May 7, 1877, the chief's name is given as Lame Deer.

It is a serious misconception to state that the only hostiles who agreed to attend the 1868 council talks were the representatives of "Sitting Bull's followers" brought in by Father DeSmet to Fort Rice on the Missouri. It is grossly unfair to the Commissioners who negotiated the treaty for Brown to imply cowardice on their part for failing to go to the Indian camps and bring them to the councils. This Sioux treaty was only a small part of a general series of major Indian negotiations being carried on throughout the West. At the same time as they were dealing with the Sioux, this commission was also responsible for meeting other tribes as widely separated as the Bannocks in the west and the Navahoes to the south. No member of the commission had any particular influence over the Sioux. For them to have attempted to go to the Powder River or Yellowstone country would not only have been a waste of time, but a very dangerous undertaking as well.

The task of coaxing the individualistic and suspicious Sioux leaders to the councils was left to native runners, Indian traders, and other men of influence such as Father DeSmet. In connection with Father DeSmet's mission to the Hunkpapa camp at the mouth of Powder River, it is not true that he "single-handedly" persuaded them to send representatives to Fort Rice, as is claimed by Colonel Brown. DeSmet was accompanied on his journey by the veteran and able fur trader, Charles E. Galpin, who had lived and traded among the northern Sioux (including the Hunkpapas) since his arrival on the upper Missouri in the early 1840s. Galpin was known and respected by these Indians, and he had considerable influence over them. The value of Galpin's assistance was openly acknowledged by Father DeSmet, as revealed in the following which he wrote to the Commissioner of Indian Affairs:

Preparations are now being made to leave Fort Rice on the first of June. Messrs. Gilpin and LaFrambois will accompany me. they are amongst the most influential gentlemen with all the Sioux tribes. Mrs. Gilpin, being of Sioux birth and a near relation to several warchiefs, excercises also a great influence among her people & will accompany her husband.

The treaty which was eventually concluded with the Sioux at Forts Laramie and Rice contained, as Article 16, the provision closing the Powder River Road or Bozeman Trail, and setting aside the lands north of the North Platte River and east of the summit of the Big Horn Mountains as unceded Indian territory. Colonel Brown defines this area to include only the lands so described that were, with but a small exception, south of the present Montana-Wyoming border. This may be the interpretation of the boundaries given by Royce in his study of Indian land cessions prepared for the Bureau of American Ethnology some years ago. But it is not the understanding which existed either at the time of the negotiations of the 1868 treaty or when these lands were taken from the Sioux in 1868. (It has already been pointed out that the Crows had been driven out of the country between the Powder River and the Yellowstone by 1859.) A report made by the 1868 government commission in January of that year recognized the Sioux claim to hunting grounds located "along Powder River and other tributaries of the Yellowstone." (This does *not* say only those tributaries south of the 45th parallel.) This same report also stated that in order to prevent further hostilities, the commission would be willing to extend the western boundary of the proposed Sioux reservation — *not the hunting lands* — from the 104 to the 106 or even 107 meridian if the Indians so insisted!

The purpose for the designation of this area as unceded hunting lands was to permit the Sioux to continue to pursue the buffalo as a means of subsistence. In 1868 and 1869, and for some years thereafter, one of the few remaining large buffalo herds on the northern plains roamed in the Yellowstone valley. To state that the Sioux were to be permitted to hunt this herd *only when it drifted south of the 45th parallel* is to place a ridiculous interpretation upon the treaty.

In the fall of 1875, after gold had been discovered in the Black Hills and efforts were being made to acquire the mineral lands from the Sioux, the Allison Commission met the combined Sioux tribes in a stormy series of councils near Red Cloud Agency. After several weeks of unsuccessful negotiations, the commission submitted as the government's final proposal, an agreement calling for the cession of not only the Black Hills but also the lands *west of a line drawn from the point where the Niobrara River crosses the Nebraska-Wyoming line to the Yellowstone River at the 107 meridian!*

The fact that such a provision was included in the proposed treaty certainly indicates that as late as 1875, the Sioux were recognized as having claims to the lands on both sides of this line as far north as the Yellowstone. Even in 1876 (when another commission rode roughshod over existing treaty provisions and forced the Sioux to give up both the Black Hills and all the hunting lands) Bishop Whipple opened the first council at Red Cloud Agency with the statement that the Indians would be required to "give up the Black Hills country, and the country *to the north.*" Unless the good Bishop was badly confused in his geography, his statement, along with the other evidence previously cited, would establish that *as long as it was in force, the 1868 treaty did not limit the unceded lands in Article 16 as extending only as far north as the present Montana-Wyoming line!*

One further statement in Colonel Brown's discussion of the 1868 treaty requires comment: It has frequently been emphasized that this document represented a complete and unrealistic surrender to the Sioux by the United States government. Brown reflects this sentiment in his remark that the treaty "closed the most direct land route to 'America'— or 'the States' as it was commonly called," imply-ing that such action was detrimental to the interests of the people of Montana Territory. If the most direct route means simply the shortest distance between two points, this may be true; but other fac-tors should be taken into consideration. For example, General William T. Sherman, although a member of the 1868 commission, was certainly not an individual who would submit to the demands of any Indian unless some practical considerations could be real-ized. In the case of this treaty, Sherman was especially concerned with facilitating the unimpeded construction of the Union Pacific line. By ending, for a time at least, the Sioux hostilities, this ob-jective was accomplished. On the matter of communications with Montana Territory, Sherman's annual report for 1868 explained the abandonment of the Bozeman Trail forts from this realistic viewpoint:

> [The Powder River] road and the posts along it had been constructed in 1865 and 1866, for the benefit of the people of Montana, but had almost ceased to be of any practical use to them by reason of the building of the Union Pacific railroad, whose terminus west of the Black Hills made it easier for the wagons to travel by an older and better road west of the mountains.
>
> For this reason and because the further extension of this rail-road, under rapid progress, would each year make the Powder River road less and less used, the commission yielded to the earnest entreaty of the Sioux, and recommended the abandonment for the time of this road.

The principal thesis of Colonel Brown's article—that the Black Hills gold rush had nothing to do with the causes of the Sioux War of 1876—is supported by detailed evidence on the hostile actions of the Sioux against the settlers in the Yellowstone Valley. It is, of course, impossible to dispute the fact that these Indians were a definite barrier to settlement in the northwest as long as they were permitted to attack and raid at will. It was one of the principal objectives of the 1868 treaty to draw these bands onto the Sioux reservation. By the winter of 1875–1876, this had not been accomplished completely, and the Army was sent to force them within the boundaries of the reserve.

Undoubtedly, had construction of the Northern Pacific not been suspended as a result of the nation-wide panic of 1873, the railroad rather than the gold rush would have brought on hostilities at a date prior to 1876. The Sioux inhabiting the lower Yellowstone Valley were strongly opposed to the construction of the Northern Pacific through what they claimed was their country. They strongly attacked the surveying parties and escorts both in 1872 and 1873. However, this hostility was not begun as early as 1871. Contrary to Colonel Brown's statement, the eastern wing of the 1871 survey *did not* lose "two men to unidentified hostile Indians on the prairies of Dakota." This writer is in possession of a series of letters written by an officer accompanying the surveyor's escort. On October 17, 1871 from Fort Rice, he reported that the expedition had returned "to this post yesterday at 3:30 P.M. *without the loss or injury of a man of the expedition,* or the serious loss of property or animals." And a little further on—"We did not see an Indian during the entire trip, nor did we see signs of more than 4 or five."

The surveying parties sent out during the following two years did see considerable signs of Sioux. The skirmishes with the railroad escorts and the raids on the settlers in the Yellowstone basin serve as the basis for Colonel Brown's assertion that Sioux "renegades" and not the Black Hills gold rush were responsible for the Sioux War of 1876. As stated earlier, there is little doubt that military action against these Indians would have been inevitable if the northwest was ever to be opened to settlement. What is left unexplained by Brown's thesis is the *timing* and the *particular circumstances* under which the war with the Sioux began!

To support his argument, Brown's article cites quotations from a report by the military commander of the Department of the Platte, General George Crook. One statement receives particular emphasis: "The occupation by the settlers of the Black Hills country had nothing to do with the hostilities which have been in progress." General Crook was hardly a disinterested or unbiased spectator towards the events of the Sioux war. At the time he wrote these words, he had just returned from the second of the two expeditions he led against the Sioux and their Northern Cheyenne allies. Crook's efforts in these campaigns had been anything but crowning successes.

When writing his report, Crook appears to have been in a rather bitter mood. Several of his remarks are not only questionable in light of the contemporary situation, but inconsistent with the General's own actions both before and after the date of his report. For example, Crook is quoted as he expresses his anger against the agency Sioux for serving (or so he charges) as the source of supply and reinforcement for the hostiles. Yet Crook had gone to these very same Indians at Red Cloud and Spotted Tail agencies in the spring of the year to urge them to serve as auxiliaries for his campaigns. And shortly after writing his annual report, Crook again went to the agencies to seek recruits for his winter expedition. It was these scouts he secured from among the agency Indians who led Mackenzie's cavalry column to the Northern Cheyenne winter camp in the Big Horn Mountains and enabled the Army to score its most spectacular success of the war. And it was these same agency Indians who acted as peacetalkers during the latter part of the winter, and brought the hostilities to a close without further bloodshed and suffering. These are hardly the actions of people who were guilty of the charges set down against them by Crook in his annual report!

Furthermore, while Crook on one hand denies a connection between the war and the gold rush, he states in the very next sentence of his report that because of violations by the Indians of the 1868 treaty, "the settlers were furnished with at least a reasonable excuse for such occupation [of the Black Hills], in that a treaty so long and persistently violated by the Indians themselves should not be quoted as a valid instrument for the prevention of such occupation."

This type of tortured reasoning has no sound basis, but it was typical of the attitude of the time. Article 12 of the 1868 treaty, requiring future cessions of the Sioux reservation to be approved by three-fourths of the male adult Indians, was thrown aside in order to secure the legal right for the prospectors to be in the Black Hills. In 1883, an attempt was made to take a sizable piece of the reservation merely by again obtaining the approval of a small number of chiefs and headmen. This time Congress, to its everlasting credit, refused to sanction another violation of the "three-fourths" clause. This difference in attitude was due to the fact that there had not recently occurred another Custer "massacre" to inflame opinion against the Sioux.

Apparently as a result of his interest in utilizing so many of Crook's statements to justify the seizure of the Black Hills on grounds other than the gold rush, Colonel Brown also overlooked a most significant remark by the General's aide, Captain John G. Bourke. Bourke wrote in his book, *On the Border With Crook,* that

> General Crook said that at the council where General Grant had decided that the northern Sioux should go upon their reservation or be whipped, there were present Secretary [of the Interior] Chandler, Assistant Secretary Cowan, Commissioner [of Indian Affairs] Smith and Secretary [of War] Belknap.

Very little is generally known about this meeting which took place at the White House during the first week in November. Contemporary newspaper reports, however, made some mention of it. What they had to say furnishes the connecting link between President Grant's order to whip both the hunting bands and the Black Hills question.

Information leaked to the reporters by participants at the meeting discloses that current Indian difficulties were prominent subjects of discussion. The presence of not only high government officials, but three military commanders (Sherman, Sheridan, and Crook), attracted immediate attention. One dispatch reported that "the military are to have more to do with Indian matters in the future than they have had in the past." Another stated:

> The president, Secretary Belknap, Generals Sherman and Crook had a private interview yesterday regarding Indian matters in general and *the Black Hills in particular.* At the close, Secretary Chandler and General Cowan were sent for and the subject was discussed further. The result of this conference is that the government will preserve a *neutral position* towards the miners who are crowding into the Black Hills in great numbers. Four hundred men left Cheyenne a few days ago for the gold fields, and it may be said positively that they will not be molested by the troops. General Crook says that miners are crowding in from all directions, and that it is impossible to keep them out.

There seems to be little question that the conference mentioned by Bourke, at which President Grant ordered the Sioux hunting bands to be driven on to the reservation, and the meeting at which the Black Hills question was discussed and Crook reported the miners could no longer be kept out, were not one and the same.

Until late in September, 1875 (barely a month before this meeting at the White House) the government was committed to a policy of using military patrols to keep miners out of the Hills, until a treaty could be made with the Sioux for the gold-bearing region. The

Allison Commission met with the various Sioux tribes in a grand council near Red Cloud Agency in September. But they were unable to secure any land cession. In fact, they were almost unable to escape from the councils with their scalps intact.

The elements among the Sioux most strongly opposed to cession were the hunting bands — Colonel Brown's "renegades." Sitting Bull, Crazy Horse, and many others of their leaders refused to even attend the meetings. Those who were present managed to keep things in a continual uproar as they expressed opposition to the negotiations and threatened the life of any Sioux who favored the sale. It was these Indians who hatched the plot, which came all too close to succeeding, to kill the commissioners. The Agency chiefs were willing to sell the Black Hills, but their asking price was far above what the Allison Commission was authorized to agree to, or the government willing to pay. Had they only to deal with the agency leaders, the government could have, eventually, come to some sort of agreement.

It was the opposition of the hunting bands — the non-reservation Indians — that broke down these important negotiations. And it was these bands, too, who were the subject of that important meeting at the White House during the first week in November. By turning the hunting bands over to the Army for punishment, the major source of opposition to the Black Hills cession would be removed. The calling in of military patrols from the route to the gold fields would permit the prospectors to enter in force. By the following spring the agency Sioux would be presented with a *fait accompli* — the Hills would be full of miners and the Indians would have to accept whatever terms the government presented to them.

Colonel Brown's emphasis on the aggressive actions by the Sioux hunting bands as a cause for the war is not new. These raids against settlers on the frontier (and friendly Indian tribes) was the reason given by the government for sending the well-known ultimatum to the Sioux which ordered them to come on to the reservation by January 31, 1876, or be considered hostile. Inspector E. C. Watkins, in a report to the Commissioner of Indian Affairs in the fall of 1875, stressed the hostile activities of the Sioux and called for their punishment by the military authorities. In their annual reports for 1876, both Generals Sherman and Sheridan stated that the Watkins report was the basis for the ultimatum and the subsequent military movement against the Sioux. What is especially interesting about these explanations is the fact that the Watkins report is dated November 9, 1875, *six days after* the meeting at the White House at which Captain Bourke says the President ordered the Army to go out and whip the Sioux! Something, obviously, is wrong here.

None of the military commanders—Sherman, Sheridan or Crook—made any mention of the White House conference in their reports. All preferred, instead, to cite the statements of Inspector Watkins and the Interior Department as grounds for the opening of hostilities with the Sioux. *Yet it was the meeting with President Grant that marked the turning point in government policy towards both the Sioux and the Black Hills.* The Commissioner of Indian Affairs was selected as the scapegoat for the failure of previous policy, including the negotiations for the Black Hills. He was removed from office, and shipped out of the country as minister to Canada. The greater voice given the military department in Indian affairs resulted in the decision to go to war against the Sioux hunting bands. Orders were given to Crook to prepare for a campaign *even before* the Interior Department came up with that scheme of sending an ultimatum to the Indians.

If one keeps in mind that it was the hunting bands who were responsible for the breakdown of negotiations for the Black Hills, and that they were also the primary objects of the Army's proposed campaigns (which eventually mushroomed into a full scale war), it is impossible to accept the statements that there is no connection between the Sioux war and the gold rush. The significant Sioux successes against Custer and Crook during that terrible summer inflamed both the public and Congress against them. The Indian appropriation bill passed by Congress late in the summer of 1876 contained the very positive provision that unless the Sioux gave up the Black Hills they would no longer be fed by the government. With no game to be found on the reservation, the buffalo almost decimated, and the hunting lands closed by the military campaigns, the Sioux leaders were forced to agree to the cession.

In a desire to reinterpret origins of the Sioux War, Colonel Brown has ignored some very essential pieces of "background data," such as the White House conference of November, 1875, which serve to link the hostilities with the pressure that was put upon the government to open the Black Hills to settlement. This enthusiasm "for setting to rest some of the myths" connected with the war led him into several serious misstatements which not only undermine his thesis but indicate that even his mastery of the "background data" is not as complete as he would have us believe. In at least one instance he has perpetuated one of the mistaken beliefs that has crept into other writings on the origins of the war. While discussing the celebrated ultimatum to the hunting bands in his concluding paragraphs, Colonel Brown comments that it is "irrelevant" to contend that compliance with the order would have forced the Indians to travel through deep snow and bitter cold, for "there is not the slightest evidence to indicate they would have complied had the weather been

Placer miners led the rush to the Black Hills gold fields, leaving denuded hillsides and upturned gravel bars in their wake. This scene by F. Jay Haynes shows such activity near Deadwood in 1877. (Haynes Foundation Collection, Montana Historical Society Photograph Archives)

perfect." Such a blanket judgment is hardly justified in light of another positive statement found in Captain Bourke's revealing volume. While narrating the events of January and February, 1876, Bourke wrote: "Telegraphic advices were received from Fort Laramie to the effect that three hundred lodges of northern Sioux had just come in to Red Cloud Agency." Further information on this response to the ultimatum is contained in a telegram dated February 24, 1876, from the Red Cloud Agent, James S. Hastings:

> Over one thousand Indians from the north have arrived *in obedience to your request* communicated to them by couriers sent from here. More are expected daily.

This piece of background data should prove a revelation not only to Colonel Brown, but also to those sentimentalists who have long complained that it was impossible for the Indians to obey the ultimatum because they could not travel during the severe winter weather. The Sioux did obey the summons. The Bourke and Hastings statements show that the flouting of the government's ultimatum was not as widespread as heretofore believed. It is true, of course, that neither Crazy Horse nor Sitting Bull complied with the message. But considering the difficulties Crook had during his campaign of March, 1876, one wonders what would have been the result had he been forced to contend with 300 lodges more of these Indians!

This rebuttal to Colonel Brown's arguments is not intended to justify hostile activities of the bands of northern Sioux in the Yellowstone region. It is intended to prove, however, that there was a good deal more to the relationship between the Black Hills question and the causes of the Sioux war than is admitted in this article. Under the interpretation held contemporaneously to those events, the Sioux were recognized as having rights in the unceded hunting lands extending as far north as the Yellowstone River. Similarly, that they were not then required to be located permanently on a reservation is evidenced by the fact that as late as 1875, Congress appropriated annuity funds "for Indians roaming" in addition to the money made available for the agency Sioux.

The Reynolds fight of March 17, 1876 and Crook's battle on the Rosebud the following June 17, were both fought within the boundaries of the unceded hunting lands as they were recognized at the time. That the Little Big Horn tragedy took place west of an invisible line that marked the boundary of the Crow reservation seems to reflect the failure of the 1868 commission (or anyone else for that matter) to either explain it to the Sioux or mark such a line. Not that it would have done any good. But as long as the government persisted in defining reservation limits by meridians and parallels that were incomprehensible to Indians, and did not utilize watercourses and other prominent landmarks, it is naive to argue that the Sioux were trespassers upon the Crow reservation.

In this connection one must point out that the Crows did not sit back quietly between 1868 and 1876, permitting the Sioux to roam unmolested through the country south of the Yellowstone. Indeed when Red Cloud came into Fort Laramie in November, 1868 (following the abandonment of the Bozeman Trail) he complained bitterly over the fact that Crows had recently raided Sioux camps in the Powder River country and killed some twenty people! What bothered Red Cloud particularly was that the Crows had been issued arms and ammunition by the Peace Commission after they signed the treaty in the spring, and they had immediately used such war material in raids against the Sioux.

When Red Cloud came to Fort Laramie the military would not supply him with arms with which to retaliate; nor would they permit the local traders to do so. The Crow-Sioux war was a perpetual conflict, dating back to before the time of Lewis and Clark. The fact that the Crows were active participants should not be overlooked simply because their war parties failed to equal the annoying effectiveness of their Sioux counterparts.

It is not disputed that the Sioux in the hunting lands raided outside the boundaries of both the reservation and the hunting grounds. But this certainly did not justify violation of the Black Hills by prospectors, as sanctioned by the government as early as November, 1875.

There is abundant evidence that elements among the non-reservation Sioux had been acting in a hostile manner for some time prior to the date when the decision was made to send the Army after them. Why was this move finally made at the particular time it was, when the Black Hills situation had reached the crisis stage? Why was it accompanied by a drastic change in the policy-making position of the Bureau of Indian Affairs? And most important, why did the military commanders fail to make any mention of the important meeting at the White House and the significant steps that were decided upon then?

Under the circumstances, the only explanation for this secrecy is that the meeting and the plans formulated at that time serve to establish a connection between the Sioux war and the Black Hills gold rush. At the time the military reports were written—in the fall of 1876—the initial shock of the Custer disaster had only begun to wear off. Some quarters were on the verge of openly questioning not only the manner in which the Black Hills were taken from the Sioux, but the whole planning and motives behind the Army's disastrous 1876 campaigns. Indian Inspector William Vandiveer, who was familiar with much that had gone on behind the scenes in connection with the war, wrote Bishop Whipple of the Sioux Black Hills Commission in October, 1876, urging that the commission's report expose the true causes of the war. He said:

> I hope it may be your lot to write the report for the commission, and that you will give a faithful review of the circumstances which led to the war. You know, as well as I do, that *this war was unnecessary and uncalled for—that the Army and not the Indians commenced it.* The responsibility should be placed where it belongs.

It was just such an accusation as this that the military commanders wished to avoid. In light of their campaign record, it is no wonder that the Generals made no mention of the fact that the war had been planned as early as November, 1875 — and by them and not the Indian Department!

1876 on the Reservations:
The Indian "Question"

by Michael P. Malone
and Richard B. Roeder

For both Indian and white residents of Montana, the Centennial year 1876 was a time of trauma and excitement, the year of the Custer battle, and the major military campaigns which preceded and followed it. Even as they were recognized with a somewhat stylized tepee in the United States Building at the Centennial Exposition in Philadelphia, the Indians were experiencing, out in Montana Territory, still another year of mounting problems and narrowing horizons. Their predicament stemmed, as always, from the unending pressure of white stockmen and miners to roll back and shrink the boundaries of their reservations. Then again, especially in this year of exploding scandals in the Grant Administration, much of the trouble arose from uncertainty, negligence, wrong-doing, and bureaucratic rivalries within the government.

Dereliction at the agencies was nothing new, of course, but it became especially notorious during the "Indian Ring" scandals of the later Grant years. Moreover, the long-standing contest over control of Indian affairs still flared between the Interior Department and the Army, whose leaders maintained they could uphold honesty at the agencies better than could political appointees. To the surprise and anguish of his old military colleagues, President U. S. Grant, in 1870 and 1871, decided in favor of civilian control of Indian affairs by launching his so-called "Peace" or "Quaker" Policy. This idealistic but tragically unworkable concept was aimed at cleaning up and revitalizing the Indian Service by allowing religious groups to nominate agents and oversee "civilization" of the reservation Indians.

*Michael P. Malone and Richard B. Roeder, "1876 On the Reservations: The Indian 'Question,' " *Montana The Magazine of Western History*, 25 (Autumn 1975), 52-61.

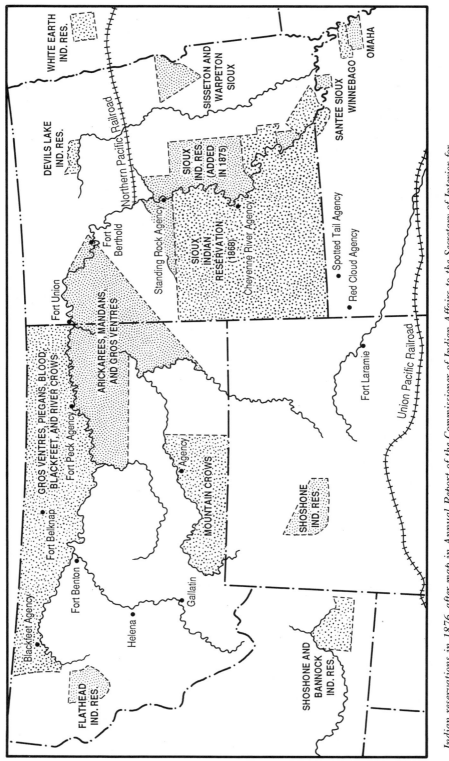

Indian reservations in 1876, after map in Annual Report of the Commissioner of Indian Affairs to the Secretary of Interior for the Year 1876 (Washington, D.C.: Government Printing Office, 1876)

In Montana, the Catholics maintained their presence on the Salish-Kutenai Reserve, while the Methodists received responsibility for all other tribes. In practice, the Peace Policy had small effect, since the Methodists made little effort to pursue it in Montana. The Territory's newspapers kept up a steady barrage of criticism at Grant's policy throughout the year, usually demanding that the "savages" be turned over to the military for more severe and summary treatment.

There were three huge Indian reserves in Montana Territory in 1876. The Salish-Kutenai Reservation covered much of the Flathead Valley. An enormous domain set aside for the Blackfeet and other northern Montana tribes reached northward from the Missouri and Marias Rivers to the Canadian boundary and westward from the Dakota border to the Continental Divide. The Crow Indians lived on a sizable reservation south of the Yellowstone River.

By 1876 the Montana Kutenai and Pend d'Oreille bands were already located on the reservation below Flathead Lake, as were some of the Flatheads. The Salish-Kutenai Agency, where considerable building was taking place, stood in the Jocko Valley. Since 1854, Jesuits had operated nearby St. Ignatius Mission.

The major problem involved the Flathead tribe. Some of them, under Chief Arlee, had moved to the Jocko by 1876, but many others, although impoverished and pressed by the increasing movement of whites into the area, refused to leave their traditional home in the Bitterroot Valley. Their chief, Charlot, a proud and honorable man, maintained that according to the 1855 treaty which his father had signed with the government, he had the legal right to remain in the upper Bitterroot. Only four years earlier, in 1872, he had refused to sign an agreement presented to him by future President James A. Garfield, which would have moved his people northward to the Jocko. Charlot was especially upset because Garfield had allowed the 1872 agreement, which Chiefs Arlee and Adolph had signed, to be published with the false inference that he, too, had signed.

There were other difficulties. During 1876 the Flatheads carried on an extended argument with Missoula County over whether their Bitterroot lands could be taxed or sold for tax delinquency. This poignant "problem" of the Flatheads would linger for fifteen more years until a sad and disillusioned Charlot finally led his people to the Jocko Reservation.

The Indian reserve which covered most of Montana north of the Missouri provoked less controversy in 1876 than did the others, mainly because it lay well to the north of Montana's white population centers. Under executive orders in 1873 and 1874, the once-hostile Blackfeet had given up some of their best lands and accepted a reservation bounded on the south by the Marias and Missouri

Rivers. These agreements opened the Sun, Judith, and upper Mussel-shell River basins to the penetration of stockmen. They also meant sadness and loss for the Blackfeet. In November, 1876, the Piegan Blackfeet moved northward to a new agency built for them on Badger Creek in the upper Marias drainage. Two Protestant ministers from Madison County who visited the agency in 1876 found it a cold, forlorn place. "It is," wrote one, "an outrage on the Indians to com-pel them to live here."

Other, smaller tribes lived east of the Blackfeet along what was to become Montana's "Highline." They received their annuity supplies at two posts erected a few years earlier by the firm of Durfee and Peck: Fort Belknap, a subagency on the upper Milk River, and Fort Peck, an agency located near the confluence of the Milk and Missouri Rivers. Gros Ventre, Assiniboine, and River Crow Indians traded at Fort Belknap, while other Assiniboines and increasing numbers of aggressive Sioux immigrants came to Fort Peck. These two posts became enmeshed in the Grant Administration scandals when, at the instigation of Grant's brother, Orvil, and others within and close to the administration, Durfee and Peck lost their lucrative traderships between 1870 and 1876.

Actually these political goings-on affected the Indians less than might be expected, because in 1876 these tribes were still roving hunters who relied more on the buffalo than on annuity goods for subsistence. The buffalo was still a viable source of livelihood because by an executive order of 1875, Grant had opened to these Indians the fine buffalo lands lying between the Musselshell, Yellowstone, and Missouri Rivers.

According to historian Edward Barry, agency conditions distressed these Indians less than did the mounting thrust into their territory of Sioux enemies from the east. In mid-1876, for instance, the govern-ment closed the Fort Belknap agency in an effort to push the Gros Ventres and Assiniboines down the Milk River to Fort Peck, where they would be near the Missouri River and "civilization." Fearing the Sioux at Fort Peck, the Gros Ventres refused to move, and in 1878 Fort Belknap was reopened to serve them once again.

The Crow Indians, traditionally friendly to whites, faced a difficult situation in 1876. Their reservation, established in 1868 on the south side of the Yellowstone River, had been under pressure from three directions: the Sioux pressed in from the east, Montana miners from the west, and cattlemen from the north and west. In 1873, respond-ing to Montana demands that the gold-rich upper Yellowstone be lopped off the western end of the Crow Reserve, federal commis-sioners had secured an agreement from the Crows that they would give up their reservation entirely and accept a new, smaller one north of the Yellowstone in the Judith Basin. However, this agreement never worked out. Stockmen and other whites raised a howl of protest over the loss of the rich Judith area, and the Mountain Crows, whose homeland lay south of the Yellowstone, refused to join the River Crows.

Thus, in 1875, President Grant threw out his earlier removal order and placed the Crows on a smaller reservation south of the Yellowstone. White stockmen and farmers ended up getting the Judith, a traditional hunting ground of the River Crows and Blackfeet, and white miners got the upper Yellowstone. Once again the Indians were the losers. Since their agency had been located east of present-day Livingston, within the detached western end of the reservation, the Crows moved eastward to a new agency on Rosebud Creek, a tributary of the Stillwater River south of present-day Columbus. There, in 1876, they were starting over once again.

Early in 1876, controversy involving the Crow Reservation erupted when Captain Edward Ball of Fort Ellis charged prominent Bozeman contractor and stockman, Nelson Story, with attempting to defraud the government and the Indians. Ball testified that Story, allegedly in collusion with Crow Agent Dexter Clapp, had offered him $1,000.00 to accept short measure and shoddy goods. The officer said that Story had double-sacked flour, so that the outer sacks could be removed to count each sack twice, and that he had included not only meat in the pork barrels, but also heads, tails, bones and trimmings. He also accused Story of branding reservation cattle as his own.

Story adamantly denied the charges, claiming that Ball held a personal grudge against him and that the officer was trying to discredit the Indian Bureau as part of the military's general effort to regain control of Indian policy. The Bozeman *Times* and the Virginia City *Madisonian* picked up Ball's accusations and publicized them, but the Madison County grand jury which investigated the case returned no indictments and, to the anger of both newspapers, absolved Story and Clapp of any wrongdoings. These charges, although never proven, typified many others of the time.

Despite all these problems, Montanans paid less heed to the native tribes than they did to hostile bands of Sioux and Northern Cheyennes still roaming along the southeastern boundaries of the territory. Pressed from the east and south, the numerous and powerful Sioux were moving into eastern Montana, pushing back the Assiniboines, Gros Ventres and Crows. A decade earlier, these Indians had fought hard under Red Cloud to close the Bozeman Road, which traversed their best buffalo lands. Then the Fort Laramie Treaty of 1868 had eased tensions by closing the road and assigned the Indians a more concentrated reservation in southwestern Dakota Territory.

A Cheyenne Indian village near Fort Keogh, about 1879. (Stanley J. Morrow, photographer, Montana Historical Society Photograph Archives)

However, after 1868, non-treaty bands such as those of Sitting Bull and Crazy Horse roamed freely off the reservation to hunt in the unceded Indian lands south of the Yellowstone in the valleys of the Big Horn, Tongue, and Powder Rivers. These Indians pressed relentlessly northward and westward, into and beyond the Yellowstone Valley, occasionally fighting openly with army units escorting Northern Pacific survey teams along the Yellowstone.

The Black Hills gold rush, which began late in 1874 and boomed through 1875 and 1876, brought this complicated problem to a head. By the end of 1875, there were roughly 15,000 miners in the Black

Hills reservation lands, and thousands of Indians were departing into the hunting areas to the northwest. When these Indians failed to obey ultimatums to return to their ruptured reservation, the Interior Department, on February 1, 1876, handed jurisdiction to the Army, thus beginning America's last great Indian war.

Montanans watched these developments with mixed feelings. The Sioux seemed capable of cutting off their potential rail and water routes down the Yellowstone River and even of mounting full scale attacks against their easternmost settlements. Yet once these Sioux interlopers were removed, most people reasoned, the broad, bountiful Yellowstone Valley might be opened to settlement, setting off a boom which would break the grip of the 1873 Panic. As prominent pioneer Peter Koch later recalled: "We all believed that now surely the time had come, when our front door was to be swung wide open, and we were to roam along the Yellowstone at will."

Residents of Bozeman, the town with the most direct interest in promoting the Yellowstone country, helped nudge that door open through some direct action. In 1875 a group of them ventured down the Yellowstone and established a trading post named Fort Pease opposite the mouth of the Big Horn River. They clearly aimed, not only at trading and prospecting, but at gaining a foothold on the Yellowstone to force out the Indians. The Sioux, however, easily kept them under siege. In February, 1876, appeals for help finally brought a relief force from Fort Ellis under Major James "Grasshopper Jim" Brisbin. (The major gained that nickname because his men laughed at his belief in Montana's agricultural potential). Brisbin found twenty men at Fort Pease; six others had been killed. He escorted them home, and their Yellowstone adventure ended in failure.

Meanwhile, General Phil Sheridan, commander of the Military Division of the Missouri, plotted a campaign against the hostile Sioux and Cheyennes. His first move against them sent a large army under General George Crook northward from Fort Fetterman, Wyoming, which ended indecisively in March. Then Sheridan decided upon the massive campaign which began to unfold in the spring of 1876. Two major cavalry-infantry columns, one led by Crook from Wyoming, the other by General Alfred Terry from Dakota, would close upon the hostile tribes from the south and east. A "Montana Column" would descend the Yellowstone to contain them from the north and west. Leading the 450-man Montana Column, Colonel John Gibbon headed out of Fort Ellis and down the Yellowstone in April. Montanans watched the departure of these, the flower of their protective armies, with grim foreboding. Said the Helena *Independent*: ". . . it ain't two to one they don't get away with Gibbon." Of course, it was not Gibbon that they got away with, but rather General George A.

Custer and much of his Seventh Cavalry, which represented the major part of General Terry's command. The outcome of this three-pronged "pincer" offensive has been told and retold so often that it need not be extensively recounted here.

First, Crazy Horse turned back Crook's column at the Battle of the Rosebud on June 17, in effect removing his force from the coming showdown. The commands of Terry and Gibbon had meanwhile met on the Yellowstone. Realizing that the major Indian concentration lay to the south, probably on the Little Big Horn River, the commanders decided to send the swift Seventh Cavalry on a sweep to strike them from the south. In the meantime, they would bring the slower infantry-cavalry forces up the Big Horn to hit the hostiles from the north.

Custer advanced up Rosebud Creek, across the divide to the Little Big Horn, and on June 25—one day earlier than the target date set by Terry—he attacked the enormous Indian encampment. In the dramatic battle which ensued, Custer and over 260 of his men died. Those surviving, under Major Marcus Reno and Captain Frederick Benteen, were rescued by the arrival of Terry and Gibbon on June 27. The victorious Indians fled southward.

Montanans learned the shocking news even before it reached nearby Dakota, and they were the first to relay it to the outside world. General Terry quickly dashed off a report and sent one of Gibbon's scouts, "Muggins" Taylor, to carry it to Fort Ellis for telegraphic dispatch to the east. When he reached the Stillwater River, Taylor met a Helena *Herald* reporter, W. H. Norton, and told him the news. Norton hurriedly wrote his report and persuaded a local rancher named Horace Countryman to take his account to Helena. Taylor arrived at Fort Ellis on July 3, turned over the dispatches to the commanding officer, and passed on the news to the Bozeman *Times*, which put out a frantic special edition that very night.

Bozeman missed the chance of originating the hottest news story of 1876, however, when the local telegrapher held the dispatches for two days before mailing them to Chicago. Countryman reached Helena with the news on July 4, just in time to dampen the festivities commemorating the Centennial of Independence. A. J. Fisk of the *Herald* immediately rushed out a special edition and wired an account of the battle to Salt Lake City, whence it passed to points east. These spotty Helena dispatches preceded the more famous ones from Bismarck, Dakota Territory, by a full day. The news, often wildly exaggerated and inaccurate, hit the nation like a bombshell, just at the Independence Day peak of the Centennial celebrations. George Custer, already a popular favorite, instantly passed into legend as a martyred hero and Montana became, at least for a moment, something more than an unfamiliar province in the wilds of the American west.

Montana reacted to the news of Custer's defeat with anger, outrage, and fear. Some observers directly criticized Custer himself. The *Weekly Missoulian* accused him of acting "in disobedience to orders," while the Fort Benton *Record* went even further, charging him with "rash and unjustifiable disobedience" and concluding that other officers had been court-martialed and shot for less. Most local commentators, however, viewed Custer sympathetically and blamed his fate on the negligence of his superiors and the shortcomings of the Grant Administration. Virginia City's *Madisonian* voiced a common frontier sentiment by denouncing "the blundering policy of a powerful government which entrusted the care of savages to the prayers of the churches rather than to the muskets of the soldiers."

Citing the Republican President's removal of Custer from command of the Dakota column after the colonel had testified about corruption in the Indian Bureau, the Democratic Helena *Independent* put the blame squarely on Grant's shoulders: ". . . the heroic Custer fell a sacrifice to Grant's remorseless hate. He sent him to the Indian country to die, and his purpose has been fulfilled."

More to the political point, the equally Democratic Bozeman *Times* contrasted the administration's military neglect of the West with its use of federal troops to occupy the defeated South: "The blame rests with the President—with the War Department—which neglects the soldiers and treats the real enemy with indifference, and uses the army to dragoon the South into the support of the Republican candidate for President."

More immediately, residents of Montana fretted about the Sioux and Cheyennes, who were still on the loose while Generals Crook and Terry seemed unable to apprehend them. Some alarmists feared a bloodbath like the one which the Sioux had inflicted on Minnesota in the early years of the Civil War. Others weighed the possibility that the Sioux might align against them with nearby Indians, like "our old friends, the Blackfeet." More realistically, many Montanans felt that Fort Ellis and Camp Baker could not adequately defend the eastern settlements. In the nervous Gallatin Valley, ordinarily reliable citizens reported seeing Sioux signal fires in the nearby mountains. Citizens in remote Fort Benton were especially apprehensive. They were afraid that, in its pursuit of Sitting Bull, the Army would push the Sioux through the Judith country toward the river town.

In the meantime, an interesting little counterpoint was being played out. A Philadelphia Quaker and noted paleontologist named Edward Drinker Cope was disregarding local fears and insisting upon outfitting an expedition into the Bears Paw Mountains in search of fossils. Despite the fact that most of the men deserted him in the field, Cope succeeded in making important finds, identifying twenty-one dinosaur species. In September, his men hauled almost a ton of bones to Carroll for shipment down the Missouri.

In 1876, however, most thoughts were on the hostile Indians, and almost everyone agreed that the Army was too undermanned and too hesitant to retaliate against the hostiles. And they agreed that major military posts must be erected at once in the Yellowstone country. General Sheridan and Delegate Martin Maginnis had been pushing Congress for three years to fund such posts, but now the shock of the Custer debacle prompted fast action. Congress provided the necessary funds, along with an increase in enlistments, and preparations began at once for construction of the Yellowstone posts. These two elaborate military bases—Fort Keogh at the mouth of the Tongue River, and Fort Custer at the juncture of the Big Horn and Little Big Horn rivers—would be completed along with smaller Fort Missoula to the west in 1877. The months following the Custer battle saw considerable activity in southeastern Montana. Terry and Crook led their large armies in slow and unrewarding pursuit of the hostiles, and other military units arrived to reinforce them. Meanwhile enthusiastic Montana contractors moved supplies for them down the Yellowstone in mackinaw boats and Diamond R freight wagons. To the anger and disgust of most Montanans, the great armies of the 1876 campaign broke up early in September and left the Yellowstone country; Crook followed the Indian bands into Dakota, and Terry and Gibbon returned their men to the forts from which they had come.

A relatively small infantry command under Colonel Nelson A. Miles, based in cantonment at the mouth of the Tongue River where the settlement soon to become Miles City began to rise, would police eastern Montana during the coming winter. This, naturally enough, looked like neglect to the edgy Montana settlements. But, beginning in October and November, the able and energetic Miles launched highly successful winter marches against the Indians which soon broke their will to fight. In October he fought a skillful series of battles with Sitting Bull north of the Yellowstone, and in November and December his troops combed through north-central and northeastern Montana, keeping the Indians under constant pressure. As the year ended, Miles headed southward up the Tongue Valley, and early in January, 1877, engaged Crazy Horse in the stand-off Battle of Wolf Mountain. Harassed by Miles in Montana and by Crook in Wyoming, the hostiles soon gave up the fight and returned to the agencies.

The Centennial year ended on a mixed note, so far as Montana's "Indian question" was concerned. While Montanans still feared the hostile bands, they also felt sure that the coming year would remove this "threat" and would open their communication routes to the east. They began to learn of the dashing Miles' successes at year's end, and they embraced him at once as their hero.

For the Sioux and Cheyennes, on the other hand, the victory over Custer provided only a brief respite. By the autumn of 1877, their war had ended. They, along with the other tribes of the region, faced a dismal future. The great buffalo hunts, already well under way in 1876, would, in the next seven years, erase the once enormous herds which had sustained the Indian way of life. Ahead, on shrinking reservations, lay years of degradation and despair.

Making a cut for the Northern Pacific Railroad in the Sweet Briar Valley, west of Bismarck, 1879   (F. Jay Haynes, photographer, Haynes Foundation Collection, Montana Historical Society Photograph Archives)

The Firewagon Road

by Robert G. Athearn

During the two decades following the building of the Union Pacific Railroad, the American public watched the further growth of this and other roads with continued fascination. Over the main lines poured thousands of passengers and untold tons of freight; along the spreading branches filtered settlers, bound for freshly-opened lands and a new life. Cities sprang up, states were created, western maps underwent continued alteration.

These changes were both dramatic and tangible, easily translated into impressive statistics that swelled the national pride. Often obscured by the clouds of steam, the shriek of whistles, and the rush to subdivide the virgin prairie, however, was the enormous change wrought on what has been termed the Indian-military frontier.

The "old" army, scattered across a land of endless distances, fragmented into ineffectual atoms, was transformed into a more economical and efficient entity by the introduction of modern rail transportation. The frontiers it had once guarded were at once made more accessible to troops and less dangerous to settlers. The same railroad that shuttled soldiers back and forth and supplied their needs also brought in hordes of settlers whose very numbers suffocated the Indian threat.

Lack of an efficient and inexpensive form of transportation had barred the way to earlier settlements in the trans-Missouri West. So had it complicated the role of the military in subduing that region. Army men were among the first to discover the high cost of supplying a population in remote areas, a discovery accentuated by the acquisition of the Southwest following the Mexican War.

Then, a few years later, with the development of mines through the West, came new demands for protection against the Indians. In the space of a few short years, military requirements in the West

*Robert G. Athearn, "The Firewagon Road," *Montana The Magazine of Western History*, 20 (Spring 1970), 2-19.

soared; along with them came unheard-of demands for appropriations. By the early post-Civil War years, Congress was asked to furnish more than five and a half million dollars annually to supply
troops in New Mexico and Arizona alone, a figure that did not include the cost of Indian agencies, the transportation of mail, or supporting territorial government.[1]

At that time the cost of shipping goods from the Missouri River
to Colorado was $1.45 per hundred pounds per hundred miles. The
Quartermaster General reported an expenditure of $3,314,495 for
Colorado military establishments in the year 1866.[2] Two years later
the Cheyenne *Leader* stated that the average cost of government transportation on the completed section of the Union Pacific Railroad
was ten and one-half cents per ton mile; in a single year the road
had saved the government nearly two million dollars. "Goods are now
brought from Omaha to this city at a saving of at least two-thirds
of the amount formerly paid for wagon rates of transportation," said
that journal.[3]

It was a well-recognized fact that transportation costs comprised
a substantial portion of western prices. The army, as well as the
civilian population, felt this keenly. During the winter of 1865-66,
for example, the garrison at Fort Sedgwick, Colorado, and the
residents of nearby Julesburg, paid $105 per cord for wood, a price
set by government contract. The wood was purchased in Denver for
about twenty dollars a cord; the actual cost of haulage added some
sixty to seventy-five dollars. The remainder was profit realized by the
contractors. The advent of rail service shattered this price structure;
wood fuel was not only cheaper, but very shortly coal was available
from the Wyoming beds.[4]

The *Leader* called the railroad one of the best investments ever
made by the United States, for it not only reduced prices but provided a key to the development of a country destined to remain in
its native condition until such facilities were available.

Viewing the newly completed road, in 1869, the Committee on the
Pacific Railroad studied a compilation of governmental military ex-
penditures for the preceding 37 years, concluding that the Indian

1. Report of the Committee on the Pacific Railroad, 1869. *Sen. Report* 219, 40th
Cong., 3d Sess. (Serial 1362), 29.

2. Ovando J. Hollister, *The Mines of Colorado,* (Springfield, Mass.: S. Bowles,
1867), 443.

3. Cheyenne *Leader,* September 12, 1868. A New York paper thought the saving
in freight charges would pay interest on the entire obligation of such a railroad. New
York *Evening Express,* October 28, 1867.

4. William M. Thayer, *Marvels of the New West* (1887; reprinted, Norwich, Conn.:
Henry Bill Publishing Co., 1890), 277.

Wars during that period had cost the nation 20,000 lives and more than $750,000,000. During 1864 and 1865 alone, the Quartermaster's department spent over twenty-eight millions for military service against the Indians in the country through which transcontinental service was planned.

The Chairman of the House Committee on Indian Affairs estimated that current expenses for military campaigns against the natives were running to a million dollars a week. Nine weeks of such campaigning would cost as much as the interest on a sum necessary to build additional lines to the Pacific Coast. The Committee con-cluded that not only were the roads an economy to be felt immedi-ately, but that their existence would replace the buffalo with cattle and grain fields, thus effecting a "final solution" to the problem of the hostile tribes.[5]

In addition to the money that could be saved by the War Depart-ment, the railroad promised to greatly simplify the logistical prob-lem of the western Army. General William Tecumseh Sherman, under whose command the plains country fell commented in 1867 that the railroads "aid us materially in our military operations by transport-ing troops and stores rapidly across a belt of land hitherto only passed in summer by slow trains drawn by oxen, dependent on the grass for food; and all the States and Territories west have a direct depen-dence on these roads for their material supplies."

He predicted that when the lines passing westward through Nebraska and Kansas reached the Rockies, and when the Indian title to the country lying between was extinguished, then the problem of Indian hostilities would be comparatively easy, for "this belt of coun-try will naturally fill up with our own people who will permanently separate the hostile Indians of the north from those of the south, and allow us to direct our military forces on one or the other at pleasure. . . ."[6]

Captain Eugene F. Ware, who had campaigned along the Platte River in 1864, later wrote: "Soon the Union Pacific Railroad was built, and the Indian problem was solved."[7]

By this overly-simplified statement, Ware meant that Sherman's prediction had come true: that the Union Pacific, in Nebraska, and what was later known as the Kansas Pacific, in Kansas, formed a long steel fence that cordoned off a vast belt of land running between the Missouri River and the Rockies. Into it poured settlers who drove

5. Report of the Committee on the Pacific Railroad, 15, 16.

6. Report of W. T. Sherman, October 1, 1867, in Report of the Secretary of War, 1867. *House Exec. Doc.* 1, Part 1, 40th Cong., 2d Sess. (Serial 1324), 36.

7. Captain Eugene F. Ware, *The Indian War of 1864* (1911; reprinted, Lincoln: Univer-sity of Nebraska Press, 1963), 405.

off the buffalo, fenced the land, and made life untenable for the tribes. It was as though a huge snowplow had wedged its way west, turning Indians to either side. While this did not occur as easily or as quickly as Ware's comment suggested, nevertheless it proved to be the ultimate course of events.

Those who anticipated the settlement of the West regarded the railroad as a key instrument for cutting away the barriers that blocked the way. As construction began in 1865, a St. Louis paper foresaw a "settlement of the Indian troubles and difficulties" resulting from the project. In a statement that characterized much of the thinking of the time, the paper argued that the money spent in placating the peaceful Indians and fighting the hostiles would alone be sufficient to build the road. Given easy, safe and cheap passage, the settlers would flow westward in great numbers, erecting new states and diluting the Indian danger as time passed.[8]

A Chicago paper took much the same point of view, asserting that the railroad builders were performing a more effective service in preventing Indian depredations than the entire army could accomplish by more direct methods. The editor predicted that an "all conquering civilization will be borne upon the wings of steam to the uttermost parts of the western plains, preparing the way for safe and rapid settlement by white men, and compelling the savages to either adopt civilization or suffer extinction."[9]

A contemporary writer used this same theme when he predicted that the locomotive's whistle would announce the coming of an "aggressive civilization" that would force the natives into a last stand for barbarism, a battle that they would lose against force of numbers, leaving them no alternative but submission or death.[10]

The Secretary of the Interior, who understood the force of the westward movement, agreed that the railroad had indeed placed Indian-White relations in what he termed "a new and interesting aspect," one that he thought demanded the concentration of Indians upon reservations to save them from annihilation.[11] It was out of this thinking that the great reservations of the northern plains finally were established.

---

8. St. Louis *Democrat*, quoted in the *Rocky Mountain News*, September 27, 1865; Chicago *Journal*, November 18, 1867; *New York Evening Post*, October 31, 1867.

9. *Chicago Journal*, November 18, 1867.

10. W. C. Church, "The Pacific Railroad," *Galaxy*, August, 1867, p. 491. Louis Simonin, a French traveler, also predicted that the Indian would have to merge with the white or be destroyed, Louis Simonin, *The Rocky Mountain West in 1867* (1867; reprinted, Lincoln: University of Nebraska Press, 1966), 142.

11. Report of the Secretary of the Interior, 1867, *House Exec. Doc.* 1, 40th Cong., 2d Sess. (Serial 1326), 7.

Residents of the West's farthest reaches observed the approach of railroads and looked forward to a day when their area would be served. In 1868, an Oregonian who had recently served his state as Surveyor General, told members of Congress that a branch line to his state would not only be of great service to its people, but would help solve some major western problems for the federal government.

Asserting that the Pacific Railroad already had demonstrated that "railroads increase population and commerce, and advance civilization, in new countries, more than all other agencies combined," he concluded that "nothing but the advancement of a permanent civilization can settle Indian wars. . . ." Should a road be constructed to Oregon, predicted the Oregonian, the number of troops in the area could be greatly reduced and the cost of hauling supplies to the remainder would be reduced as much as eighty per cent. The government, he contended, would profit even if it granted the bonds necessary for construction—he suggested thirteen millions worth—for it would probably save as much as three million dollars a year. In no time at all the cost of such a road would be thus recovered.[12]

Arguments by the white population of the West, to the effect that the coming of railroads would aid the army in "solving" the Indian problem, were not lost upon the natives. Many of them objected to the appearance of the "firewagon," as they called the steam locomotive, because they feared its power and were mystified by its noisy functioning. More thoughtful men among Indian leaders foresaw that the ultimate effect of this new technology would be detrimental to their people. But to the average tribesman that form of danger probably appeared to lie in the distant future and therefore was not matter for today's concern.

Even though there were large numbers of Indians on the plains, it was difficult for the leadership to organize a great fighting force to campaign any distance from the home country. The powerful and capable Sioux, who would long resist white encroachments, could have given the rail builders a great deal more trouble than they did had the threat seemed more immediate. For years their hunting parties had ranged the country where the Union Pacific proposed to lay its first tracks, but some of the more conservative and more philosophically inclined leaders undoubtedly held that there were still plenty of buffalo to be found north of that country. In any event, there appeared to be no great disposition on the part of the majority to wage an all-out war over this issue.

---

12. P. J. Pengra, *Oregon Branch of the Pacific Railroad* (Washington, D.C.: McGill & Witherow, [1868]), 1-15.

Small war parties sporadically harassed surveyors and later, the rail layers, as they moved westward along the Platte River. Union Pacific officials objected to such sniping and continually asked for more military protection. In the spring of 1867, Thomas C. Durant told General Grant that such raids were interfering seriously with surveyors who were trying to lay out the line in what is now Wyoming. He warned that unless the Indians could be kept away from these men, there was a danger that surveying would have to be suspended.[13]

Samuel Reed, one of the railroad's engineers, admitted that the natives were decidedly hostile, that "some men have been killed and a large amount of stock lost." However, he said, the attacks had merely caused delays, not a work stoppage.[14]

T. J. Carter, a Government Director of the Union Pacific, also spoke of the matter but he, too, used terms no stronger than "embarrassment" as opposed to language that suggested any possibility of abandoning the project.[15]

Most of the attacks were raids executed by roving bands of Indians who frequently picked off isolated individuals or very small groups of workers. For example, Nebraska papers carried a story in May, 1867, describing the killing of an engineer from one of the surveying parties at work in Wyoming. Significantly, the Indians did not attack the party itself, or its military escort, but swooped down upon two men who had separated themselves from the group, killing one of them.[16]

During the next month, similar strikes were made, in each case the targets being small and isolated groups. In one instance, a stagecoach carrying a single passenger was attacked, but there were no casualties.[17]

About the same time a band of 25 or 30 raiders threatened a group of railroad workers, but elected not to attack. Instead they cut off an army deserter who was trying to leave the country and killed him before the workers could come to his rescue.[18]

Occasionally Indians became bolder and attacked working parties, but in most cases no great numbers on either side were involved in the incidents. One of the most publicized of these events was the foray

---

13.   T. C. Durant to U. S. Grant, May 23, 1867. Tuttle Correspondence, 1867-1869, Union Pacific Archives, Omaha, Nebraska (hereafter UP).

14.   Report of Samuel B. Reed, September 1, 1867. Leonard Collection, University of Iowa Library, Iowa City.

15.   T. J. Carter to Orville Browning, July 23, 1867. Report of the Government Directors, *Sen. Exec. Doc.* 69, 47th Cong., 1st Sess. (Serial 2336), 33-34.

16.   Plattesmouth, Nebraska *Herald,* May 29, 1867.

17.   Ibid., June 12, 1867.

18.   Ibid., June 19, 1867.

near Plum Creek in August, 1867, in which several men were killed. In this instance the Indians used tools left by section hands who were repairing track a few miles west of present Lexington, Nebraska, to remove spikes and bend the rails sufficiently to derail any train that made its way along the road. The Indians had cut the telegraph line and some half-dozen men had been sent out by hand car to discover why messages had ceased to flow along the line.

When their vehicle hit the road block, and spilled its occupants, some 40 Indians came out of the tall grass where they had hidden and launched an attack. At the height of the action, a freight train of about 25 cars came along and it, too, was wrecked, killing the engineer and fireman. The conductor, who was injured, ran back to Plum Creek and spread the alarm.

The next day a group of armed civilians returned to the scene and found the Indians still celebrating by riding around the site with streamers of calico taken from the wreckage tied to the tails of their horses, while others attended to two barrels of whiskey that had been part of the cargo. When the leader of the celebrants was picked off by the first shot fired, his followers promptly fled and the rescue party set about cleaning up the wreckage. One of the workers, who had been aboard the hand-car, lived to tell the tale, even though he had been scalped. Retrieving his lost hairpiece, he had it tanned and carried around later to show, and horrify, his acquaintances.

The Plum Creek affair was, therefore, more bizarre than most of the raids against the road and it attracted considerable attention at the time.[19] In this instance, the Union Pacific could not cry out for additional troops or criticize the government for laxity in its protection, because the road itself was somewhat at fault for sending out such a small party when Indians were known to be in the area. Andrew J. Poppleton, a company attorney, admitted that this was the case when he later discussed the claims for damage that had arisen out of the event. He told President Oliver Ames that a suit involving some $9,000 in claims for property lost by shippers probably would go against the road, due to its own negligence. Laconically he noted that the matter undoubtedly could be settled for fifty cents on the dollar, and he recommended that such a course be followed.[20]

Complaints over Indian harassments mounted during 1868. During that year, as the workers moved across western Nebraska and approached Cheyenne, their isolation was more apparent to wandering bands of Indians who never lost an opportunity to attack if the

---

19. Michael Delahunty, "The Plum Creek Railroad Attack, 1867," *Nebraska History,* 7 (April-June 1924), 38, 39.

20. Andrew J. Poppleton to Oliver Ames, August 26, 1870, President's Office, Letters Received, August 1870-January 1871, UP.

odds were right. The Cheyenne *Leader* complained about the situation periodically, asserting that the government had granted lands for railroad construction for the purpose of opening and developing the western country, and it therefore had the responsibility of protecting those who had answered the call. It was perfectly clear to the editor that the railway and Indians could not exist together. "One of them must relinquish," he insisted. "If the railroad is to succeed, the Indian must retire, but if the Indian is to rule, there can be neither railway nor settlements."[21]

Late in April a mass meeting was held at Cheyenne to complain about the government's laxity in protecting the rail route, at which time a committee was appointed to memorialize Congress on the subject. Anticipating the arrival of General Sherman on one of his inspection tours, residents called for yet another meeting to discuss the matter with him.[22]

Without giving any figures, the editor of the *Leader* assured his readers that between their city and North Platte, the Indians were said to be thicker than fiddlers in Hell.[23] He bitterly criticized the "feeble, listless opposition offered by the U.S. troops," and predicted that all-out war was an immediate prospect for those unfortunate enough to live in the region.[24]

In response to the complaints, Sherman promised that Generals Alfred Terry and Christopher Augur would protect the Union Pacific "with jealous care," and that they would round up all the wandering bands of Sioux in the region, after which these Indians would be herded northward to reservations where they would be fed by the army.[25]

While Sherman's comments were formal and gave the appearance that he was not nearly as concerned about the situation as were editors along the line of the road, his interest in the project was nevertheless real and of long duration. He argued that although the Union Pacific was in private hands, it had more than the usual claim for protection because of the government's pecuniary interest in the work. Aside from this, it promised to be of great assistance to the army and he shepherded rail workers from the Indians with the concern of a mother bear for her cubs.

In 1868, General Christopher C. Augur reported to his superiors that he had placed detachments of troops at every station between Fort Kearney and Cheyenne, plus some more at Forts Sanders and

---

21. Cheyenne *Leader*, April 30, 1868.
22. Ibid.
23. Ibid., June 22, 1868.
24. Ibid., August 29, 1868.
25. Report of W. T. Sherman, November 1, 1868, in Report of the Secretary of War, 1868, *House Exec. Doc.* 1, 40th Cong., 3d Sess. (Serial 1367), 7.

Steele in Wyoming.[26] When more soldiers were needed, Frank North organized four companies of Pawnee Indian scouts, fifty men to a company, to patrol the line. As his brother, Luther, commented, the tribes knew that the road meant the extinction of their way of life and they resented it.[27]

Despite their sporadic raids, however, the Indians were not a major problem or a real deterrent to construction crews. General Augur stated that due to the precautions taken by the army, no serious attempt at interference with construction occurred in 1868.[28] Editors and concerned residents of towns along the road did not share his viewpoint. To them, even the smallest of interruptions to this great work could not be tolerated.

Before the Union Pacific reached Promontory in Utah, it began to influence both the Indians and the disposition of troops in the West. In August, 1868, posts along the Bozeman Trail that ran along the Big Horn Mountains and into Montana, were abandoned. The action is still heralded by pro-Indian historians as a great victory for the Sioux and as a great defeat for the army. As Sherman correctly pointed out, those posts, built in 1865 and 1866 for the benefit of travelers to Montana, "had almost ceased to be of any practical use to them by reason of the building of the Union Pacific railroad . . ."

The trail never had been used by any regularly organized freight lines, but rather was fortified in response to heavy pressure for a shortcut into the mining country. The route north of the Utah communities was much shorter and along it lived Indians less hostile than the Sioux. While the army was capable of keeping open the Bozeman Trail, the expense of doing so, considering the traffic it bore, was needless.[29]

Some of the troops formerly stationed at forts in that area were transferred to Fort Fred Steele, in Wyoming, and the rest were sent back to Omaha. It was here that the economy effected by the road was demonstrated. General Augur reported that it was now cheaper to winter the soldiers at Omaha than to build new quarters in the

---

26. Sherman's Report of October 1, 1867; Report of C. C. Augur, October 14, 1868, in Report of the Secretary of War, 1868, *House Exec. Doc.* 1, 40th Cong., 3d Sess. (Serial 1367), 22.

27. Copy of an address delivered by Captain Luther North at Chadron, Nebraska, June 21, 1933, Luther Heddon North Papers, Nebraska State Historical Society, Lincoln.

28. Report of C. C. Augur, October 14, 1868.

29. Report of W. T. Sherman, November 1868, in Report of the Secretary of War, 1868. *House Exec. Doc.*, 1, 40th Cong., 3d Sess. (Serial 1367), 3. See also, Robert G. Athearn, *William Tecumseh Sherman and the Settlement of the West* (Norman: University of Oklahoma Press, 1956), 198.

more remote West and to supply them.[30] Should the occasion arise, detachments could be sent forth by rail at any time of year.

In commenting upon the completion of the Kansas Pacific to Denver, in 1870, General John Pope remarked that the existence of the new road greatly simplified the number and location of military posts under his jurisdiction. It also revealed to the army the most suitable sites for permanent establishments along the route. Henceforth, supplies and men could be shuttled rapidly from point to point, saving both time and money.

In the General's words: "It becomes practicable, therefore, to conduct military operations with facility over the larger part of this department (of the Missouri), to receive immediate intelligence, and to concentrate troops rapidly." He heartily endorsed the policy of maintaining larger—hence more economical—posts along rail lines from which points troops could be dispatched into hostile country during the campaigning season and wintered at the larger bases where facilities were better and the morale was higher.[31]

The new mobility now open to the military was not lost upon the Indians who were also impressed by the speed and efficiency of the railroads. In 1879, at the time of the Ute uprising in Colorado, troops were moved in from both east and north to help quell the disturbance.

During that operation, a small incident occurred that went almost unnoticed in the exciting events of the day. Passengers on a southbound Utah and Northern train noticed two rifle-carrying Indians come aboard. Upon inquiry as to their destination, the warriors said they were headed for Salt Lake City where they planned to take the Union Pacific eastward to some point in Wyoming from which place they planned to join the Colorado Utes in their struggle with the bluecoats. Apparently no move was made to halt these reinforcements; contemporary newsmen expressed amusement at the resourcefulness of the natives in utilizing modern facilities in moving to the front.

From the time the Union Pacific construction crews first pushed westward, a regrouping of troops was commenced in the western country. General Sheridan reported, in 1869, that elements of two cavalry and three infantry regiments were stationed at strategic points on the road from Omaha Barracks to Camp Douglas near Salt Lake City.[32]

---

30.   Report of Augur, October 14, 1868, p. 23. See also George A. Crofutt, *Crofutt's New Overland Tourist* (1878; reprinted, Omaha: Overland Publishing Co., 1880), 88; and W. F. Rae, *Westward by Rail* (New York: D. Appleton & Co., 1871), 93.

31.   Report of General John Pope, Headquarters, Department of Missouri, October 31, 1870. Report of the Secretary of War, 1870. *House Exec. Doc.* 1, Part 2, 41st Cong., 3d Sess. (Serial 1446), 11.

32.   Report of Philip H. Sheridan, November 1, 1869, in Report of the Secretary of War, 1869, *House Exec. Doc.* 1, Part 2, 41st Cong., 2d Sess. (Serial 1412), 36.

During the years that followed, smaller posts continually gave way to larger and more permanent bases. Recognizing that such establishments not only offered protection—and hence encouraged settlement—but that they were of economic value, Denver called loudly for consideration. A local editor asked for a large depot to supply military posts in Colorado and neighboring communities, arguing that it was not only necessary and economical, but that "our people have a right to some of the patronage of the government."[33]

Although the spread of rail transportation lessened governmental expenses over known routes, it also tended to push the frontiers of settlement outward, generating new demands for protection. In 1870, Secretary of War William Belknap admitted that the railroad across the plains had saved the American people much money, but "with the opening to settlement of the wilder portions of the country, army posts are pushed further and further into the wilderness, and as the stations are extended the expenses of transportation are and will remain very great."[34]

This, however, was part of America's westward expansion and it was the railroad that made such growth possible. As new posts were required in more remote areas, older forts nearer the tracks were broken up and abandoned. Troops would continue to be stationed near the Union Pacific for a few years. but their days were numbered. As settlers poured in, towns grew, and a white population bulked large in the land, the Indians moved back.

In the autumn of 1872 General Philip Sheridan noted the rapid expansion of rails and said that no additional protection had been necessary for the Union Pacific or the Kansas Pacific that year. Already the roads had begun to have their effect on the central plains. The deeper thrust into unsettled areas, mentioned by Secretary Belknap, was made possible by the entering wedge driven through Nebraska and Kansas.

The frontier movement, which had moved forward for over two hundred years, now gathered momentum; soon it would break into a gallop. Before long the Northern Pacific would accelerate its drive through the Dakotas and Montana, injecting new hordes of farmers into Indian country.

In 1872, Francis A. Walker, Commissioner of Indian Affairs, predicted that this development "will of itself completely solve the great Sioux problem, and leave ninety thousand Indians ranging between the two transcontinental lines as incapable of resisting the

---

33. *Rocky Mountain News,* July 30, 1870.
34. Report of the Secretary of War, 1870, *House Exec. Doc.* 1, Part 2, 41st Cong. 3d Sess. (Serial 1446), vii.

Government as are the Indians of New York or Massachusetts." He predicted that army columns moving north from the Union Pacific and south from the Northern Pacific would crush the Sioux and their allies "as between the upper and nether millstones."[35] He was correct, as to the feasibility of his millstone theory. That the events that followed would completely solve the Sioux problem was true only from the white man's point of view.

As the railroad network spread in the West, recognition of its utility to the military arm grew. During 1877 Union Pacific officials talked of building a branch across Wyoming and into Montana. General George Crook, then commanding the Department of the Platte with headquarters at Omaha, gave his enthusiastic endorsement to such a plan. Not only would such a line save money and open up new country to settlers, but it would "have a most salutary and positive effect in settling our Indian troubles."[36]

The Government Directors of the Union Pacific agreed with Crook, holding that wherever railroads went "the Indian question is practically settled." They supported their contention with the argument that "from the vast domain covered by the Union Pacific Road, its connecting lines, and the settlements included by them, Indian troubles have disappeared, and the cost of the Indian service, generally, has been greatly reduced."[37]

Among the generals, none seemed more impressed by the rapid settlement of the railroad West than was Phil Sheridan. In 1878 he called the emigration to Kansas unparalled, while that entering Nebraska, Colorado, Utah and Wyoming was "not far behind in acquiring population." He guessed that some two millions of settlers had recently spread across the plains and mountain areas from Texas to Montana, where they were busily engaged in farming, mining and ranching. From their efforts, including that of town building, had emerged a whole new segment of the American economy "and the millions obtained by the sweat of their brow adds much more to trade, commerce, and prosperity of the world." His wonderment grew as he concluded that "all this comes from the development of a coun-

---

35. Report of General Philip H. Sheridan, October 12, 1872, in Report of the Secretary of War, 1872, *House Exec. Doc.* 1, Part 2, 42d Cong., 3d Sess. (Serial 1558), 36; Report of the Commissioner of Indian Affairs, 1872, in Report of the Secretary of the Interior 1872, *House Exec. Doc.* 1, Part 5, 42d Cong., 3d Sess. (Serial 1560), 397.

36. George Crook to J. H. Millard (Government Director of the Union Pacific), October 9, 1877, Reports of the Directors of the Union Pacific Railroad Company, 1864 to 1886, *Sen. Exec. Doc.* 69th, 47th Cong., 1st Sess. (Serial 2336), 136.

37. Ibid., 128.

This photograph, taken at Fort Sanders, Wyoming, in July 1868, documents the close rela-tionship between military and railroad men. Pictured from left are Sidney Dillon (Union Pacific); unknown; Lt. Gen. Philip H. Sheridan; Mrs. J. H. Potter; Brig. Gen. Frederick Dent; Mrs. John Gibbon; Col. John Gibbon; John Gibbon, Jr.; Ulysses S. Grant; Katie Gibbon; Mrs. Kilburn; Allie Potter; Grenville M. Dodge (chief engineer, UP); Lt. Gen. William T. Sherman; Lt. Col. Adam L. Slemmer; Maj. Gen. William S. Harney; Thomas C. Durant (UP vice-president); and Lt. Col. Joseph H. Potter. (National Park Service)

try which only ten years ago was the land of the Indian, the buffalo, and the elk."[38]

In 1882, as Sheridan watched the Utah and Northern enter Montana, he commented that this and similar extensions of main lines not only developed new country but wrought a change in the western army. He reiterated the conviction that this additional service made more obvious the desirability of abandoning small posts and concentrating the men in larger units. Instead of a scattering of weak and isolated western forts, the army now could maintain large garrisons that were not only cheaper to supply, but at these places the

---

38.   Report of General P. H. Sheridan, October 25, 1878, in Report of the Secretary of War, 1878, *House Exec. Doc.* 1, Part 2, 45th Cong., 3d Sess. (Serial 1843), 38.

discipline was better, not to mention the improved daily living conditions of the soldiers. "I have already selected points with a view
to such a concentration," he wrote, "as soon as the condition of
Indian affairs will admit of the withdrawal of troops from the more
remote places."[39]

The General was aware of his own great enthusiasm for railroads
in the West and he was almost apologetic for constant references to
it in his reports. But, as he explained in one of them, this new instrument of steel was already a significant factor in reshaping military
strategy on the high plains; its use was regarded as being a prime
significance in the solution of the army's most urgent current
problem — the American Indian.[40]

General Pope also recommended the policy of concentrating
troops at larger posts. In 1879 he suggested the elimination of several
smaller outposts on the ground that they no longer fulfilled any important military object. For example, he said, Forts Larned and Hays,
in Kansas, and Fort Lyon, in Colorado, had by now outlived their
original usefulness because of the coming of the railroad. The country in which they had been located originally as defensive positions
was now so well settled that there was little likelihood of any successful Indian uprisings in those parts. Such places were, to use Pope's
words, "out of position;" that is, they were so far away from potential
Indian trouble that it would be difficult to transport their garrisons
to areas where trouble was apt to occur.[41]

George W. McCrary, Secretary of War, agreed that the revolution
of the rails had left the War Department with a large number of
useless military reservations. The advance of settlement had con-
verted what were once vital military sites into property that had
become "simply a source of expense to the United States."[42]

William T. Sherman, the redoubtable man who now held the rank
of General of the Army and was its senior officer, read the reports
of his subordinates with interest. Having followed the progress of
railroad construction since the laying of the first Union Pacific rails
at Omaha, he was perhaps the greatest rail enthusiast among army
men. More than once he had recalled with pride that the Union
Pacific's first locomotive had borne his name and he was aware that
the little 22-ton engine had made history on the plains of Nebraska.

39. Report of General P. H. Sheridan, October 20, 1882, in Report of the Secretary
of War, 1882, *House Exec. Doc.* 1, Part 2, Vol. I, 47th Cong., 2d Sess. (Serial 2091), 80.

40. Report of Philip H. Sheridan, October 22, 1880, in Report of the Secretary
of War, 1880, *House Exec. Doc.* 1, Part 2, 46th Cong., 3d Sess. (Serial 1952), 56.

41. Report of General John Pope, October 3, 1879, in Report of the Secretary of
War, 1879, *House Exec. Doc.* 1, Part 2, 46th Cong., 2d Sess. (Serial 1903), 83.

42. Report of the Secretary of War, 1879, *op. cit.*, iv.

By 1880 the General, now nearing retirement age, concluded that western railroads had "completely revolutionized our country in the past few years." He agreed with the findings of his subordinates that these roads had wrought a complete change in the plains military situation by rendering useless the many small posts that once had guarded wagon and emigrant routes. He supported the recommendation that many of these places should be abandoned in favor of larger establishments where men and stores could be concentrated, to be dispatched by rail to any point of trouble. He suggested that the new forts might well be located at intersections of railroads, to make them as versatile as possible. He believed that some of them should be near the nation's borders.

The revolution, of which Sherman spoke, had so thoroughly met the problems of internal protection that future fortifications fell more into the category of national defense than at any time since the founding of the nation.[43] His beliefs coincided with those of the journalist, Albert Richardson, who had earlier talked of the role of the railroads in national defense and had labelled the locomotive as "the true apostle of the Monroe Doctrine."[44]

As Sherman viewed the nation's newer defensive posture, and looked back over the years since the conclusion of the Civil War, he commented upon the changes that had taken place in that relatively short span of time. At the beginning of the period, the trans-Mississippi West was, to use his words, "occupied by wild beasts, buffalo, elk, antelope, and deer, and by wilder Indians." But, through the courage of the western settlers, a great change had taken place and "this vast region has become reduced to a condition of comparative civilization."

The General explained one of the principal reasons for such a rapid change: "Three great railroads now traverse the continent, with branches innumerable, and a fourth is making rapid progress. States, Territories, cities, and towns have grown up; neat cattle have already displaced the buffalo; sheep and goats have replaced the elk, deer, and antelope; and crops of wheat, rye, barley, and oats are now grown in regions believed hitherto to be desert or inaccessible." This advance of settlement and this taming of the land, he said, "is the real cause of the great prosperity which now blesses our country and swells the coffers of our national Treasury."[45]

43.   Report of General W. T. Sherman, November 10, 1880, in Report of the Secretary of War, 1880. *House Exec. Doc.* 1, Part 2, 46th Cong., 3d Sess. (Serial 1952), 4.

44.   Richardson, quoted in the *Rocky Mountain News*, May 30, 1866. See also New York *Evangelist*, October 31, 1867, and the New York *Evening Mail*, November 12, 1867.

45.   Report of W. T. Sherman, November 6, 1882, in Report of the Secretary of War, 1882. *House Exec. Doc.* 1, Part 5, Vol. I, 47th Cong., 2d Sess. (Serial 2091), 5.

Nor was the nation at large the only beneficiary. The army itself, thought Sherman, faced a new and happier day because of the technological advance provided by rail service. For years western assignments had meant a life of privation and even suffering for both men and officers. Himself a hardened campaigner of many years, Sherman had seen the conditions under which his troops lived in these remote posts and he reacted strongly to the situation. During one of his inspections, in 1866, he stopped at Fort Sedgwick in eastern Colorado. After examining the men's quarters, the General called them "hovels in which a negro would hardly go," adding that if southern slaveholders had kept their field hands in such quarters "a sample would, ere this, have been carried to Boston and exhibited as illustrative of the cruelty and inhumanity of the masters."[46]

But, by the early eighties, thanks to the spread of rail service, said Sherman, many of these posts were being abandoned and the men were stationed at places where living conditions were much superior, where schools were available, and where the constant effort merely to keep alive no longer dominated daily life.

Gone, too, were many of the long and time-consuming marches across arid stretches. "Now almost every post in the army has railroad communication near, with mails, and connection by telegraphy to all parts of the world," he wrote. "In my judgment, the condition of the Army, officers and men, is incomparably better and more comfortable than it was twenty years ago." With all these advantages, thought the old General, army life would be sufficiently attractive to encourage enlistments by a larger and better group of men.[47]

Henry Poor, who grew famous for his late nineteenth century railroad publications, shared Sherman's view that military utilization of rail service had national implications. "The facility with which troops can, by its use, be thrown either upon the Pacific or into the interior of the continent, relieves it (the army) from the necessity of maintaining permanently large bodies . . . at points likely to be menaced," he wrote in 1879. The railroads to the Pacific, and all their branches, he concluded, had even eliminated the necessity of a large standing army "with all the vast expenditure and evils resulting from such an establishment."[48]

Military men, starved for appropriations and struggling against congressional tendencies to reduce the army, doubtless thought Poor had carried the idea of rapid transit too far.

---

46. "Protection Across the Continent," *House Exec. Doc.* 23, 39th Cong., 2d Sess. (Serial 1288), 6-8.

47. Report of General W. T. Sherman, November 3, 1881, in Report of the Secretary of War, 1881, *House Exec. Doc.* 1, Part 2, Vol. I, 47th Cong., 1st Sess. (Serial 2010), 39.

48. Henry Poor, "The Pacific Railroad," *North American Review*, 128 (June 1879), 670.

From the earliest days of Union Pacific construction, the army had looked forward to the development of railroads as an answer to many of its western problems. As construction crews of various roads spread their iron network across the barrenness beyond the Missouri River, there developed a warm relationship between railroaders and military men. Although the land grant roads were obliged to carry government traffic at half rate, and during the 1870's the Secretary of the Treasury withheld even this amount pending the outcome of litigation over the matter, the roads cooperated with military officials.

Not only did they provide transportation on regularly scheduled trains, but special service was available for any emergency. For example, in the autumn of 1879 Sidney Dillon directed his General Manager at Omaha to carry soldiers immediately to any point on the line when the situation demanded it. "The resources of the road are at the service of the Government for the protection of the settlers," he wrote.[49]

In another instance, during the presidency of Charles Francis Adams, Jr., the railroad's chief executive recommended the issuance of passes to one of the army officers. Although the road had severely restricted this practice, Adams explained his action with the comment: "As you are aware, we are under considerable obligation to officers of the army . . . , and they certainly are not an over-paid set of men."[50]

The War Department went to great lengths to show its appreciation for such ready cooperation on the part of the Union Pacific and other land grant roads. In 1878, after the government had for several years withheld money due landgrant railroads for transportation, the Secretary of War intervened in behalf of the roads. He argued that Congress had "greatly embarrassed" the operations in his department and he strongly recommended that the legislators rescind their actions, thus allowing the roads to collect money due on military accounts.[51] Although the legislators failed to respond to the request, and the matter was later settled in favor of the roads

---

49. Sidney Dillon to S. H. H. Clark, and Dillon to P. H. Sheridan, October 21, 1879, President's Office, Letters Sent, May 1879-February 1880, UP.

50. Charles Francis Adams, Jr. to S. R. Callaway, January 11, 1886, Adams-Callaway Correspondence, UP.

51. Report of the Secretary of War, 1878, *House Exec. Doc.* 1, Part 2, 45th Cong., 3d Sess. (Serial 1843), x. See also Edward H. Rollins to Lot M. Morrill (Secretary of the Treasury), September 9, 1876. Secretary and Treasurer, Letters Sent, June-November 1876, UP. The action of which the Secretary complained was a provision in the army appropriation act of June 16, 1874, that prohibited the payment of any money appropriated by the act from being used to pay land-grant roads for services rendered to the government.

through court action, the secretary's gesture was appreciated by the companies involved.[52]

In addition to the conveniences brought about by rail transportation, the army was ever aware that it had, over the years, saved a considerable sum of money by using the new facilities. For the first seven years of rail service on the Union Pacific alone, beginning in July, 1866, the government had spent slightly over $5 million for the haulage of troops and supplies. The cost of wagon transportation over the same routes was estimated at nearly $16 millions, or a difference of about 66 per cent.

Troops were carried by rail at approximately five cents a mile (throughrates) as opposed to twelve and a half cents by stagecoach. The average rate for through freight, by rail, was nineteen cents a hundred pounds per hundred miles; by wagon this would have ranged from $1.45 to $1.99 for the same distance. Here the government estimated that it had saved some $6 million.[53]

Since a number of military posts that existed during the 1870's and 1880's did not have rail service, and were served by stagecoach and wagon, the War Department had dramatic comparisons in transportation costs available with the issuance of each annual report. In 1873, for example, American railroads carried nearly 73,000 military personnel as compared to approximately 2,000 transported by wagon and stagecoach. Most of those using the older method of travel were in the West where rail service was still in its infancy. In that year the Union Pacific carried just under 6,200 military passengers.[54]

Although the figures for those carried by western railroads rose during the ensuing years, due to new construction, so did the statistics for horse-drawn vehicles. As late as 1880 the Quartermaster General reported that the army had forty-five contracts for wagon transportation and, during the preceding year, this method had moved over 4,000 passengers, and nearly 32,000 tons of supplies. [55]

52.   At the United States Pacific Railway Commission hearings in 1887, Union Pacific counsel John F. Dillon testified that "with very trifle exception, since the act of 1873, the Government has never paid to the Union Pacific Company the half transportation money which by the terms of the contract is due from the Government to the Company for Government services. And this is true not only prior to 1875, when it was expressly judged by the Supreme Court of the United States that this amount was due to the Company in cash, but it is equally true since that time . . . ," Testimony of John F. Dillon, Reports of the United States Pacific Railway Commission, 1887, II, *Sen. Exec. Doc.* 51st, 50th Cong., 1st Sess. (Serial 2505), 824.

53.   Report of Quartermaster General M. C. Meigs, January 28, 1873. *House Exec. Doc.* 169, 42d Cong., 3d Sess. (Serial 1567), 1-4. See also, Reports of the Government Directors for 1874 and 1876.

54.   Report of Quartermaster General M. C. Meigs, October 10, 1873. In Report of the Secretary of War, 1873. *House Exec. Doc.* 1, Part 5, 43d Cong., 1st Sess. (Serial 1597), 108.

55.   Report of Quartermaster General, 1880 in *House Exec. Doc.* 1, Part 2, 46th Cong., 3d Sess. (Serial 1952), 318–19.

Despite such an increase in wagon haulage, the great propor-tion of military traffic was by rail. In 1882, for example, the Union Pacific alone carried approximately that much army freight, while other roads hauled a proportionate amount. In that year the Union Pacific also transported nearly 12,000 military personnel and over 4,000 animals.[56]

Not only were new areas opened to settlement by the advent of rail service, but a good deal of country was occupied beyond its reach, in anticipation of such building. The army, therefore, was obliged to provide protection for ever-increasing numbers of communities that grew up in more remote regions and until railroads reached them transportation facilities were of the horse-drawn variety.

As early as 1883 the picture began to change considerably. In that year both the Northern Pacific and the Santa Fe had completed their main lines, opening vast sections of the West. The Denver & Rio Grande connected Salt Lake City to Denver in that year, while only months earlier the Utah and Northern had been finished from Salt Lake City to a connection with the Northern Pacific, in Montana.

With the completion of these and other principal western roads, such as the Southern Pacific, the country beyond the Missouri River was soon interlaced with trunk and branch lines that served a large part of what so recently had been a barren land. General Pope called this rapid spread of railroads to be "one of the wonders of this western country," saying that it seemed to progress without cessation. He predicted that "it will be but a short time before the whole region will be a network of railroads, and all Indian reservations of Indian country will be so easy of access from them that troops can be con-centrated so soon that any hostilities on a large scale can be dealt with almost as soon as begun."[57]

By the late 1880's the so-called Indian Wars were practically ended; only the final death struggle of the tribes remained to be enacted dur-ing the next few years. Already an era had passed; not only were there no "wild" Indians to be seen along that great swath the Union Pacific and Kansas Pacific had cut westward across the plains, but even the military forts that had once protected the roads were disappearing.

As early as 1871, Forts Kearney and Sedgwick were abandoned. The former, located in central Nebraska, had guarded the old Cali-fornia trail since 1848; the latter, first named Camp Rankin, was established in 1864 on the south bank of the Platte River in north-eastern Colorado to protect wagon travel. A half dozen years later North Platte Station, originally built as Camp Sergeant and intended

---

56. Report of Quartermaster General, 1882, in Report of the Secretary of War, 1882, *House Exec. Doc.* 1, Part 2, Vol. I, 47th Cong., 2d Sess. (Serial 2091), 259.

57. Report of General John Pope, October 2, 1882, in Report of the Secretary of War, 1882, p. 101.

to protect Union Pacific construction crews working near the junction of the North Platte and South Platte Rivers, also was closed down. Fort McPherson, established in 1863 near the present town of North Platte, Nebraska, saw the last of its troops march out in the spring of 1880. By then the only important Nebraska post west of Omaha that remained was Fort Sidney. Established in 1867 along the line of the Union Pacific. it was active until 1894.

Wyoming posts were similarly rendered unnecessary by the growth of settlement along the Union Pacific. Fort Sanders, near modern Laramie, was built in 1866 to protect the stagecoach route; by 1882, having outlived its usefulness as a sentinel along the main travel route, it was closed. To the west, in central Wyoming, lay Fort Fred Steele. Located near the crossing of the North Platte River in the spring of 1868, to protect the railroad workers, it functioned for less than two decades, being abandoned in the autumn of 1886. Only Forts Laramie and Bridger remained; both lived on until 1890. Fort Laramie was not on the line of the road, but this old post, occupied by the army in 1849, served as a guardian of the westward passage for over four decades. Bridger, rebuilt as a military post in 1858 at the time of the Mormon War, served in a similar capacity.

The story of the Kansas posts was much the same. West of Forts Leavenworth and Riley, both of which were built in the days before the railroad, lay such posts as Harker, Hays and Wallace. Harker, built in 1864, guarded both the old stage route to Santa Fe and the Kansas Pacific railroad construction crews; it was the first to go, being abandoned as early as 1873. Wallace, erected in western Kansas in the autumn of 1865, was no longer needed in 1882; by then the surrounding countryside was undergoing heavy settlement.

Hays, established in west central Kansas during 1865, and built especially to guard Kansas Pacific workers, lasted until 1889. During that autumn the editor of a Kansas newspaper noted that the government had called for the post's abandonment and, having served there during the early days of its history, he recalled its importance as a military station.

Commenting upon the rapid development of western Kansas that had taken place during the intervening years, he spoke of the changes that had taken place. "In this brief period the Indians have been sent from this region to stay, and the civilization of the white man shows here in its splendor," was his testimony to the accomplishment of the railroads.[58]

---

58. W. S. Tilton of Wa-Keeney, Kansas, *Western Kansas World*, September 7, 1889. See also Francis Paul Prucha, *A Guide to the Military Posts of the United States, 1689-1895* (Madison: University of Wisconsin Press, 1964).

REALITY ON THE PLAINS.—[See Poem, Page 618.]

Harper's Weekly, *July 29, 1876, p. 617.*

PART TWO
Fighting the Sioux War

This second section opens with a critical biography that appeared more recently in *Montana*. Paul Andrew Hutton, a prominent military historian, explores the frontier career of Lieutenant General Philip H. Sheridan, who was the nation's chief Indian fighter during America's pell-mell settlement of the post–Civil War West. Hutton's capsule biography depicts Sheridan as a proud agent for the advance of white, Christian civilization and no friend to the Indian. Clearly perceiving the inextricable relationship between Indian livelihood and the great bison herds, Sheridan applauded and supported destruction of the shaggy beasts. In 1876 Sheridan dictated the strategy of the Sioux War, saw to its eventual success, and broke Sioux resistance, thus opening their lands to white settlement.

A simplified but common view of the Great Sioux War holds that by focusing on the half dozen major northern clashes beginning with the Powder River fight on March 17, 1876, and ending with the Tongue River or Wolf Mountain battle on January 8, 1877, the story of this terrible war is told. In truth, these military encounters comprise but a third of the combat story. By the army's own official tallies, most notably Sheridan's 1882 *Record of Engagements With Hostile Indians Within the Military Division of the Missouri,* and the Adjutant General's 1891 *Chronological List of Actions, &c, With Indians,* some twenty-two armed fights occurred in every corner of the war zone over the course of two years.[1]

The first of these episodes came within weeks after President Ulysses S. Grant officially unleashed the United States Army on the

---

1.   Military Division of the Missouri, *Record of Engagements With Hostile Indians Within the Military Division of the Missouri, from 1868 to 1882, Lieutenant-General P. H. Sheridan, Commanding* (Washington, D. C.: Government Printing Office, 1882; reprint, Bellevue, Neb.: Old Army Press, 1969), 49-75; Adjutant General's Office, *Chronological List of Actions, etc., With Indians from January 15, 1837 to January, 1891* (Fort Collins, Colo.: Old Army Press, 1979), 60-64.

Sioux. In 1875 white citizens from Bozeman constructed a small trading post called Fort Pease on the Yellowstone a few miles below its confluence with the Bighorn River. Traders at the post never realized any profits, however, because the small outpost was under a virtual siege by Sioux warriors continuously. The Sioux even made life-threatening adventures of routine daily searches for food and fuel. So stressed were the traders that in mid-February 1876 they appealed to Bozeman for relief. Edgar I. Stewart, an eminent mid-twentieth century Custer scholar, chronicles Major James Brisbin's successful relief expedition to Fort Pease, a sortie that represented the first recorded demonstration against the Sioux in a protracted war. Stewart's essay appeared in *Montana* in 1956.

Assistant Surgeon Holmes Paulding accompanied Colonel John Gibbon's Montana Column during its summer campaign along the Yellowstone, and he was one of the doctors who tended wounded survivors of the Little Bighorn fight. Paulding sent his mother seven letters from the campaign, five of which were previously unpublished before Thomas R. Buecker skillfully presented them in an article appearing in *Montana* in 1982. The Paulding letters are loaded with gritty insights on the Yellowstone campaign occurring in early and mid-1876.

Father Peter J. Powell's "High Bull's Victory Roster," which appeared in *Montana* in 1975, looks at an equally valuable grouping of souvenirs gathered by Northern Cheyennes from the Little Bighorn battlefield, but which were lost again when Colonel Ranald Mackenzie's cavalrymen sacked Dull Knife's village on November 25, 1876, in the southern Bighorn Mountains. Among Seventh Cavalry relics collected by the Powder River expedition's victors were leather-bound memoranda books kept by several of the first sergeants of Custer's companies. The final soldier entries in a couple of these books were poignantly dated on the very eve of the Little Bighorn fight. One book also contained ledger drawings rendered later by several Cheyenne warriors who sought to chronicle their own exploits before and during the war.

Many years after the ledger was recaptured, it was shown to two aged Cheyenne combatants. The Cheyennes distinctly recalled the exploits depicted in the drawings and identified the ledger's Indian owner, Crazy Head, who was killed during the November battle. With gut-wrenching frankness, Father Powell recounts the Dull Knife fight and the destruction of the Cheyenne village. Northern Cheyenne art and material culture never recovered from the loss inflicted that dark wintry day in 1876.

Don Rickey, Jr., concludes this section with an essay appearing in *Montana* in 1963. Rickey recounts the tenacious campaign of Colonel Nelson Miles up the Tongue River in early January 1877 and his fight at Wolf Mountain with Sioux and Cheyennes, some of whom were refugees from the Dull Knife battle only six weeks earlier. Miles maneuvered skillfully against Crazy Horse's warriors, and when a blizzard halted the fighting, he controlled the field. The Indians were uprooted again, and an end to the war was nearer at hand.

Lieutenant General Philip H. Sheridan, the army's chief Indian fighter, stands at center in this photograph taken in New Orleans in 1865. (Courtesy of Paul Andrew Hutton)

Phil Sheridan's Frontier

By Paul Andrew Hutton

They buried Philip Henry Sheridan, commanding general of the United States Army, on August 11, 1888, in Arlington Cemetery. His grave, on a high, green knoll near the Custis–Lee Mansion, faces eastward toward the city of Washington. Lavish eulogies poured forth from that city, where Congress had tardily voted him a fourth star only weeks before his death, and from throughout the nation. They rang with the familiar names of battle sites— Stones River, Missionary Ridge, Winchester, Cedar Creek, Five Forks, Appomattox—that had established Sheridan as the youngest member of the Union's trinity of great captains. But strangely absent from this outpouring of mournful praise was any mention of the task that had dominated the first seven and last twenty years of the general's career—the conquest of the American frontier.

Phil Sheridan had been, in fact, the republic's preeminent frontier soldier. He had commanded a larger frontier region—the vast Division of the Missouri—for a longer period of time than any other military officer in the nation's history. He had given overall direction to the final, and greatest, Indian campaigns waged on this continent. Between 1867 and 1884, his troops fought 619 engagements with the western Indian tribes, completing the subjugation of America's native peoples and the conquest of their lands, which had been set underway almost four hundred years before. At the same time he actively promoted the movement of hunters, stockmen, miners, farmers, and railroaders into these newly appropriated regions, using his military power and political influence to bring some order to this rapid, oftentimes chaotic, expansion westward. The American West during the 1870s and 1880s was in a real sense Phil Sheridan's frontier.

Sheridan's origins gave little hint of the vital role he was to play in his adopted nation's future. The exact place and date of his birth

*Paul Andrew Hutton, "Phil Sheridan's Frontier," *Montana The Magazine of Western History*, 38 (Winter 1988), 17-31.

is unknown. He confused the issue himself claiming both Albany, New York, and Somerset, Ohio, on various official documents, before finally deciding that Albany on March 6, 1831, sounded best. It seems almost certain that he was born either in County Cavan, Ireland, where his parents were tenant farmers, or on the boat en route from Liverpool. He was an infant when his parents, John and Mary Sheridan, settled in the hamlet of Somerset, Ohio.[1]

Sheridan's later life was greatly influenced by the education he received in Somerset's one-room schoolhouse. He particularly admired an itinerant educator named Patrick McNaly, a drunken brute who believed that education could be beaten into students. Sheridan recalled with admiration that the Irishman consistently punished every "guilty mischief-maker" by whipping the whole class when unable to identify the actual culprit. This effective tactic made a deep impression on young Phil, as did the overall power of education. "The little white schoolhouse of the North made us superior to the South," he later remarked, "Education is invincible."[2]

At fourteen, his schooling over, Sheridan secured a position as clerk in a local general store at two dollars a month. He rose quickly to become bookkeeper in Somerset's largest dry-goods shop, a mighty responsibility for one so young, for almost all business was transacted on credit. Although dedicated to his bookkeeping chores, the lad was often lost in daydreams of martial glory, especially after the outbreak of the Mexican War. His greatest hero as a youth had been Somerset's revolutionary war veteran who was trotted out every Fourth

---

1. In a letter from Michael Sheridan, Philip's younger brother and military aide, to his older brother John, reference is made to the fact that in his memoirs, the general was using "the Albany statement as given by mother. . . . " Clearly, Mary Sheridan had always lied about the place of her son's birth, and the family simply continued the subterfuge. This certainly is an understandable action considering the strong anti-Irish sentiment at the time the Sheridan family arrived in the United States. Once Philip became a famous soldier this deception took on important political ramifications, since he could not run for President unless native born. Michael Sheridan to John Sheridan, January 31, 1888, William F. Drake Collection, enclosed in William F. Drake to author, February 23, 1987. For more on this topic, see Paul Andrew Hutton, *Phil Sheridan and His Army* (Lincoln: University of Nebraska Press, 1985), 2-3; Richard O'Connor, *Sheridan the Inevitable* (Indianapolis: Bobbs-Merrill, 1953), 18-19; *Personal Memoirs of Philip Henry Sheridan, General United States Army, New and Enlarged Edition with an Account of his Life from 1871 to his Death in 1888 by Brig.-Gen. Michael V. Sheridan* (2 vols., New York: D. Appleton and Company, 1902), 1:1-2. This author, in a burst of premature certitude, only recently and incorrectly wrote that Albany was the place of birth. See Paul Andrew Hutton, "Philip H. Sheridan," in Paul Andrew Hutton, ed., *Soldiers West: Biographies from the Military Frontier* (Lincoln: University of Nebraska Press, 1987), 78-99.

2. H. C. Greiner, *General Phil Sheridan As I Knew Him, Playmate-Comrade-Friend* (Chicago: J. S. Hyland, 1908), 353.

of July to be admired by the citizenry. "I never saw Phil's brown eyes open so wide or gaze with such interest," noted his boyhood chum Henry Greiner, "as they did on this old Revolutionary relic." On another occasion Greiner and Sheridan interrupted their play to gawk admiringly at a tall, carrot-topped West Point cadet who was courting one of the young ladies at Somerset's St. Mary's Female Academy. The lady, Ellen Ewing, would eventually marry that fledgling soldier from nearby Lancaster, and her beau, lanky William Tecumseh Sherman, made a deep impression on young Phil Sheridan.[3]

Learning that the 1848 appointee from his district to West Point had failed the entrance examinations, Sheridan hurriedly appealed to Congressman Thomas Ritchie offering to fill the vacancy. The congressman, who knew Sheridan's father well, promptly returned a warrant for the class of 1848, which elated Sheridan but horrified his family. Not only was West Point generally viewed by westerners as a bastion of aristocracy, special privilege, and militarism, all out of keeping with the ideals of the republic, but it was also firmly Episcopalian. John Sheridan took Phil in hand to the Church of Saint Joseph where Dominican Father Joshua Young advised: "Rather than send him to West Point take him out into the back yard, behind the chicken coop, and cut his throat."[4]

John Sheridan brooded over this sound if drastic advice for some time, but finally relented and allowed the boy to go. Phil traveled to the military academy with future general David S. Stanley. Stanley remembered Sheridan as "small and red faced, [with] long black wavy hair, bright eyes, very animated and neatly dressed in a brown broadcloth suit." At the academy, the long locks were soon shorn and the simple suit replaced by the "plebe skin," or brown linen jacket, of a freshman cadet. Poor Sheridan, Stanley noted, was "the most insignificant looking little fellow I ever saw."[5]

West Point was an unhappy place for Sheridan. Gray buildings melded into a rocky landscape under foreboding wintry skies, reinforcing the discipline and monotonous regimen of cadet life. The traditional hazing frayed his volatile temper, and his grades suffered. The refined mannerisms and aristocratic temperament of the southern clique that dominated academy social life irritated him. While he found solace in the company of three other Ohio cadets—George Crook, John Nugen, and Joshua Sill—his rural, Irish-Catholic, Whig roots left him constantly insecure and ill at ease.

---

3. Ibid., 19; Lloyd Lewis, *Sherman: Fighting Prophet* (New York: Harcourt, Brace and Company, 1932), 47.

4. Lewis, *Sherman*, 47-48; Sheridan, *Personal Memoirs*, 1:7-8.

5. David S. Stanley, *Personal Memoirs of Major-General D. S. Stanley, U.S.A.* (Cambridge, Massachusetts: Harvard University Press, 1917), 17-18.

His frustrations broke forth late one afternoon on the drill field in September 1851. Virginian William R. Terrill ordered Sheridan to align himself properly in the ranks. Instead of obeying the order Sheridan lunged at Terrill with his bayonet. When Terrill reported the incident to his superiors, Sheridan sought him out and attacked him, but this time with his fists. An officer intervened and saved the wiry, five-foot-five Sheridan from a thrashing by the much larger Virginian. Saved from expulsion by a previously unblemished record, Sheridan received only a year's suspension. Unrepentant, he harbored deep resentment against all those involved in the incident. He brooded for nine humiliating months back at his Somerset bookkeeping job before returning to West Point in August 1852, where he compounded his poor grades with a bitter attitude that left him only eleven demerits away from expulsion when he graduated thirty-fourth in a class of fifty-two in July 1853.[6]

Brevet Second Lieutenant Sheridan was assigned to the First Infantry and ordered to Fort Duncan, Texas, perhaps the most desolate and primitive post on the frontier. Nevertheless, he found the fort an improvement over West Point and busied himself with amateur ornithology and hunting expeditions. He was soon transferred to his friend George Crook's regiment, the Fourth Infantry, and sent to Fort Reading, California, at the northern tip of the Sacramento Valley. The region was overrun by the dregs of humanity in search of a quick fortune in the goldfields. The miners and squatters terribly abused the local Indians, while their political representatives — most notably ambitious young Isaac Stevens, governor of Washington Territory — pushed through specious treaties to force the tribes off their coveted lands.

Crook, who had been in the Pacific Northwest since 1853, characterized the situation as "the fable of the wolf and the lamb." It was not infrequent, Crook noted, "for an Indian to be shot down in cold blood, or a squaw to be raped by some brute," and the white criminals to escape unpunished. Then, when the Indians were pushed beyond endurance and struck back, the soldiers "had to fight when our sympathies were with the Indians." Sheridan's sympathies, however, were not with the "miserable wretches" native to the region, for he felt

---

6. Sheridan, *Personal Memoirs*, 1:9-14; Official Register of the Officers and Cadets of the U.S. Military Academy, West Point, New York, June 1849, June 1850, June 1851, June 1852, June 1853, United States Military Academy Archives; John L. Hathaway, "Recollections of Sheridan as a Cadet," in *War Papers Read before the Commandery of the State of Wisconsin, Military Order of the Loyal Legion of the United States* (Milwaukee: Burdick, Armitage & Allen, 1891), 270-74.

their "naked, hungry and cadaverous" condition to be the natural result of the overthrow of savagery by civilization.[7]

A gold discovery and influx of miners at Colville, Washington Territory, finally drove the Yakima and Rogue River Indians to war. Sheridan marched north in October 1855 with a detachment of 350 regular troops and a regiment of Oregon mounted volunteers under the command of Major Gabriel Rains. Sheridan's introduction to Indian fighting was a dismal affair, with the Yakimas easily avoiding the pursuing troops. On one occasion Sheridan, in command of the advance column, pursued a party of fleeing Indians for two miles before discovering them to be a company of Oregon volunteers. Winter snows mercifully ended the campaign, and Sheridan spent the next few months at Fort Vancouver.

While the reorganized troops were busy preparing for a spring invasion of the Walla Walla Valley, the Yakimas struck the first blow on March 26, 1856, attacking white settlements at the Cascades, a vital portage on the Columbia River. With forty dragoons and a small cannon, Sheridan rushed upriver to the rescue aboard a little steamboat. Although they outnumbered the soldiers, the Indians only skirmished before withdrawing when more troops arrived on March 28. Slightly wounded by a Yakima bullet that grazed his nose before killing a soldier standing beside him, Sheridan had his first victory over the Indians and his first military honor when General Winfield Scott commended him in general orders.[8]

After his victory at the Cascades, Lieutenant Sheridan and his troops occupied the nearby village of the Cascade tribe, easily rounding up the demoralized Indians. The Cascade men protested their innocence, but Sheridan found freshly burned powder in several of their old muskets. He hauled thirteen of the men before Colonel George Wright, and a drumhead court-martial immediately sentenced nine of them to death. The soldiers fastened a rope to a nearby cottonwood tree, stacked two barrels underneath, and unceremoniously hanged the Indians. Among those executed was Tumult, a Cascade Indian who had warned several settlers of the impending attack and had guided an elderly white man to safety. Sheridan noted with satisfaction that this "summary punishment inflicted on the nine Indians, in their trial and execution, had a most salutary effect on

---

7.　Martin F. Schmitt, ed., *General George Crook: His Autobiography* (Norman: University of Oklahoma Press, 1946), 16; Sheridan, *Personal Memoirs,* 1:44-45, 70.

8.　O'Connor, *Sheridan,* 49-51; Sheridan, *Personal Memoirs,* 1:90; William N. Bischoff, "The Yakima Campaign of 1856," *Mid-America,* 31 (April 1949), 163-208; Turner F. Levens, "When Sheridan Was in Oregon," *Washington Historical Quarterly,* 16 (July 1925), 163-85.

the confederation, and was the entering wedge of disintegration."[9] Somerset schoolmaster McNaly's legacy was ever the directing influence in Phil Sheridan's use of force to effect the will of his government.

Sheridan's remaining years in the Pacific Northwest were spent quietly at the Grande Ronde Indian Reservation, guarding the several tribes who lived there. He learned the Chinook language while there, aided no doubt by Frances, a Rogue River Indian girl who lived with him on the reservation. This liaison, however, seemed to have no moderating influence on his prejudice toward the natives. He was proud of the harsh tactics he employed on the reservation to suppress traditional customs. "We made," he later noted

> a great stride toward the civilization of these crude and superstitious people, for they now began to recognize the power of the Government. . . . I found abundant confirmation of my early opinion that the most effectual measures for lifting them from a state of barbarism would be a practical supervision at the outset, coupled with a firm control and mild discipline.[10]

It was difficult to concentrate on the duties at hand, for the news from the East was increasingly worrisome. Pony Express riders carried the sober details of Fort Sumter westward across the plains to western posts. Sheridan fretted that the war would end before he could return east. He was delighted to depart Portland in September 1861 as a newly minted captain in the Thirteenth Infantry and was anxious to see action, confiding to a friend that if the war lasted long enough he might "have a chance to earn a major's commission."[11] The small-framed, thirty-year-old frontier captain was a latecomer to the war. Ulysses S. Grant had already won fame as the victor at Fort Henry and Fort Donelson, William T. Sherman was now in command of a division, and George Crook's political connections had secured him the colonelcy of an Ohio volunteer regiment by the time Sheridan took command of a desk at General Henry W. Halleck's Missouri headquarters. His bookkeeping skills paid rich dividends as the young staff officer quickly straightened out the confused accounts of Halleck's predecessor, General John C. Frémont.

---

9. Sheridan, *Personal Memoirs*, 1:89; Levens, "When Sheridan Was in Oregon," 167-68, 170-71.

10. Sheridan, *Personal Memoirs*, 1:119-20; Fred Lockley, "Reminiscences of Mrs. Frank Collins, Nee Martha Elizabeth Gilliam," *Quarterly of the Oregon Historical Society*, 17 (December 1916), 367-68; Grace E. Cooper, "Benton County Pioneer-Historical Society," *Oregon Historical Quarterly*, 57 (March 1956), 83-93.

11. Whitelaw Reid, *Ohio in the War: Her Statesman, Her Generals, and Soldiers* (2 vols., New York: Moore, Wilstach and Baldwin, 1868), 1:500.

Sheridan's impressive staff service brought him to General Sherman's attention. He recommended Sheridan be given command of one of the Ohio volunteer regiments, but the governor declined to make the appointment. Russell Alger, the future Secretary of War, then a captain in the Second Michigan Cavalry, succeeded where Sherman had failed, using his considerable political influence back home to have Sheridan appointed colonel of his regiment. On May 27, 1862, Sheridan jumped from regular army captain to volunteer army colonel, beginning one of the most meteoric rises in American military history.

The new colonel fought a masterful battle at Boonville, Missouri, against a force over four times the size of his own, prompting General William Rosecrans and four of his brigadiers to telegraph Halleck that Sheridan deserved a promotion and was "worth his weight in gold."[12] Promoted to brigadier general of volunteers in September 1862, Sheridan quickly won a high reputation in army circles for his bulldog tenacity and reckless courage. His fierce counterattack at Stones River turned seeming defeat into an important but grisly Union victory and won him a second star in the volunteer army. It remained for his bold charge up Missionary Ridge, however, to secure him General Grant's esteem and guarantee his future. The press would dub Sheridan's assault on the seemingly impregnable Confederate positions on the crest of Missionary Ridge in November 1863 as the miracle at Missionary Ridge.

General Grant, who had watched the assault in amazement, was delighted. "Sheridan showed his genius in that battle," Grant later declared,

> and to him I owe the capture of most of the prisoners that were taken. Although commanding a division only, he saw in the crisis of that engagement that it was necessary to advance beyond the point indicated by his orders. He saw what I could not know, on account of my ignorance of the ground, and with the instinct of military genius pushed ahead.[13]

When Grant went east in March 1864 as commander of all Union forces, he took Sheridan with him to command the Army of the Potomac's cavalry. Sheridan quickly defeated Confederate cavalry commander J. E. B. Stuart at Yellow Tavern and earned an independent command in the Shenandoah Valley. With orders to block the

---

12. W. S. Rosecrans, C. C. Sullivan, G. Granger, W. L. Elliott, and A. Asboth to Henry Halleck, July 30, 1862, Box 1, Philip H. Sheridan Papers, Library of (hereafter Sheridan Papers).

13. Bruce Catton, *Grant Takes Command* (Boston: Little, Brown, 1968), 90.

advance of General Jubal Early's Confederates up the valley and seal off the rebel breadbasket once and for all, Sheridan won battles at Winchester and Fisher's Hill and secured a brigadier's star in the regular army as a reward.

His greatest triumph, however, came at Cedar Creek. Sheridan was fourteen miles to the north, at Winchester, when his army was taken by surprise on October 19, 1864. Galloping to the sound of the guns, he rallied his routed forces to crush Early's Confederates. "Sheridan's Ride," as it was called, became one of the most memorable episodes of the Civil War, soon celebrated in poem, story, and painting.

With the rebel army destroyed, Sheridan and his "robbers," as his army was thereafter known, ravaged the Shenandoah Valley so that it would never again support an invading army from the south. A crow, Sheridan boasted, would have to carry his own rations when crossing Virginia's most bountiful valley. "I do not hold war to mean simply that lines of men shall engage each other in battle . . .," Sheridan declared, in defining the strategy he would apply both in the Shenandoah and later on the frontier. "This is but a duel, in which one combatant seeks the other's life; war means much more, and is far worse than this." The key to strategic success in war lay in ravaging the enemy's homeland, depriving him of the resources to make war, and destroying the will of the people to resist, "for the loss of property weighs heavy with the most of mankind; heavier often, than the sacrifices made on the field of battle." As he later advised Prussian Count Otto von Bismarck in 1870:

> The proper strategy consists in the first place in inflicting as telling blows as possible upon the enemy's army, and then causing the inhabitants so much suffering that they must long for peace, and force their government to demand it. The people must be left nothing but their eyes to weep with over the war.[14]

President Abraham Lincoln had hesitated to agree to Sheridan's Shenandoah command, believing the general too young and inexperienced. The president had once described Sheridan as "a brown, chunky little chap, with a long body, short legs, not enough neck to hang him, and such long arms that if his ankles itch he can scratch them without stooping." Lincoln now confessed that he had always thought a cavalryman should be "six feet tall, but five feet four seems about right," he declared, subtracting an inch from Sheridan's already diminutive size. His re-election hopes given a timely boost by the vic-

---

14. Sheridan, *Personal Memoirs*, 1:487-88; Hutton, *Phil Sheridan and His Army*, 204.

tory at Cedar Creek, the president promoted Sheridan to major general in the regular army.[15]

Realizing that the war would soon be over, Sheridan hurried south to rejoin Grant. At Five Forks his troops destroyed the right flank of Lee's army, and at Appomattox he blocked the Army of Northern Virginia's line of retreat. On Sunday, April 9, 1865, thirty-four-year-old Phil Sheridan, the Union's finest combat commander, walked with General Grant into the McLean house at Appomattox to accept the surrender of Lee's army.[16]

The war over, Grant immediately sent Sheridan to the Texas border with orders to provide material and moral support to the forces of Benito Juárez in their struggle with Maximilian, the puppet of the French emperor, Louis Napoleon. Sheridan relished the opportunity to confront French troops in battle, but the Department of State restrained him. Sheridan still aided Juárez by declaring huge quantities of arms and ammunition as surplus or condemning and depositing them on the Rio Grande for Juárez's troops. The French soon abandoned Maximilian, and the imperialist adventure swiftly moved to its melancholy finale.

Although preoccupied with border affairs, Sheridan kept a wary eye on civil matters in Texas and Louisiana. He distributed troops at critical points to suppress night-riding white terrorists and assist civilian authorities in enforcing the law. Before the war, Sheridan's mind, as he put it, had never "been disturbed by any discussion of the questions out of which the war grew" and he had been animated at the outbreak of the rebellion only to preserve the Union. The war had radicalized him, so that by the time of Appomattox he was one of the most stridently Republican and bitterly anti-Southern generals in the army. Enraged by the various vagrancy and apprentice laws — Black Codes — enacted in Texas, Sheridan angrily declared that they resulted in "a policy of gross injustice toward the colored people on the part of the courts, and a reign of lawlessness and disorder ensued." Although hardly enlightened in his racial views, Sheridan determined that he would protect the blacks. Now that they had been given their

15. *Army and Navy Journal*, 13 (March 11, 1876), 506; O'Connor, *Sheridan*, 233.

16. For Sheridan in the Civil War, consult his memoirs as well as O'Connor, *Sheridan*; Joseph Hergesheimer, *Sheridan: A Military Narrative* (Boston: Houghton Mifflin, 1931); Edward J. Stackpole, *Sheridan in the Shenandoah: Jubal Early's Nemesis* (Harrisburg, Pennsylvania: Stackpole, 1961); Stephen Z. Starr, *The Union Cavalry in the Civil War: The War in the East from Gettysburg to Appomattox 1863-1865* (Baton Rouge: Louisiana State University Press, 1981); Robert Thomas Zeimet, "Philip H. Sheridan and the Civil War in the West" (doctoral diss., Marquette University, Milwaukee, Wisconsin, 1981); Lawrence A. Frost, *The Phil Sheridan Album* (Seattle: Superior Publishing, 1968).

freedom, "it was the plain duty of those in authority to make it secure" and "see that they had a fair chance in the battle of life."[17]

Sheridan further angered unreconstructed Texans. When asked by a reporter at Brownsville, Texas, what he thought of the Lone Star state, Sheridan acidly replied: "If I owned hell and Texas, I would rent Texas out and live in hell!"[18] Sheridan also argued with Texas Governor James Throckmorton over troop assignments. The governor wanted troops transferred from the interior of the state to protect frontier settlers from raiding Comanches. Sheridan refused to move any men, noting that "if a white man is killed by the Indians on an extensive Indian frontier, the greatest excitement will take place, but over the killing of many freedmen in the settlements, nothing is done."[19]

Sheridan's determined defense of blacks in Texas and Louisiana, his bitter disputes with local politicians, his forceful suppression of white terrorism, and his enthusiastic application of the Reconstruction policies of the congressional Radical Republicans, led President Andrew Johnson to dismiss him from his command on July 31, 1867.[20] Reassigned to command the Department of the Missouri, which included present-day Kansas, Oklahoma (Indian Territory), New Mexico, and Colorado, the embittered Sheridan would find the task of frontier defense equally difficult work, but far more congenial to his temperament.

Peace on the frontier was tenuous at best. Although the 1867 Treaty of Medicine Lodge had established reservations for the Cheyennes, Arapahos, Kiowas, Comanches, and Kiowa-Comanches in the Indian Territory, the Indians had in general failed to settle on the reservations. Congress had been preoccupied with the impeachment of President Johnson and had failed to appropriate the necessary funds to meet the government's treaty obligations. It hardly surprised Sheridan when a Cheyenne war party raided white settlements along the Saline and Solomon rivers in Kansas in August 1868. Sheridan thought that the only way to ensure a lasting peace was to see the Cheyennes "soundly whipped, and the ringleaders in the present

17. Sheridan, *Personal Memoirs*, 1:121-23; 2:231-33, 262.

18. *Army and Navy Register*, 4 (November 3, 1883), 8-9. For a response by a Texan, see Virginia Eisenhour, ed., *Alex Sweet's Texas: The Lighter Side of Lone Star History* (Austin: University of Texas Press, 1986), 88-89.

19. Hutton, *Phil Sheridan and His Army*, 25.

20. For Sheridan and Reconstruction, see Joseph G. Dawson III, *Army Generals and Reconstruction: Louisiana, 1862-1877* (Baton Rouge: Louisiana State University Press, 1982); William L. Richter, *The Army in Texas During Reconstruction 1865-1870* (College Station: Texas A & M University Press, 1987); James E. Sefton, *The United States Army and Reconstruction, 1865-1877* (Baton Rouge: Louisiana State University Press, 1967).

trouble hung, their ponies killed, and such destruction of their property as will make them very poor."[21]

Sheridan determined on a winter campaign to crush the Indians. Although campaigning against Indians during winter was hardly a novel idea, Sheridan's campaign was universally greeted as a bold, innovative plan. He was convinced that his well-fed and well-clothed troopers could challenge the severe climate long enough to strike a decisive blow. Winter limited the Indians' mobility, their greatest advantage over the soldiers. With their ponies weakened by scarce fodder they would seek the comfort of their traditional winter camps and be lulled into a false sense of security. Distance and climate had always protected them, but the westward advance of the railroads had ended that advantage, allowing supplies to be shipped rapidly to distant depots and stockpiled for prolonged campaigns.

Sheridan was well aware of the vital role to be played by the railroads in bringing order and peace to the frontier, and he was determined to remove the Indian barrier that impeded the rapid advance of the lines. Thus, he concentrated his forces against the Cheyennes, Arapahos, and Sioux who ranged near the Kansas Pacific and Union Pacific lines and paid only passing attention to the Kiowas and Comanches, who traditionally raided south into Texas and New Mexico. Self-interest and past fellowship tied the soldiers and railroaders together, for most of the railroad construction bosses, surveyors, and engineers were former soldiers with close ties to the military establishment. Grenville M. Dodge, chief engineer of the Union Pacific, had commanded an army corps during General Sherman's Atlanta campaign. William J. Palmer, president of the Kansas Pacific, and W. W. Wright, superintendent of the same line, were both former Union army generals. These personal relationships naturally resulted in close cooperation between the soldiers and the railroadmen. Military escorts for surveying parties and construction crews were readily provided, and Sheridan often made large troop transfers to oblige the needs of the railroads.

This alliance was only natural considering the heavy federal investment in the railroads. It was in the best interests of the government, the military, the capitalists, and the people to have the roads completed as rapidly as possible. For the military, the lines promised rapid and inexpensive transport of troops and supplies and consolidation of numerous scattered posts. More importantly, the transcontinental lines would split the northern Indian tribes from the southern ones, spell doom for the great buffalo herds, and bring

---

21. Philip H. Sheridan, "Report, In the Field, Fort Hays, Sept. 26, 1868," Box 83, Sheridan Papers.

in more settlers. In 1867, General Sherman correctly foresaw that the completion of the transcontinental railroad was "the solution of the Indian question."[22]

Throughout late 1868 and early 1869 Sheridan directed a masterful winter campaign against the Cheyennes and allied tribes. In sharp encounters at the Washita in November 1868, at Soldier Springs the following month, and at Summit Springs in July 1869, Sheridan' s troopers broke the power of the Cheyennes and compelled them to settle on a reservation in Indian Territory. The campaign won Sheridan an enviable reputation as an Indian fighter.[23]

After Grant took office as president in March 1869, he appointed Sheridan lieutenant general and gave him command of the Division of the Missouri. This vast command extended from Sheridan's Chicago headquarters on the east to the western borders of Montana, Wyoming, Utah, and New Mexico on the west and from the Canadian line on the north to the Rio Grande on the south. Most of the Indian population of the United States lived within the boundaries of Sheridan's division: Sioux, Northern Cheyennes, Southern Cheyennes, Kiowas, Comanches, Arapahos, Utes, Kickapoos, and Apaches all battled Sheridan's troopers. Before he left his frontier post to become commanding general of the army in 1883, Sheridan planned and directed the greatest Indian campaigns of the century.

Sheridan's pragmatism and elastic ethics made him the perfect frontier soldier for an expansionist republic. He ruthlessly carried out the dictates of his government, never faltering in his conviction that what he did was right. He viewed all Indians as members of an inferior race embracing a primitive culture. He felt them to be inordinately barbarous in war, which he attributed to a natural, ingrained savageness of the race. They formed, in Sheridan's mind, a stone-age barrier to the inevitable advance of white, Christian civilization. Sheridan not only favored this advance, but he also proudly saw himself as its instrument.

---

22. Grenville M. Dodge, *Personal Recollections of President Abraham Lincoln, General Ulysses S. Grant, and General William T. Sherman* (Council Bluffs, Iowa: Monarch Printing Company, 1914), 195.

23. For Sheridan's winter campaign, see Hutton, *Phil Sheridan and His Army*, 28-114; William H. Leckie, *The Military Conquest of the Southern Plains* (Norman: University of Oklahoma Press, 1963), 88-132; De B. Randolph Keim, *Sheridan's Troopers on the Borders: A Winter Campaign on the Plains* (Lincoln: University of Nebraska Press, 1985); Robert M. Utley, ed., *Life in Custer's Cavalry: Diaries and Letters of Albert and Jennie Barnitz, 1867-1868* (New Haven, Connecticut: Yale University Press, 1977); Stan Hoig, *The Battle of the Washita; The Sheridan-Custer Indian Campaign of 1877-69* (Garden City, New York: Doubleday, 1976); John M. Carroll, ed., *General Custer and the Battle of the Washita: The Federal View* (Bryan, Texas: Guidon Press, 1978).

Although he denied uttering it, the infamous quote that "the only good Indian is a dead Indian" became synonymous with Sheridan and his Indian policy. Although the sentiment certainly did not originate with the general, it nevertheless has the ring of typical Sheridan rhetoric.[24] Exactly as he had done in the Shenandoah Valley in 1864, Sheridan proposed to undermine the Indians' economy and impoverish them, as well as kill warriors in battle. Sheridan believed that the essential first step in his total war against the Indians was the destruction of the great buffalo herds. Not only did buffalo provide a rich commissary for the plains tribes, but the herds also gave the Indians reason to continue their traditional seasonal movements, which led them off their reservations and into collision with whites. Several treaties, such as the 1868 Fort Laramie Treaty with the Sioux, gave the Indians the legal right to hunt in certain areas off the reservation so long as the buffalo ranged in sufficient numbers to justify the chase. Sheridan hoped to quickly reduce the buffalo population and thus terminate this hunting right.

The general applauded the activities of the white hunters who began slaughtering the buffalo in the early 1870s for their hides. In 1875, when the Texas state legislature was considering a bill to protect buffalo in Texas, Sheridan protested. Instead of outlawing the slaughter, Sheridan declared, the legislature should strike a bronze medal with a dead buffalo on one side and a discouraged Indian on the other and bestow it on the hunters. "These men have done in the last two years, and will do more in the next years, to settle the vexed Indian question, than the entire regular army has done in the last thirty years," the general declared.

> They are destroying the Indians' commissary; and it is a well known fact that an army losing its base of supplies is placed at a great disadvantage. Send them powder and lead, if you will; but for the sake of a lasting peace, let them kill, skin, and sell until the buffaloes are exterminated. Then your prairies can be covered with speckled cattle, and the festive cowboy, who follows the hunter as a second forerunner of civilization.[25]

After the destruction of the southern herd during the early 1870s, Sheridan worked to ensure the same fate for the northern herd. In 1881, when the government considered protecting what was left of the herds, Sheridan vigorously opposed such action. "If I could learn that every buffalo in the northern herd were killed I would be glad,"

---

24. Sheridan, *Personal Memoirs*, 2:464-65; Hutton, *Phil Sheridan and His Army*, 180.

25. John R. Cook, *The Border and the Buffalo: An Untold Story of the Southwest Plains* (New York: Citadel Press, 1967), 163-64.

Philip H. Sheridan encouraged the wholesale slaughter of the remnant buffalo herds in hopes their annihilation would force the Sioux and other Northern Plains Indian tribes to remain on their reservations. Here photographer L. A. Huffman shows a hunter taking buffalo hides and tongues in northern Montana in the early 1880s. (Montana Historical Society Photograph Archives)

the general wrote the War Department. "The destruction of this herd would do more to keep Indians quiet than anything else that could happen. Since the destruction of the southern herd, which formerly roamed from Texas to the Platte, the Indians in that section have given us no trouble."[26]

---

26. Sheridan to the Adjutant General, October 13, 1881, Box 29, Sheridan Papers.

Sheridan's sponsorship of several civilian hunting parties onto the plains — such as the millionaire's hunt of 1871 and the Grand Duke Alexis hunt in 1872 — furthered his policy of exterminating the buffalo while at the same time he curried the favor of powerful, influential citizens. An avid sportsman, Sheridan liked to combine business with pleasure on these western jaunts. Nevertheless, they were a calculated part of his overall strategy to defeat the defiant western tribes.[27]

With their economic base destroyed, western Indian tribes would have no choice but to retire to the reservations allotted to them by the government. Sheridan believed the concentration of the tribes and their segregation from the whites to be essential to the establishment of order on the frontier. He thus agreed with the reservation policy and supported President Grant's so-called Peace Policy out of loyalty to his old commander, but he vehemently disagreed with what he viewed as the overly mild treatment of the Indians on the reservation. "An attempt has been made to control the Indians, a wild and savage people, by moral suasion," Sheridan noted in 1874, "while we all know that the most stringent laws have to be enacted for the government of civilized white people."[28]

The Civil War had taught Sheridan how easily the social order could be disrupted, and he had come to believe that the application of force was essential to guarantee stability. "I have the interest of the Indian at heart as much as anyone, and sympathize with his fading out race," Sheridan wrote, "but many years of experiences have taught me that to civilize and christianize [*sic*] the wild Indian it is not only necessary to put him on Reservations but it is also necessary to exercise some strong authority over him." Sheridan believed that only the army could exercise this control, and he repeatedly but futilely recommended that supervision of Indian affairs be transferred from the Department of the Interior back to the War Department where it had been until 1849.[29]

---

27. For Sheridan's hunting expeditions, see Henry E. Davies, *Ten Days on the Plains*, ed. Paul Andrew Hutton (Dallas: DeGolyer Library/Southern Methodist University Press, 1985); William E. Strong, *Canadian River Hunt* (Norman: University of Oklahoma Press, 1960); Strong, *The Grand Duke Alexis in the United States of America* (New York: Interland Publishing, 1972). Also see David A. Dary, *The Buffalo Book: The Full Saga of the American Animal* (Chicago: Swallow Press, 1974); Tom McHugh, *The Time of the Buffalo* (New York: Alfred A. Knopf, 1972); and Wayne Gard, *The Great Buffalo Hunt* (New York: Alfred A. Knopf, 1959).

28. Sheridan to J. T. Averill, January 28, 1874, Box 10, Sheridan Papers.

29. Sheridan to War Department, July 11, 1872, Box 7, Sheridan Papers. For Sheridan on Indian policy and transfer, see Paul A. Hutton, "Phil Sheridan's Pyrrhic Victory: The Piegan Massacre, Army Politics, and the Transfer Debate," *Montana The Magazine of Western History*, 32 (Spring 1982), 32-43.

The Indian Bureau's protection of Indians that Sheridan believed were guilty of depredations frustrated him, while the lack of a firm national consensus on the righteousness of his Indian campaigns deeply troubled him. During the Civil War, a grateful nation applauded his every action, but now he drew bitter criticism for pursuing similar tactics against the western Indians. The public condemnation of his direction of Custer's 1868 Washita fight and Baker's 1870 Piegan massacre on the Marias deeply wounded Sheridan.

Sheridan could never fathom why so many opposed his methods. His experience in previous Indian campaigns where conventional military methods had been employed and failed had convinced him by the early 1870s that the army could not "successfully fight Indians on the principle of high-toned warfare; that is where the mistake has been." "In taking the offensive," he once explained to Sherman in defense of his methods,

> I have to select that season when I can catch the fiends; and if a village is attacked and women and children killed, the responsibility is not with the soldiers but with the people whose crimes necessitated the attack. During the war did any one hesitate to attack a village or town occupied by the enemy because women and children were within its limits? Did we cease to throw shells into Vicksburg or Atlanta because women and children were there?[30]

Sheridan could not cope rationally with eastern criticism, repeatedly relying on a string of Indian atrocity tales to discredit those who opposed his tactics. He pointed to "good and pious ecclesiastics" as the agents of frontier disorder, castigating them as

> the aiders and abettors of savages who murdered, without mercy, men, women and children; in all cases ravishing the women sometimes as often as forty and fifty times in succession, and while insensible from brutality and exhaustion forced sticks up their persons, and, in one instance, the fortieth or fiftieth savage drew his saber and used it on the person of the woman in the same manner.

He viewed his soldiers as defenders of female virtue — the heart of civilization — who sacrificed everything to destroy "murderers and rapers of helpless women." Sheridan repeatedly trotted out these atrocities — committed by Cheyennes during the 1868–1869 war — in his debates with the eastern humanitarians. "I do not know exactly how far these humanitarians should be excused on account of their

---

30. Sheridan to William T. Sherman, May 9, 1873, Division of the Missouri, Letters Sent, Records of U.S. Continental Commands, Record Group (RG) 393, National Archives, Washington, D.C. (hereafter NA).

ignorance," he wrote in 1869, "but surely it is the only excuse that gives a shadow of justification for aiding and abetting such horrid crimes."[31]

This use of such graphic diatribes gives some insight into Sheridan's background, his unconventional nature, and his quick reliance on any tactic to discredit his enemies. No story was more traditional in American history or more effective in rallying support to the western army than the plight of captive frontier women. Unmarried until age forty-four and then taking a wife young enough to be his daughter, Sheridan fully subscribed to Victorian notions of man as woman's protector. He was mortified when unable to save the captive Clara Blinn and her child, who the Arapahos murdered at the Battle of the Washita in 1868; and he was elated at Custer's 1869 rescue of two women held by the Cheyennes during the same campaign. Nonetheless, he saw these women as forever tainted by their captivity. In 1872, Sheridan refused to authorize the payment of five ponies to ransom Mary Jordan from the Cheyennes. "I cannot give my approval to any reward for the delivery of this white women," Sheridan declared. "After having her husband and friends murdered, and her own person subjected to the fearful bestiality of perhaps the whole tribe, it is mock humanity to secure what is left of her for the consideration of five ponies."[32] Mrs. Jordan's captors murdered her.

Sheridan's bizarrely convoluted logic dictated that the Indians be destroyed *before* such outrages could occur, *before* the social fabric could come undone, *before* the race could be polluted. It was a no-win situation for Sheridan. "We cannot avoid being abused by one side or the other," he mused in 1870. "If we allow the defenseless people on the frontier to be scalped and ravished, we are burnt in effigy and execrated as soulless monsters, insensible to the suffering of humanity. If the Indian is punished to give security to these people, we are the same soulless monsters from the other side."[33] Sheridan consciously, even combatively, made his decision to support the settlers who resided on the extended frontier line encompassed by his military division:

> My duties are to protect these people. I have nothing to do with Indians but in this connection. There is scarcely a day in which I do not receive the most heart rendering [sic] appeals to save settlers . . . and I am forced to the alternative of choosing whether I shall regard their ap-

---

31. *Annual Report of the Secretary of War,* [1869] (2 vols., Washington, D.C.: Government Printing Office, 1869), 1:47-48.

32. Sheridan to Sherman, November 30, 1872, Box 8, Sheridan Papers. For the details of this tragic episode, see Minnie Dubbs Millbrook, "The Jordan Massacre," *Kansas History,* 2 (Winter 1979), 218-30.

33. Sheridan to Sherman, March 18, 1870, Box 91, Sheridan Papers.

peals or allow them to be butchered in order to save myself from the
hue and cry of the people who know not the Indians and whose families
have not the fear, morning, noon, and night, of being ravished and
scalped by them. The wife of the man at the center of wealth and
civilization and refinement is not more dear to him than is the wife
of the pioneer of the frontier. I have no hesitation in making my choice.
I am going to stand by the people over whom I am placed and give
them what protection I can.[34]

Such sentiments endeared Sheridan to the westerners, who soon
came to regard him as their special advocate. They saw the question
clearly. "Shall we Williampennize or Sheridanize the Indians?" asked
the Columbus, Nebraska, *Platte Journal* in 1870. An angry Texan's letter in 1870 to the Chicago *Tribune* clearly expressed the position of
many westerners: "Give us Phil Sheridan and Send Philanthropy to
the devil![35] But Indiana Congressman Daniel Voorhees spoke for many
in the East when he rose in the House to denounce the "curious spec-
tacle" of President Grant "upon the one hand welcoming his Indian
agents in their peaceful garments and broadbrims coming to tell him
what they have done as missionaries of a gospel of peace and of a
beneficent Government, and upon the other hand welcoming this
man, General Sheridan, stained with the blood of innocent women
and children!" Wendell Phillips, the famed Boston reformer, could not
have agreed more, declaring at an 1870 Reform League meeting: "I
only know the names of three savages upon the Plains—Colonel Baker,
General Custer, and at the head of all, General Sheridan."[36]

Undeterred, Sheridan planned and directed a series of harsh campaigns during the 1870s that broke the back of Indian resistance and
opened the frontier to rapid white occupation. In the largest of these
campaigns, the Red River War of 1874–1875 on the southern plains
and the Great Sioux War of 1876–1877 on the northern plains, he
employed the same overall strategy that had succeeded in his
1868–1869 winter campaign. In each case he attempted to employ
winter as an ally—although both campaigns saw summer fighting—
and to have converging columns trap the Indians. Recognizing the
difficulties of distance and terrain, he never expected these columns
to meet or work in concert. Rather, they would keep the Indians insecure, off-balance, and constantly moving. In neither of these cam-

34. Ibid.

35. Columbus, Nebraska, *Platte Journal*, June 29, 1870; Chicago *Tribune*, April
25, 1870.

36. Francis Paul Prucha, *American Indian Policy in Crisis: Christian Reformers and the
Indian, 1865-1900* (Norman: University of Oklahoma Press, 1976), 50; Robert Winston
Mardock, *The Reformers and the American Indian* (Columbia: University of Missouri Press,
1971), 71-73.

paigns did the Indians suffer much loss of life in battle, but rather were defeated by starvation, exposure, stock and property losses, and constant insecurity. These campaigns reaffirmed the effectiveness of Sheridan's philosophy of total war, for it was concern over the suffering of their families that brought the warriors in to the reservations to surrender. If Indian women and children had been allowed to find sanctuary on the reservations—which they were not—or if the soldiers had been prohibited from attacking the Indian villages, then Sheridan's strategy could not have been successful. Only by making war on the entire tribe—men, women, and children—could Sheridan hope for quick results. Although brutal, this strategy was eminently successful.[37]

So wedded to his converging-columns, winter-campaign strategy, Sheridan often refused to consider alternatives. Sheridan's conservatism, combined with his underestimation of the tenacity, courage, and ability of his Indian foes, could lead to disaster, as it did at both the Rosebud and Little Big Horn in 1876. In these most conventional of battles, where large numbers of troops and Indians maneuvered for control of open battlefields, the Indians simply out-generaled Crook and Custer. Only after Sheridan turned to occupying the Sioux hunting grounds, to constant harassing tactics, and to military control over the agencies did the Indians suffer defeat as a result of starvation and exhaustion.

Sheridan, who during the Civil War had proven to be quite original in his approach to military problems, failed for the most part to provide innovative or imaginative leadership for the frontier army. The long shadow cast by the Civil War was part of the problem. Instead of looking to the future, Sheridan and many other army officers were far more captivated by the glorious past. The conflict on the western frontier was simply not a "real" war to the men who had won their stars in the great struggle of 1861–1865. Traditionalism set the tone of Sheridan's little frontier army.

After the Great Sioux War the nature of Indian campaigning changed. Sheridan's soldiers no longer marched into strange country against a foe of unknown numbers. Instead, his troopers ringed the Indian reservations with their forts, guarding against outbreaks. Clearly on the defensive, the Indians never could muster much strength. "Indian troubles that will hereafter occur will be those which arise upon the different Indian reservations," Sheridan declared in 1879, "or from attempts made to reduce the number and size of these reservations, by the concentration of the Indian

---

37. The best overview of these campaigns remains Robert M. Utley, *Frontier Regulars: The United States Army and the Indian, 1866-1891* (New York: Macmillan, 1973).

tribes."[38] The characteristic type of campaign after 1877 was the pursuit of Indian fugitives over a large expanse of territory. Such was the case with Chief Joseph's Nez Perce band in 1877 and with the Northern Cheyennes of Dull Knife and Little Wolf in 1878.

To guard against these outbreaks Sheridan could muster few troops. In the Departments of the Missouri, the Platte, and Dakota, he had but one man for every 75 square miles of territory, while in the Department of Texas he had but one for every 120 square miles of territory. His infantry companies averaged forty men, while the cavalry and artillery did only slightly better with sixty and fifty men, respectively. Sheridan complained that three or four of his companies were "expected to hold and guard, against one of the most acute and wary foes in the world, a space of country that in any other land would be held by a brigade."[39]

Keeping the peace on the Indian frontier remained Sheridan's primary duty throughout his years as commander of the Division of the Missouri, but even when there was Indian unrest his troops were quickly pulled from the frontier to meet various threats to national order. Sheridan and his troopers were called to duty, for example, during 1875 when he was placed in charge of Louisiana, during the tense election crisis of 1876, and during the railroad labor strife of 1877. Indian wars were already anachronistic to Gilded Age Americans, and the requirements of frontier expansion were usually subordinated to more pressing political or economic needs in the East.

Sheridan spent much of his time with the establishment, construction, maintenance, and abandonment of forts within the Division of the Missouri. A parsimonious Congress never appropriated enough funds to build vital new posts or to keep established forts in even a modest state of repair. Western communities competed for forts, depots, or headquarters offices, and some frontier community boosters even fabricated Indian scares to bring in troops, with a resulting gain to the local economy from construction and supply contracts. Sheridan often confronted irate citizens, congressmen, and even his own officers over troop transfers or the location, construction, and budget of forts and depots. Sheridan guarded his meager resources, spending funds only on those projects that he considered in "the public interest." He resented accusations that his actions retarded development in the western territories, for just the opposite was true. When Montana's territorial delegate chided Sheridan over his refusal to construct new posts, the general angrily reminded him

---

38. *Annual Report of the Secretary of War,* [1879] (2 vols., Washington, D.C.: Government Printing Office, 1879), 1:45.

39. Ibid.

that "nearly everything done for the opening of a way to Montana for the last two years has been ordered by me, or on my recommendation."[40]

Sheridan was one of the West's greatest boosters, actively promoting western lands and constantly encouraging settlement. Despite his warm approval of the activities of western capitalists, he never sold his favor to any business interest and his name was never tainted with scandal. He was quick to point out to frontier promoters that "if the wishes of the settlers on the frontier were to be gratified, we would have a military post in every county, and the Army two or three hundred thousand strong."[41] He had enormous power over the frontier economy, and when he could justifiably do so he worked to assist struggling western communities. One of his proudest accomplishments was to "have been connected with the great development of the country west of the Mississippi river by protecting every interest so far as in my power, and in a fair and honorable way, without acquiring a single personal interest to mar or blur myself or my profession."[42]

Along with his promotion of western growth, Sheridan also developed a deep interest in the cause of conservation during his final years as commander of the Division of the Missouri. He had long had a special interest in the Yellowstone National Park region and had sponsored several exploring expeditions into the area. During an 1882 trip to Yellowstone National Park, Sheridan was enraged to learn of the slaughter of the park's wildlife by hide hunters. He was further disturbed to learn that the Department of the Interior had granted monopoly rights to develop the park to a company affiliated with the Northern Pacific Railroad. In contradiction to his earlier encouragement of the slaughter of the buffalo and his long support of the Northern Pacific, Sheridan now vigorously raised his voice in opposition. "The improvements in the park should be national," he declared in 1882, and if the Department of the Interior could not operate and protect the park, he would. "I will engage to keep out skin hunters and all other hunters," he told the administration, "by use of troops from Fort Washakie on the south, Custer on the east, and Ellis on the north, and, if necessary, I can keep sufficient troops in the park to accomplish this object, and give a place of refuge and safety for our noble game."[43]

---

40. Sheridan to Martin Maginnis, June 9, 1874, Division of the Missouri, Letters Sent, RG 393, NA.

41. Sheridan endorsement, March 13, 1873, Box 9, Sheridan Papers.

42. *Proceedings of the State and Assembly of New York, on the Life and Services of Gen. Philip H. Sheridan, Held at the Capitol, April 9, 1889* (Albany: James B. Lyon, State Printer, 1890), 53, 63.

43. Philip H. Sheridan, *Report of an Exploration of Parts of Wyoming, Idaho, and Montana in August and September, 1882, Made by Lieut. Gen. P. H. Sheridan* (Washington, D.C.: Government Printing Office, 1882), 17-18.

Sheridan also proposed a bold plan to expand the park's bound-aries by over three thousand square miles to incorporate vital wildlife habitat. The general quickly enlisted powerful allies to block the monopolists, expand the park, protect its animals, and transfer its con-trol to the army. George Bird Grinnell, editor of *Forest and Stream,* vol-unteered his journal to assist him. John Schuyler Crosby, Sheridan's former aide who was now territorial governor of Montana, also entered the fray on the side of his old commander, as did Missouri Senator George Vest, chairman of the Senate Committee on Territories.

As part of his crusade to protect Yellowstone National Park, Sheridan organized a presidential excursion to the park during the summer of 1883. President Chester Arthur's trip, which was guided by Sheridan and accompanied by Secretary of War Robert Lincoln, Senator Vest, Governor Crosby, and other dignitaries, attracted wide publicity. It resulted in blocking efforts by the railroad to run a spur line into the park, reducing the company's leases in the park from 4,400 acres to only 10 acres, and defeating an attempt to return the park to the public domain. Sheridan failed to expand the park, but in August 1886 he had the satisfaction of ordering a company of the First Cavalry to take charge of the park, inaugurating thirty-two years of able military administration. When Sheridan rode to Yellowstone's rescue he achieved the finest moment of his last years and secured a national treasure for posterity.[44]

On November 1, 1883, General W. T. Sherman retired from the army and Phil Sheridan moved to Washington to assume the posi-tion of commanding general. By law, however, Sherman's four stars retired with him, leaving Sheridan with the rank of lieutenant general. Sheridan found his new position frustrating, for the office was devoid of any real authority. The commanding general had no vital respon-sibilities in time of peace, because various bureau chiefs actually ad-ministered the army and reported directly to the secretary of war. Despite his relative youth, Sheridan's health had been slipping for years and he now withdrew more and more from the public limelight to spend time with his wife, Irene Rucker Sheridan (they were married in 1875), and their four young children. He spent much of this time working on his memoirs, which he completed in March 1888.

When seen in public Sheridan was more often than not in civilian clothes. His oddly shaped figure had grown increasingly portly, his

44. For Sheridan and Yellowstone, see Paul A. Hutton, "Phil Sheridan's Crusade for Yellowstone," *American History Illustrated,* 19 (February 1985), 10-15; Thomas C. Reeves, "President Arthur in Yellowstone National Park," *Montana The Magazine of Western History,* 19 (Summer 1969), 18-29; Jack Ellis Haynes, "The Expedition of President Chester A. Arthur to Yellowstone National Park in 1883," *Annals of Wyoming,* 14 (January 1942), 31-38.

face reddened and fleshy and his hair white. The New York *World* described him as if a character in a low comic opera: "He wore upon the back of his round, bullet head an old fashioned silk hat about two sizes too small. He wore a short, light, yellow-gray overcoat which had only two buttons and they were ready to fly off from the undue strain of Sheridan's round figure. The trousers were a gray plaid and fitted very snugly to the General's fat legs."[45]

On May 22, 1888, just after his return from Chicago to inspect the site for Fort Sheridan, the fifty-seven-year-old general collapsed from a severe heart attack. A string of heart attacks of increasing seriousness followed. This news prompted Congress to revive the grade of general of the army, and President Grover Cleveland promptly signed the commission so that Sheridan joined Washington, Grant, and Sherman in holding the four-star rank. His spirits buoyed by the promotion, even though his body was now frail and emaciated, he requested that he be taken to his seaside cottage at Nonquitt, Massachusetts. Throughout July he calmly waited, looking out over the lovely summer sea of Buzzard's Bay, as his condition worsened. He faced the end without fear or despair, for Sheridan knew neither. He had dealt in death all of his adult life—he was too familiar with it to fear it when it came for him on the Sabbath evening of August 5, 1888.

His legacy, as with all of humankind, is a mixed one. Hardly cerebral, he nevertheless possessed a truly continental vision for the republic. He was determined to open up the West and unite it with the rest of the nation. He could be cruel and vindictive in this enterprise, and this found expression in his frontier military policies. Knowing nothing but a soldier's life, Sheridan tended to view every situation in light of how military power could establish order. Deeply affected by the chaos of Civil War, he was quick to apply force against all those who opposed his government's wishes—be they unreconstructed rebels in the South, striking laborers in the East, or Indians in the West.

Despite his racism, brutality, and conservatism he was in many ways the perfect soldier for his times. He ruthlessly carried out the dictates of his government, confident that his harsh tactics brought on a quicker peace and thus an end to warfare for all. He conquered and subjugated the Indians, opening their rich lands to a wildly expansive and exploitative generation. He then sought, in his simple, blunt way, to impose order on that mad push westward and was at times somewhat successful.

---

45. O'Connor, *Sheridan*, 349.

By the time Phil Sheridan passed from the scene his frontier was gone as well. That final, rapid push westward—in all its brutality and all its glory—remains his great legacy. "He was," as the Bard said, "a man, take him for all in all, I shall not look upon his like again."

Major Brisbin's Relief of Fort Pease

By Edgar I. Stewart

In 1875, a group of traders from Bozeman constructed a trading post—Fort Pease—on the left bank of the Yellowstone River opposite and a few miles below its confluence with the Big Horn.[1] Never a military post, it was hoped that this would become an important factor in the economic life of the territory when the river traffic— expected to develop with the coming of the steamboat to the river— should fully materialize.

But for the moment, the founders of Fort Pease, Montana Territory, contented themselves with a more immediate pursuit, the securing of wolfskins, and trading. For the few months that the fort was in active operation it was used entirely as a trading post.

The small development, consisting of a series of log huts connected by a palisade of cottonwood logs enclosing an area some 200 feet square, was built on land which the Sioux claimed as their own. Since these Indians regarded the establishment as an invasion of their hunting grounds, the garrison was in a state of siege almost from the beginning. Individual members could leave the protection of the friendly stockade only at the risk of their lives. The Sioux, shortly, became so bold and insolent as to threaten the post itself with attack. So constant was the Sioux siege that members of the garrison secured daily food and fuel only with great difficulty and danger.

*Edgar I. Stewart, "Major Brisbin's Relief of Fort Pease; A prelude to the bloody Little Big Horn Massacre," *Montana The Magazine of Western History,* 6 (Summer 1956), 23-27.

1. See "Fort Pease, The First Attempted Settlement in Yellowstone Valley," by Clyde McLemore, *Montana The Magazine of History,* 2 (January 1952), 17-31 for a good detailed account of the life of this trading post.

On the tenth of February, the Bozeman *Times* reported the arrival, two days before, of B. F. Dexter. He had left Fort Pease on the twenty-second of January, in company with seventeen other men, most of whom had merely transferred their activities to other places (although a few came on to Bozeman).

Dexter reported that during the month of January almost continuous fighting had gone on between the members of the garrison and the Indians. On one occasion, three trappers had been surprised in camp on Pryor's Creek by the Indians and had lost all of their possessions, horses, equipment, and even their coats. The men—the newspaper referred to them as "the boys"—had been occupied in preparing supper, and the Indians had been able to approach within ten feet before their presence was discovered. Dexter reported that about three hundred Indians were in the party that attacked the three men and said that the usual proportion was about one hundred Indians for every white man. Although he stressed the large size of the Indian parties he apparently did not regard the situation as being too serious, for at the same time, he announced his intention of returning to Fort Pease about the first of March. His plans called for prospecting on Goose Creek and ultimately making his way to the Black Hills.[2]

On the eighteenth of February, 1876, the Bozeman *Avant-Courier* noted the arrival of a party of seven men from Fort Pease. This group included Taylor Blivins, previously reported killed by the Sioux, and P. W. McCormick. The two reported that they had been discouraged by the constant hostility of the Sioux, which prevented much progress either in hunting or trapping. Otherwise, they believed that they would have done quite well. They said that forty-one men remained at the fort. The number was sufficient, in their estimation, only to hold off the hostile Indians until a relief column could be organized and sent to the assistance of the post.[3]

Based on this information, appeal for military aid and assistance was immediately telegraphed to Brigadier General Alfred H. Terry, at U. S. Army Department Headquarters in St. Paul.

With approval of the Department Commander having been granted, Major James Brisbin (known to his troops as "Grasshopper Jim" because of his fervent belief in the agricultural possibilities of Montana Territory) who only recently had assumed command at Fort Ellis, left that fort, February 22, with a battalion consisting of Companies F, G, H, and L of the Second United States Cavalry. This also included a detachment of twelve men of Company C of the Seventh

---

2. Bozeman *Times*, Feb. 10, 1876.
3. Bozeman *Avant-Courier*, Feb. 18, 1876.

James Sanks Brisbin, a major of the Second Cavalry from 1868 to 1885, commanded the Fort Pease relief expedition in early 1876 and enjoyed a prominent role throughout the Great Sioux War. (Montana Historical Society Photograph Archives)

Infantry, under command of Lieutenant Quinton. They were in charge of both a Gatling gun and a twelve pounder "Napoleon" gun. Fifteen civilian volunteers from the town of Bozeman and a train of supply wagons, completed the complement, total strength of which was 14 officers, 192 enlisted men, and 15 citizens.

The column marched fourteen miles the first day out, crossing the divide between Fort Ellis and the Yellowstone River by way of Bozeman Pass. The next day they covered twenty-two miles, probably camping that night a short distance below the present site, the city of

Livingston. On the twenty-fourth, they marched fifteen miles, then forded the river to the right bank, moving down two miles more before going into camp.[4]

On the twenty-fifth, seven miles brought them to the "Bowlder." (Lewis and Clark called it "Rivers Across" from the fact that Big Timber and Boulder creeks enter the Yellowstone River from opposite sides of the stream.) An additional eight miles brought them to "Point of Rocks" on the Yellowstone. They apparently covered another five miles before going into camp. The next day, the twenty-sixth, saw only a short march, eleven miles being covered in the course of which they crossed Bridger Creek. Although signs of Indians in the vicinity were strong, and the members of the command were alerted to the possibility of being "jumped" by the Sioux, they were surprised and relieved when none of the hostiles elected to stand their ground or attack. Thus the column was able to pass through without any molestation.[5]

On the twenty-seventh, the military party made two crossings of the river, both being made on ice. Major Brisbin's expedition camped that night not far from the present town of Columbus, near the junction of the Stillwater with the Yellowstone River. Here Lieutenant Schofield, with 25 citizens and 30 Crow Indians, joined the command. He had been sent on, in advance, to visit Crow Agency and enlist the services of as many citizens and Indians as he could. The next morning an additional 24 Crows came in, bringing the number of scouts to a total of 54, an extremely welcome addition to the command, since the Crows were the inveterate and hereditary enemies of the Sioux. These additions were made despite the efforts of some persons who had preceded the soldiers to the Agency, carrying unfavorable reports as to the purposes of the expedition with the aim of discouraging any prospective volunteers. Such "gratuitous advice" it was remarked was "not appreciated by the military."[6] Reports reaching Bozeman from Fort Pease indicated that the Indians had disappeared with the coming of cold weather. Other opinion expressed was that Brisbin's column would experience little difficulty "in finding the Sioux and getting a fight out of them."[7]

By the first of March, the column had reached Baker's Battleground and pushing on, had crossed to the right bank of the river before going into camp. Here, near the mouth of Pryor Creek, while the

---

4. The itinerary of Brisbin's march, as well as his telegram from the mouth of the Big Horn, are to be found in *House Exec. Doc.*, 44th Cong., 1st Sess., No. 184, pp. 49-51.

5. Bozeman *Times*, March 16, 1876.

6. Bozeman *Times*, March 2, 1876.

7. Bozeman *Times*, March 2, 1876.

horses of Company G were being watered, the ice broke and a number of the animals were pitched into the wintry stream. All were rescued except three horses, two Indian ponies, and a mule which were swept under by the extremely swift current and drowned. This was the only accident suffered during the expedition."[8]

The next day the party covered twenty miles, camping that night near the base of Pompey's Pillar. On the third of March, they again crossed the river, and marched on Stanley's trail of 1873 for a distance of twenty miles before making a dry camp at a point about six miles back from the stream.

On March 4, the Military "rescue" party arrived at Fort Pease, having covered sixteen miles in a march which involved two crossings of the river. Brisbin's detachment camped outside the stockade. On investigation they found only nineteen survivors—eighteen white men and one negro. Six men had been killed and eight wounded by the Indians. Fortunately, the remainder had escaped by making their way to the settlement through Sioux infested country. Major Brisbin found no Indians and learned that none had been seen recently. But there was plenty of evidence that small parties were in the vicinity. The expedition discovered five war lodges, estimated to have housed about sixty-two warriors, located at the mouth of the Big Horn River. Their occupants were said to have fled south "with the utmost precipitation when they saw the cavalry column."[9] Indicative of their haste was the fact that they left moccasins, medicine bags, and axes in camp. It was the opinion of rescued and rescuers alike that these Indians had been watching the men at the fort, hoping to pick off any who ventured out or who dared attempt a return to the settlements.

Brisbin's scouts brought in a mass of contradictory reports. Some felt that the Sioux were abandoning the immediate vicinity of the Big Horn and Little Big Horn Rivers and moving farther eastward to the Rosebud. Others reported a heavy trail of at least five hundred hostiles going north toward the Musselshell River.[10] Since these were heading in the direction of Fort Peck, the opinion was expressed that they were Sioux who were returning to that Agency to await the departure of the troops before again taking the warpath.[11] Scouts were recalled and again sent out in all directions. But they were unable to discover further signs of the presence of hostile Indians in the immediate vicinity, although some scouted as far as the mouth of the Little Big Horn.

---

8. Bozeman *Avant-Courier,* March 17, 1876.
9. Bozeman *Avant-Courier,* March 17, 1876.
10. Bozeman *Avant-Courier,* March 17, 1876.
11. Bozeman *Times,* March 16, 1876.

In the meantime, the fort was evacuated, and all of the traders started back with Brisbin's detachment. (Some of them apparently with considerable reluctance.) All valuable property was removed with the idea of transporting it to a place of comparative safety. For some unknown reason, one gun—a field piece—was left behind and the flag was also left flying.

Major Brisbin, apparently in a state of indecision, seems to have wanted to scout further, in the hope of discovering the exact whereabouts and strength of the enemy. But he was prevented from doing this because of an acute shortage of forage for the livestock. This fact, along with the advent of bad weather, compelled an immediate return to Fort Ellis. The party traversed much the same route followed in coming out.

The first day, they covered only eight miles, twice crossing the river in the course of an eighteen mile march. The fine weather, which had prevailed until the day before their arrival at Fort Pease, was now bitterly cold. Members of the command suffered considerably from exposure. The cold, coupled with shortage of forage, was especially hard on the animals, many of which gave out and had to be abandoned while others were shot.[12]

On the night of March 8, the column camped near Pompey's Pillar. Two nights later, it was at the mouth of Canyon Creek, about eight miles above the present city of Billings. On the twelfth, the expedition reached Countryman's Ranch, near the mouth of the Stillwater. On the fifteenth they crossed the Yellowstone River for the last time, crossing to Hot Spring Creek and moving upstream twelve miles before going into camp.

Major Brisbin and Captain Tyler there left the column in command of Captain Ball, while they pushed on ahead to Fort Ellis. The ambulance in which they were riding broke through the ice while crossing Boulder Creek, throwing both men to the water. The chilled officers sat up all night, drying their clothes and blankets.[13] They arrived at Fort Ellis on the fifteenth, two days ahead of the column.

The expedition covered a total of 398 miles, of which 208 had been on the outward march while the return journey had covered only 190 miles.[14]

On arriving at Ellis, the troops found that during their absence orders had arrived for another movement eastward, a part of the campaign against the Sioux and Northern Cheyenne Indians that was to culminate in the famous Battle of the Little Big Horn, where Custer

---

12. Bozeman *Times*, March 16, 1876.
13. Bozeman *Times*, March 16, 1876.
14. *House Exec. Doc.*, 44th Cong., 1st Sess., No. 184, pp. 50-51.

and his command perished. The four companies of the Second Cavalry were about to retrace the journey just completed.

On the day that Major Brisbin's expedition arrived at Fort Ellis, five companies of the Seventh Infantry were to leave Fort Shaw in northern Montana, en route to Fort Ellis, to participate in that disastrous "Custer" campaign.

In another part of Montana Territory, Colonel J. J. Reynolds, with a cavalry detachment from both the Second and Third Cavalry regiments, had just attacked an Indian camp on the Little Powder, succeeding only in making a grand fiasco of the whole affair.

Thus the Master of the Tragedy was beginning to bring together various, ominous threads. Soon these would be woven into a bloody patchwork on the desolate ridges above the Little Big Horn. The tortured bodies of George Armstrong Custer and his troopers would add the warp and woof to make the Nation's most famous and most repatched Indian battle a part of the tapestry of history—a crazy quilt pattern which even today defies credulity.

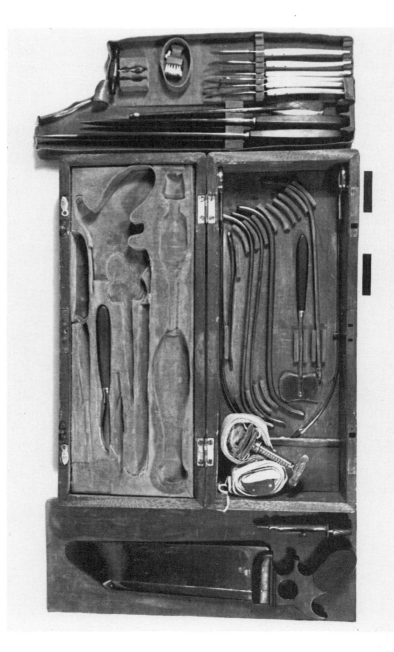

This Civil War-era medical instrument case is typical of those used during the Great Sioux War. (Donated in 1917 by Dr. C. B. Miller, Somers, Montana, Montana Historical Society Museum)

A Surgeon at the
Little Big Horn

Edited by Thomas R. Buecker

In all the annals of western history, hardly a single event can match the notoriety that attaches to the Battle of the Little Big Horn, the legendary "Custer's Last Stand." Due to the oft-discussed actions of Lieutenant Colonel George A. Custer, the trend of interest in the Sioux Campaign of 1876 has centered on the fate of the Dakota column, largely composed of that most famous of cavalry regiments, the Seventh Cavalry. However, the Dakota column was but one of three launched by the War Department into the Yellowstone and Powder River countries in search of the "hostiles" that fateful summer of 1876.

Entering from the west was the Montana column, under the command of Colonel John Gibbon, Seventh Infantry. His column consisted of four companies of the Second Cavalry and six companies of the Seventh Infantry, totaling twenty-seven officers, 408 enlisted men, and forty-five scouts and civilian teamsters. Moving down the Yellowstone, Gibbon's command was the only force in the field during the first few weeks of the summer campaign. Following General Alfred H. Terry's orders to remain on the north side of the river, Gibbon's soldiers advanced leisurely along the Yellowstone before connecting with the Dakota column. Although the command struggled through the unpredictable Montana spring weather, the expedition many times took on the air of a country outing for the men, particularly the officers of the command. One of the officers, the only surgeon assigned to the column, was 1st Lieutenant Holmes O. Paulding, Assistant Surgeon, U.S.A.

Holmes Offley Paulding was born on October 7, 1852, in Washington, D.C., to a distinguished family. His father and great-uncle were ranking naval officers, and his mother was a member of the promi-

*Thomas R. Buecker, "A Surgeon at the Little Big Horn," *Montana The Magazine of Western History*, 32 (Autumn 1982), 34-49.

nent Offley family of Georgetown. After studying medicine in the
Columbian University in Washington, Paulding received appointment as an Assistant Surgeon on November 10, 1874. After accept-
ing his appointment, he was assigned for duty in the Department
of Dakota, first stationed at Fort Snelling, Minnesota, and then at
Fort Abraham Lincoln, Dakota Territory.[1] While at Fort Lincoln, he
had ample opportunity to become well-acquainted with George
Custer and became a member of the "Custer Clan." In late October
1875, the army transferred him to Fort Ellis, near Bozeman. From
there, he accompanied Gibbon's column during the entire period
it was in the field—from April 1 to September 29, 1876.

Paulding proved to be an impatient member of the expedition.
He did not understand Gibbon's cautious advance down the Yellowstone and complained of the lack of action and monotony that
characterized most of this phase of the campaign. Writing his mother
after the first month in the field he stated: "I wish we would go
somewhere away from here instead of purposelessly fooling around
in sagebrush bottoms all summer." He, along with other members
of the expedition, did not fully appreciate, or was unaware of, key
factors that would affect the outcome of the Sioux War of 1876. They
had no idea of the location, much less the number, of the hostiles
they were expected to defeat. The lack of this pertinent information
greatly contributed to Custer's defeat and to the Army's failure in
the summer campaign.

Throughout most of the period of his duty with the Montana column, Dr. Paulding wrote letters to his mother in Washington. (At the
same time, he kept a diary that has been published, which greatly sup-
plements these letters and furnishes information of a nature that he
probably preferred not to write to his family.)[2] The letters [which follow]
present an excellent example of the observations and feelings of a participant in the most celebrated campaign of the western Indian wars.

1. Information on Paulding's service is found in his Appointment, Commission,
and Personal File (2228 A.C.P. 1883) in the records of the War Department, Office
of the Adjutant General Record Group, (RG) 94, National Archives, Washington, D.C.
(hereafter NA).

2. The original of the diary is found with the William J. Ghent Papers at the Library
of Congress, Washington, D.C. A more accessible, and footnoted, version of the diary
is found in Barry C. Johnson, "Dr. Paulding and His Remarkable Diary," *Side Lights
of the Sioux War* (London: English Westerners Society, 1967), 47-69.

3. Fort Pease was a small stockade built by a group of Bozeman traders in 1875.
It was described as a series of log huts surrounded by a cottonwood palisade 200
feet square. The post was under a virtual state of siege by the Sioux during the winter
of 1875-1876, until it was relieved by a cavalry column under the command of Major
Brisbin. Gibbon's column remained in camp here from April 21 to May 9. See Edgar
I. Stewart, "Major Brisbin's Relief of Fort Pease," *Montana The Magazine of Western History,*
6 (Summer 1956), 23-27.

Expedition against Sioux
Camp at Fort Pease[3]
April 21st 1876

My Dear Mother

We camped last night about three miles above here, at the mouth of the Big Horn, and this morning a Scout brought us in dispatches from which we learned as the most important items that Gen. [George] Crook had gone back after losing some men and a great deal of stock and suffering severely in other ways, to recuperate and that he was to start again about May 15th.[4]

We are left the only force in the field, and Custer is to come over from Lincoln and perhaps part of [Colonel W.B.] Hazen's command from Buford, all to concentrate about this part of the country.[5] As we crossed the Yellowstone, the last ford just above the Big Horn the scouts sent in word that they had found fresh Indian signs, but as yet we havent seen any. Our orders are now to stay here and fortify the place and wait further supplies &c, which will keep us in this miserable hole for from thirty to forty days. The old stockade makes a pretty good corral for our stock, none of it having been burned except one building. We are supplied for nearly 45 days and will by that time have down another train and go on further. Our camp is just outside the stockade on a sage brush alkali plain full of carcases, old skins and other filth from the previous occupants of the place, and it will be a wonder if they dont get typhoid fever when the rains begin. So far the weather has been good and we have got along very nicely. The main source of annoyance being the fords of the river which have been steadily growing deeper. I dont think we can cross again below here as our last one nearly swept the horses off their feet and reached up to the saddles, since which the Big Horn has joined its large current with the Yellowstone and nearly doubled the size. I suppose however that if Gibbon gets it in his head to try it again nothing will demonstrate its unpracticability short of drowning one or two dozen men, unless he waves his hand and spreads the waters asunder like Col & Bvt Gen Moses. [Major James] Brisbin

---

4. Striking the first blow of the 1876 campaign, a large column under General Crook left Fort Fetterman, Wyoming, in March to search the Powder River country for hostiles. Although a large village was destroyed, severe winter conditions forced Crook to withdraw to his base and delay further operations until late spring.

5. Fort Abraham Lincoln was established in August 1872, near Bismarck, Dakota Territory. Fort Buford was established on June 15, 1866, near the Missouri River and near the mouth of the Yellowstone in western Dakota Territory. See Francis Paul Prucha, *A Guide to the Military Posts of the United States, 1789-1895* (Madison: State Historical Society of Wisconsin, 1964), 53, 63.

has been quite decent & pleasant this time though he is like the 5th wheel of a coach & has nothing to do and no command except merely nominally that of the Cavalry battalion. he cant ride a horse & goes booming along in a spring wagon away out of sight.[6] Throughout the trip he seems to have made a point of treating me with great consideration and though I may be uncharitable in connecting the two items, I am going to send him home tonight with the party who take in this letter on sick leave on account of chronic rheumatism &c. &c. . . . .

Your affec. Son
Holmes Offley Paulding

Yellowstone Expedition
Camp at "Fort Pease" mouth of Big Horn
April 24th 1876

My dear Mother

. . . Our means of sending mail are so precarious that I doubt if half ever get anywhere. A white man is liable to get drowned at the fords, picked up by Sioux, or to desert for some more genial clime, and one of the Crows cant be relied on much, owing to various peculiarities, one of which consists in a habit they have when suddenly alarmed by any thing of throwing away every single thing— blankets, robes, saddle and clothes and putting out completely stripped except their rifle and cartridge belt, as hard as the pony can travel. These things have a tendency to render their carrying the mail 250 miles a trifle uncertain as to its general results. I am feeling rather blue and lonesome this evening— since we left Ellis I have lived with [2nd Lt. Charles F.] Roe[7] and we have messed together, and today his Company and Captain [Edward] Ball[']s left for a scout up the Big Horn to old Fort C.F. Smith and return, a trip of 150 miles.[8]

---

6.   Brisbin at the time was suffering from rheumatism to such an extent that he was on crutches and unable to mount a horse. He insisted on accompanying the expedition, and rode in an ambulance most of the time. Paulding went with the earlier spring march to relieve Fort Pease, and this reference to Brisbin must result from incidents then.

7.   Roe, 2nd Cavalry, commanded the company in the absence of both the captain and first lieutenant, and was a messmate of Paulding. Later, Matthew Carroll, a civilian in charge of transportation with the column, joined their mess.

8.   Companies H & F, 2nd Cavalry, under the command of Capt. Edward Ball, left on the 24th for a seven-day scout via the Big Horn River, old Fort C. F. Smith, and Tullock's Fork. The scouting detail returned on May 4, having seen large numbers of wild game, but no hostiles. See Lt. E. J. McClernand, Second Cavalry, Acting Engineer Officer, "Journal of the Marches Made by the Forces under Colonel John Gibbon, Commanding the Expedition down the Yellowstone, between the First Day of April and the Twenty-ninth Day of September, 1876," *House Exec. Doc.* 1, Part 2, Vol. II, 45th Cong., 2d Sess. (Serial 1796), Appendix PP, 1361-76.

I tried every way to go with them & Gen Brisbin,[9] as well as Roe and Ball applied to have me do so, but Gibbon refused. I suppose he thinks that any trifling assistance I might render toward smoothing over or preventing the death of half a dozen common soldiers or junior officers would not justify my absence in case of the Comdg Genl being seized with a sudden attack of wind on the stomach. From all the reports of our scouts we have reason to think this scouting party will stand the best sort of a show for jumping or being jumped by the Indians. There is an immense herd of buffalo, thousands and thousands of them, blackening the plains of the Big Horn Valley from 30 miles up to the base of the mountains where Fort Smith is and these herds are all on the stampede from below on the Yellowstone and through the Rosebud bottom, over the divide . . .

We reached here in the evening of the 21st and a courier who had joined a day or two before brought dispatches for us to stay here until further supplies should be sent down, after which we are to cooperate with Crook and Custer, making probably an all summer job of it. Our camp is made in front of the old stockade on the plains, a sage brush desert enclosed by the bluffs ½ mile distant to the West with the river just east of camp and the opposite bluffs within gunshot distance overlooking us. . . .

We dont have much to do in the way of amusement here. Gibbon dont want me to go off after deer or buffalo, which would carry me some distance away, for, as he feelingly says if I should get shot they would'nt have any doctor & might want one.[10] I hope I will get a small perforation if we have a fight, just for spite. I would rather be shot than have any of the men so injured as to require operations impossible of performance by one *unassisted* surgeon, for I cant conceive of anything worse than to know what should be done for a man and not be able to do it. I go out some times a mile or so with my shot gun and get ducks, geese or chickens. I got a rara avis for this region the other day, a canvas back duck, which may have wandered four or five miles up in the air & sailed from Chesapeake Bay to the mountains to furnish me a dinner.

April 29th
We havent had a mail for some time until last night. Two men came in with a mail which had started some days ago, but one man got nearly drowned and had to go back with a played out horse . . . I have been amusing myself making a bed stead out of cotton wood,

---

9. Brisbin had been brigidier general of volunteers during the Civil War.

10. The lack of activity in this part of the campaign led many, including Dr. Paulding, to hunt in order to break the monotony and supplement field rations, not fully appreciating the danger.

my only tools being a dull axe and a scalping knife.[11] but the bed stead
is bully and keeps off wood ticks quite well. These wood ticks are about
the size and appearance of bed bugs but when they fasten to a horse
or other animal, swell to the size of this.

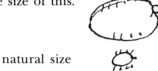

natural size

They are a great annoyance, get on the horses while grazing and climb
into everybody in camp with great energy. I see that a board has been
ordered to buy Kentucky horses for the battalion at Fort Ellis. I hope
it will send out the plugs soon as they are much needed. If there are
any good horses I may sell my pony and get one. It will be a good
spec. for horses are the staff of life out here and a good one can be
sold after some years use at twice the price for one in the east.
American horses being rare here as everyone uses a "Broncho" (California horse) "Cayuse" (cross between an Indian and American horse)
or an Indian pony.

                                                        May 1st
   Ball[']s command with Roe and the other boys has just got in and
had a nice trip. Saw no Indians at all and lots and lots of game. They
say the Elk came in among their horses while grazing and they got
all the meat they wanted. They report that the Big Horn Valley is the
most lovely in Montana. How I wish I could have gone with them. We
sent a party of the Indians down to the Rosebud River and they got
back yesterday saying they saw no signs of Sioux. The valley of the
Rosebud and Yellowstone on back sides filled with herds of buffalo
quietly grazing as if not disturbed at all for a long time—I wonder
where they are? Probably have gone north of the Missouri to their
"Agencies" or across the line.[12] I wish we would go somewhere away
from here instead of *purposelessly* fooling around in sage brush bottoms all summer. I am going out hunting with one of our scouts—
Muggins Taylor[13]—in a day or two, after big game. A courier leaves

---

   11.   Lt. Bradley noted in his diary, "The men are rendering their stay here as pleasant as possible by raising their beds off the ground, building shades of boughs over
their tents, etc.," James H. Bradley, ed. by Edgar I. Stewart, *The March of the Montana
Column* (Norman: University of Oklahoma Press, 1961), 72.

   12.   Many officers held the belief that the hostiles would flee north to Canada where
the army had no jurisdiction to pursue.

   13.   H. M. "Muggins" Taylor served as a scout from April 3 to September 30, and
was hired at the Crow Agency. He carried the first word of Custer's defeat to the outside world, via the Helena *Daily Herald*, after the battle.

immediately with mail so this scribble must terminate. Weather
lovely—all well and doing nothing. Love to all

Your affec. Son
Holmes Offley Paulding

Yellowstone River between Rosebud
& Tongue r's. M.T. June 14th/76

My dear Mother

Soon after my last letter to you (May 22nd)[14] they stopped sending
Couriers in with mail so that there has been no opportunity since
of sending a word to any one. Tommorrow two companies of Cavalry
will go up as far as Fort Pease and a Courier will leave them then
to take in the mail. We just returned yesterday from a long march
of about 2 weeks down nearly to the Powder River part of our command did reach Powder river and there met Gen. Terry who had come
up with a steamer, it being not far from the Missouri, and the same
day our party arrived. Gen Custer with the 7th Cav. (entire 12 companies) came marching in, down the Powder river valley with the band
playing and guidons flying from each troop. Our fat friend Gen.
Brisbin was with the party that first reached Gen. Terry. This party
has gone down the river since we left Fort Pease, taking some small
boats they found there & when we got within about 2 days march
of Powder river, Brisbin experienced an unaccountable liking for
water and got out of the ambulance (in which he has been riding
all the way from Ellis) to go with the boats that one day. The conse-
quence was that instead of camping with us that night, the long headed old chap who had knowledge that they could not be far off & must
be within easy reach by boats since they can travel 75 or 100 miles
a day in the current, went on down & sure enough he succeeded in
getting in the first word with Terry, before Gibbon should see him.[15]
Terry came up in the steamer next day and hearing that we had seen
an Indian camp near the Rosebud, which we cautiously had not
attempted to disturb,[16] ordered us all back & so coming up with
Custer on the other side of the river. I am going on too fast, having,

---

14.   Paulding's letter of May 22 is missing from this series.

15.   Gibbon's lack of aggressive activity in the early stage of the campaign led Major
Brisbin to make this early report to General Terry. Paulding also noted in his diary:
"Brisbin of course accomplished his object in getting in the first word with Terry
& Gibbon is very hot about it apparently," Johnson, "Dr. Paulding," 59.

16.   On May 27, Lt. Bradley discovered a village some twenty-five miles south of
the camp, but Gibbon did not choose to advance on it. See John Gray, *Centennial Campaign: The Sioux War of 1876* (Fort Collins, Colo.: Old Army Press, 1976), 83-84.

I believe, skipped all the time getween my last letter (May 22) & the time when we started down toward Powder river, but at odd intervals I have written a sort of letter to Jake Doyle[17] which I send with this, and I have asked him to tell you the little news there is in it as I dont expect to get time to write at all here. The morning of May 23, a war party came over this side of the river & caught 3 of our men near the bluffs. They killed & mutilated these men and then rode off pursued by a party of our Cavalry, but they might as well hunt for a needle in a hay stack as Indians in the bad lands. I was sent out with a small party to bring in the bodies and we buried them in camp just after sunset.[18]

During the ceremony there were about 200 Sioux on the bluffs across the river watching us & riding around in plain sight. A large camp was found up the Rosebud about 18 miles off, but our genial C. O. did not deem it advisable to attack it, a chance any other commander would give any price for, and after laying there for 10 days with the Indians showing themselves everyday in plain sight, as though they knew what a harmless concern they were dealing with, he as last began to do something. *not* to cross the command in boats & attack — but to *go away*. and this he did, keeping on down the river till we met Terry & were turned back as soon as he heard of it.[19]

Our C. O.'s excuse was that he had rec'd orders from St. Paul to guard *this* side of the Yellowstone. There's literal obedience for you.[20] This whole trip has been a miserable farce and everything has been as disagreeable as idiotic, pig headed stupidity could make it. We started out with as little as we could make last for 2 months, and here we are at least 22 days hard marching from home even if we started now, but theres no knowing how much longer we may stay out. We have all got into a way of grumbling, it is bad for all of us, taking away interest & causing distrust of everybody and worse than all it tends to make one disagreeable and sour. If it keeps up much longer I am afraid the whole Cavalry outfit will lose all traces of good nature they started with.[21]

---

17.   Doyle was probably a civilian acquaintance of Dr. Paulding in the East.

18.   While on an unauthorized hunt, two enlisted men and one civilian were attacked and killed by hostiles within sight of the camp. They were the only casualties, by hostiles, from the Montana column, Johnson, "Dr. Paulding," 54-56.

19.   Probably because of an aborted attempt to cross the swollen Yellowstone several days earlier, on May 17, Gibbon did not elect to cross and pursue the band sighted.

20.   On April 1, before leaving Fort Ellis, Gibbon had received telegraphic instructions from Terry cautioning him not to go south of the Yellowstone, that his objective was to prevent the Indians from getting away to the north, and to keep between the Indians and the Missouri, Gray, *Centennial Campaign*, 73.

21.   There are strong indications that the lack of decisive action and other disagreements caused friction among some of the officers of the column, Johnson, "Dr. Paulding," 57-58.

So far we have lost as many men doing nothing as Crook did in his winter campaign & a hard fight. One of our men coming down with a mail party was shot by one of his own party who took him for an Indian in the darkness one night.[22] I guess I wont think over the disagreeables any more & if I have another chance to avoid such an affair as this trip I will do it in preference to going along.

The weather has been in the main very lovely and the scenery various. In the valley there are stretches of mile upon mile as level as a parlor floor covered with long fine grass & groves of cottonwood in full leaf. The valley is in many places from four to six miles wide from the river to the bluffs. back of the bluffs you strike the badlands, a horrible desert wilderness of soft black sliding earth & sandstone bluffs, with the whole country cut off by impassible crevices & ravines. There is quite a lot of hunting, although the game is more plentiful further up the river. I often wish I could send home some of the things I picked up in the way of pets but so far I have lost everything. It is you know next to impossible to carry along anything alive in army wagons. The other day I ran down a young antelope with great long legs, it stood half as tall as I am. Kept it 3 or 4 days when I had to go with the Cavalry and when I got back it was dead. We also had a lot of young sage chicks, wild goslings, horned toads, war & bald eagles, and a young buffalo but they are all dead or lost some way through constant marching . . . having missed our golden opportunity to catch Indians (a hard thing to do in summer) they wont be able to do much & we may either go home very soon or else spend the rest of the summer chasing a few scattered bands around & through the mountains. Give my love to all and dont be worried about me as I can stand it as long as the rest can. Affec.

Your Son
Holmes Offley Paulding

In the Field
Little Big Horn River M.T.
June 28 1876

Dear Mother

A mail is to start for some where tonight and as it may get East and as I know how fast bad news travels I must just send a line to let you know that nothing has happened to me or to our battalion.

---

22. On the night of May 20, the sergeant of the guard accompanying a supply train from Fort Ellis was accidentally shot by one of his sentries. He died a short time later, Matthew Carroll, "The Diary of Matthew Carroll," *Contributions to the Historical Society of Montana* (10 vols., Helena: State Publishing Company, 1896), 2:229.

We reached here yesterday morning to find that Custer's command had attacked an immense village extending along the valley from here up and down several miles each way.

His command divided into 3 battalions attacking at different points on the 25th. He, with five whole companies, was literally annihilated, not an Officer or man escaping. Reno's battalion of 3 Co's made two or three charges, despirately from the other end of the village but were driven back to the river and up the bluffs nearly 400 feet high & very steep & suffered a loss of about 50 killed and the same number wounded. We had been making forced marches to reach here, seeing the smoke from timber set fire by the Indians to drive out our men, & reached here the morning of yesterday.[23]

The Sioux had seen us and being short of ammunition had left their village in a great hurry the night before, of course we did not chase them which we might have done & destroyed them with even our small force. The trouble with Custer was he did not know what he was attacking and failed to surprise the camp, so when he was moving along concealed the Indians seem to have out flanked and surrounded him. More than half of that gallant regiment is dead among them several dear friends of mine—Custer, Cook, Keogh, Jack Sturgis, Porter, Yates, Tom and Boss Custer and all the other poor fellows, among them too was my old friend Dr. Geo. Lord. About 300 or 350 dead & 50 badly wounded of Reno's outfit. After driving Reno on the bluffs subsequent to the massacre of Custers battalion, the Indians surrounded him & fought from all sides all day of the 26th. About dark we were seen coming up the valley 8 or 10 miles off when we went into camp that night & then the Indians ran away.

My hands are full of work[24] and we are going to try & fight our way out of this beginning in an hour. Dont anticipate any serious resistance as we are prepared & reinforced by the remains of the 7th and have a gattling gun battery of 3 guns.

I will write to you more at length as early as possible. am now writing on a medicine pannier for which they are waiting to pack on a mule. Give best love to all at home and believe me my dear mother.

Your loving Son
Holmes Offley Paulding

---

23.   Large volumes of smoke were noticed also by Terry's force on the 26th when they were twenty miles or so from the site of the village. The soldiers thought the smoke was from the 7th Cavalry destroying the village. See Charles Roe, *Custer's Last Battle* (1927; reprinted, Fort Collins, Colo.: Old Army Press, 1973), 5.

24.   Lt. John F. McBlain, who was then an enlisted man in the 2nd Cavalry, wrote in 1896, "Everything possible was done for Reno's wounded. Dr. Paulding, our surgeon, was here, there and everywhere, and did all in his power to alleviate the suffering . . . ," John F. McBlain, "With Gibbon on the Sioux Campaign of 1876," *Cavalry Journal*, 9 (June 1896), 147.

In the Field
Yellowstone opposite Big Horn
July 2nd 1876

My Dear Mother

I have just returned tonight to our permanent camp near Fort Pease, after a short but terrible trip with pack animals on which we started from this point on June 24th. . . .

We had marched several hundred miles & were down near the Powder river, when the steamer "Far West" (well named) with Gen. Terry and staff on board came up the Yellowstone and ordered us back to this point. we marched along & reached here the night of the 28th of June[25] and the next day the steamer came up and crossed us over to the eastern side of the river whence we marched toward the mouth of the Little Horn where we were to meet Custer's column on the 26th.

He was coming down near the base of the mountains heading the various streams, in search of Indians, & finally to come down the Little Horn to where it empties into the Big Horn about 40 miles from here, and we were to meet him there. It took us till nearly night of the 24th to cross our battalion of about 200 Cavalry & 200 Infantry and we camped only 8 miles away on Tullocks Fork. The next morning we broke camp early & marched over a high mountainous divide about 21½ miles before striking water which we were finally compelled to make for on account of the suffering of the Infantry so struck down to the Big Horn River. At this point I told Gen. Terry the Infantry could go no further without 2 or 3 hours rest. They were straggled back on the road exhausted & faint & I spent some hours with my men carrying them water.[26] Finally got them into camp, when the Cavalry moved over a ridge two miles along to make their camp for the night. The Infantry was to remain there for a rest of 2 hours & then follow them & I was ordered to stay with them as Dr. Williams[27] of Gen. Terrys staff went ahead with the Cavalry. It soon began to rain and as we marched into camp, nearly dark, we could see the Cavalry moving about for a night march undertaken on account of our scouts having come in with a report that there was a big smoke about 20 miles up the Little Horn river whose mouth was 16 miles

---

25. Paulding is in error on the date. The command actually reached the crossing point of the Yellowstone on the evening of the 23rd. McClernard, "Journal of the Marches," 1370.

26. The march of the 25th was described by General Terry as one of the severest tests, in the way of marching, that American soldiers had ever suffered, McBlain, "With Gibbon," 142.

27. Asst. Surgeon John W. Williams was the chief medical officer of Terry's staff during the campaign and stayed with headquarters most of the time, Gray, *Centennial Campaign*, 272.

above our camp. I was reluctantly compelled to stay with the Infantry, and after a frugal but hearty meal of hard tack & grease, took out
the 2 or 3 hours before daybreak in trying to sleep as well as I could
lying in the wet grass under a tree from which the rain pattered into
my face & neck. At 2 A.M. we were up and started marching until 9
when we came in sight of the Cavalry. It had marched in the inky
darkness until after 1 o'clock and made but 12 miles when it had to
stop to rest and graze until just before we came. We caught up with
them on the high bluffs north of the mouth of the Little Horn (I will
here digress to say the steamer with a co. of Infantry and a Napoleon
12 pounder was to meet us at this point and was already on her way
up the river where no steamer ever went before)[28] Well, when we came
up we found them halted and awaiting a report from some of our
scouts who had gone from Powder River up with Gen. Custer. Three
of them had tried to get into camp the night before but had been
driven away by the sentries who thought them hostile and had swum
across the Big Horn where they were at that time opposite to us. Our
remaining scouts tried to induse them to recross & deliver any word
from Custer, but they said they were tired, sick and very much afraid
and would'nt come over. They yelled across the river that the day before
Custer had attacked a village 14 or 15 miles up the Little Horn, where
we could see the several immense columns of smoke, that he had been
led into a trap & surrounded. The village consisting of 1900 lodges
& over 8000 warriors, who had whipped him, shot down his men like
buffalo & that there were no white men left except for a few who had
got into the heavy brush and timber & that the Indians had set fire
to it to drive them out or burn them & that they did not think any
one was left, also that these Indians would come on down & attack
us and do the same with us as they had with Custer who had twice
as many men as our column, the whole 12 Cos. of the 7th Cavalry
being with him for the first time in the history of the regiment, united,
all newly remounted & splendidly equipped.

We of course could not credit so preposterous an idea as that, of
any number of Sioux whipping that gallant regiment,[29] so concluded

---

28. Terry ordered Capt. Grant Marsh to go up the Big Horn to the mouth of the
Little Big Horn by June 26. Being unfamiliar with the river, up which no steamboat
had ventured before, the *Far West* actually went thirteen miles above the mouth of
the Little Big Horn. On June 28, the boat was at its assigned point of landing, Gray,
Centennial Campaign, 187-88.

29. Although the Crow scouts reported Custer's defeat and annihilation, none
of the officers with Terry's column believed it. Gibbon later wrote, "I do not suppose
there was a man in the column who entertained for a moment the idea that there
were Indians enough in the country to defeat, much less annihilate, the fine regiment of cavalry which Custer had under his command." See Michael Koury, ed., *With
Gibbon on the Sioux Campaign of 1876* (Bellevue, Neb.: Old Army Press, 1970), 26.

that he had been trying to surprise the camp, perhaps 200 or 250 lodges, and while sneaking down some ravine at night without flankers had been discovered & had a volley poured in from the sides of the ravine above, which would have killed some of his advance guard & would perhaps have driven him back on his main column. but that as a matter of course they had gone in & cleaned out the village, and that the smoke we saw was from the burning up of lodges and plunder. We expected to find a guard left behind with my dear old friend Dr. Lord in charge of the wounded & Williams & I pictured to ourselves how glad he would be to have us come in and help him through. Custer, we supposed would be scattered over the country pursuing the fugitives.

Our scouts (20) however, had a big scare on & said they were afraid to go ahead, or even ride with the advance guard with Terry and the staff. They were ordered to the rear, and after talking together for a few minutes, turned tail and galloped off deserting us entirely.

We thought at the very worse Custer might have underestimated the force he was attacking & had perhaps fortified to await reinforcements, so we pushed ahead, sweeping up the valley as fast as we could go with the Inf'y (which is simply an encumbrance of the worst kind in chasing Indians)

We marched ahead nearing the fires until within 8 miles of them when we had gone nearly 26 miles, and at that point two men were sent out to try and communicate with Custer under a reward of $200 each in case of success.[30] At the same time Roe's company—F, 2nd Cav. was ordered up on the bluffs, under which the main column was marching to flank the outfit & see what he could. the valley was 3 or 4 miles wide between the river & the bluffs which rose to a height of some 200 or 300 feet, and formed the edge of a wide plateau or bench, from which a lovely & extensive view could be had of the surrounding country. After Roe had gone up Gen. Brisbin told me I could go with him & ride along the bluffs, so I trotted up there. As I rose to the edge of the plateau I saw 2 Indians disappear into a ravine a little to the right of me & behind me & I went ahead & told Roe. We soon saw Indians riding up from ravines ahead of us toward an elevated ridge which made the southern boundary of the plain, galloping up & down in small parties along its edge & concentrating in a body of 20 or 30 at the highest point ahead. Some of them seemed to be trying to get behind us so as to see the size of the main column & made a circuit of several miles. We kept in toward the

---

30. Muggins Taylor and Henry Bostwick were the two scouts sent out. They traveled on opposite sides of the Little Big Horn and both returned to the column having run into large numbers of hostiles. See Edgar I. Stewart, *Custer's Luck* (Norman: University of Oklahoma Press, 1958), 300-301.

largest body & being in some doubt as to whether they might not
be some of Custer's Ree Indians, tried to communicate with them.
We had reached the edge of a wide (300 or 400 yards) ravine or dry
creek & sent ahead 3 men to try to find out what they were, and as
we followed down out of sight, heard a few shots & went ahead and
up the opposite side on a trot. It was then nearly dark and we were
met by the 3 men who said that while we were coming through the
ravine, they had got up near enough to wave a hankerchief and had
been shot at 4 times, so returned. Then about 5 miles ahead of us
& opposite the fires (which we could see were burning timber but
no lodges in sight) three large bodies of men, maybe 300 in all, rose
up on the edge of the bluff and rested there, just on the crest, closely
huddled together & looking in the distance like squadrons of cavalry,
only seeming to me, larger in number & disposed rather more irreg-
ularly than usual with animals galloping up & down the line.[31] Behind
the main body & scattered over the plain for more than a mile, but
so nearly on a level with us as hardly to be distinguished were other
animals, moving slowly & raising considerable dust. The question
now was whether what we saw meant Indians or soldiers. As to those
nearest us, the small scattered bands; there was no doubt they were
Sioux, hanging about to annoy & pick up ponies &c. A party of them
ran down the valley to pick up or cut off part of a band of stray horses
our column had driven up before it from the brush along the river[32]
& another party of 16 ran around in front of us yelling in Sioux for
us to "Come On" — Our column halted in the valley over a mile wide
behind us. Roe sent down 2 or 3 messengers describing what he had
seen, but was ordered to halt & at dark to rejoin which he soon did.

When we got back we told just what we had seen & all the cavalry
at least was anxious to go on right then and there & not give them
a chance to get off without a brush, which would make them cut loose
their plunder anyhow. Instead of doing so, the Camp disposed itself
for a night attack & slept.

Early next morning— the 27th, we moved on over the bluffs, the
entire command, toward the village, or what was left of it. It was but
a few miles away & of course on reaching it, not an Indian was seen,
all having got away during the night. When we got there we found
ourselves on the side of an immense village that had covered the valley
for at least 8 miles up & 2 or 3 miles across. It had been hastily abandoned the night before from appearances. Where each tepee had

---

31.   Roe later recorded that the apparent troops they saw were Indians dressed
in the clothing of Custer's men, Roe, "Custer's Last Battle," 7.

32.   As McBlain described this bold action: "Their audacity was somthing wonderful, but no firing could be permitted for fear of hitting some one in the advance
party or in the main column," McBlain, "With Gibbon," 145.

been were left piles of undressed robes, hatchets, axes, tin cups, camp & equipage such as is used by soldiers, Indian & Cavalry saddles, spurs, hobbles, cut up blue clothing, dead ponies & a good many wounded cavalry horses limping around. Two lodges had been left up and were filled with 16 dead Indians. Most of them seemingly Chiefs & other Indian bodies had been recently buried around the outskirts of the village & in scaffolds, with their ponies killed near them. Some bodies of white men were also found and also heads (which had been cut off and dragged around by throngs [*sic*]. I rode on one flank and picked up part of a buckskin jacket marked "Porter", a bullet hole under the right shoulder, from which the blood had streamed down told the fate, a pair of gloves marked "Yates" 7th Cav.", the under clothing of Lieut. Sturgis & other things.[33] Feeling sick at heart we went on caring little how soon we shared the same fate. No signs of a fight having occured *in the village* were to be seen, but Lieut. Bradley in ascending with a scouting party the ridge, across the Little Horn from us, send over word he had found 200 dead bodies of white men along the crest and in looking with our glasses we could see the remains of about 40 horses & men in a little clump on top of a knoll, where they had made their last stand. Custer was among the party. We found our Indians had told us what they thought the truth. Keeping on up the valley with scouts ahead, we were soon met by Lieut. Hare and 2 other officers of the 7th Cav.[34] & learned from them the particulars as to Reno's charge & conflict on the plains: While Custer was attacking with 5 cos. from the other side that they had been driven back across the river & up the bluffs & corralled there where they still remained with the remnants of the other 7 cos. & pack animals. They had heard nothing from Custer from the time he made his charge, about noon on the 25th to that time (morning of the 27th) that they had plenty of food but were getting short of ammunition and that until the night before they had got no water being under constant fire for two days & away up on high steep bluffs under which the river ran whose opposite bank was lined with rifle-men to keep them from getting down. They had been surrounded by a body of Indians numbering 3000 or 3500 men and there was no chance of escape. Indeed they could not show their heads above ground without being shot at from the surrounding hillocks. It seems

---

33.   The clothing mentioned belonged to 7th Cavalry personnel all killed with Custer's command: 1st Lt. James E. Porter, Co. I, Capt. George W. Yates, Co. F, and 2nd Lt. James G. Sturgis, Co. M. Sturgis was temporarily assigned for duty with Co. E. Kenneth Hammer, *Biographies of the Seventh Cavalry* (Fort Collins, Colorado: Old Army Press, 1972), 121, 171, 222.

34.   Paulding later, in his letter of July 8, stated that there were two officers: 2nd Lt. Luther Hare, Co. K, and 2nd Lt. George Wallace, Co. G.

that the night before the Indians had suddenly drawn off & allowed them to get water & a little sleep & to attend to their wounded of whom there were about 50 on the hill. Our coming explained why the Indians had left. They must have run short of ammunition from the terrific fire they kept up for 2 days and were afraid to await our attack. Dr. Williams & I were ordered up to Reno's position immediately to give Dr. Porter[35] who had accompanied the expedition from Bismarck, relief. He was the only one of the 3 M.D.s surviving[36] and we found a horrible sight & did all we could for the wounded of whom only 50 had got in, the rest being killed or carried off by the Sioux. None of the officers knew what had become of Custer, his staff & 5 cos. with him until we told them that *all* had been killed, not a man escaping to tell the story. They had lost more than ½ their regiment, about 330 men & 14 officers. How we got away with the remainder & the wounded I will have to defer until another chance arrives to write a letter. We are back at a safe place now and are all played out, myself included and everything is going on as though nothing had happened. Of course we dont realize what has occurred yet. We have made forced night marches and are entirely wore out and it has been with great effort I have written what you will find here.

A Curier left us the night of the 27th and I sent by him a few hasty lines to let you know I, at least, had'nt "gone up the spout." He had a hard time getting in, was chased by 40 Indians, took the brush & swum the Big Horn & I dont know whether my letter was lost or not so send this. It must go right away & there is no time to write more so good bye. We have reason to think Crook struck their Camp yesterday[37] & if so he must have gotton away with it since they had so little ammunition left after the fight. The mail leaves again in a few minutes so again good bye.

Affec. Your Son
Holmes Offley Paulding

---

35.   Acting Assistant Surgeon Henry Porter, a civilian contract surgeon, was post surgeon at Camp Hancock, on the opposite side of the Missouri from Fort Lincoln, where he received a three-month contract for duty with the Sioux campaign, Hammer, *Biographies,* 10-11.

36.   The two other surgeons were Assistant Surgeon George Lord, killed with the Custer Battalion, and Acting Assistant Surgeon James DeWolf, killed during Reno's retreat to the bluffs, Hammer, *Biographies,* 9-10.

37.   Up to July 8, the Montana and Dakota columns knew nothing of Crook's operations or whereabouts during the critical middle stage of the campaign.

Terry's Indian Expedition
Camp on Yellowstone mouth Big Horn
July 8th 1876

My Dear Mother,

On the night of the 2nd I wrote you about the Little Horn affair but had not time to finish before the Steamer left with the mail. A Courier leaves tomorrow so I will endeavor to finish the account. I believe I got as far as our arrival at the site of the Indian encampment when we found signs of the recent battle. As we proceeded up the valley, we found a lot of dead Indians lying in scaffolds, under trees & in 2 lodges. Saw nothing of any white men except a very few bodies & some heads evidently dragged from a distance. The bodies may have been of wounded or captured men tortured. Our small party of scouts from across the river send word that they had just found 28 white men (soldiers) lying dead in a ravine crossing the bluffs opposite & a mile or two behind, where we then were. soon after they reported a total of 196 which afterward swelled to 204 dead, all except the first 28 being found along the summit of the bluff and about 40 in one group which was on a little knoll higher than the rest where they had made a last stand & among which were recognized Gen. Custer, Tom Custer (Capt), a brother of Gen. Custer who accompanied him on the trip named Boston Custer, Calhoun his adjutant and bro-in-law, Capt. Cooke (reg't adj) & Capt. A. E. Smith.[38] We were shortly after met by Lts. Hare and Wallace of the 7th Cav. who rode down to us and shook hands and from them learned the particulars of the whole thing, or such as they themselves knew at that time. Major Reno, to whose battalion they belonged, was at the time we arrived corralled on the summit of the bluffs across the river about 3 miles or more from where Custer had fought, having been driven there on the first day of the fight, and had with him 7 companies, or what was left of them. The particulars are brief as we learned them from these officers & from one of our Crow scouts named "Curley" who had been with Custer until the fight was over or nearly so,[39] and who had escaped by mixing with Sioux after all the Whites were killed

---

38. 1st Lt. William W. Cooke was the regimental adjutant of the 7th Cavalry. Capt. Thomas Custer commanded Co. C, and 1st Lt. James Calhoun of that company was in temporary command of Co. L. Algernon Smith of Co. A was in temporary command of Co. E. Because of the absence of many 7th Cavalry officers (half were on leave or detached service), Custer shifted around the officers present for duty to fill company command positions, Hammer, *Biographies*, 8, 45, 75, 76.

39. By his own admission, Curley was not in the fight, but watched it from a hill some distance off, Stewart, *Custer's Luck*, 478-80.

but 5, one of whom was then wounded, were about as follows. Custer with his regiment had been marching with a pack train up the Yellowstone but 20 or 30 miles back near the mountains where he could cross all the streams near their head and scout them. He was to meet our column at the mouth of the Little Horn on the 27th but on the 23rd struck a fresh trail of Indians moving & lit out after them, instead of waiting as they should have done to strike when we should be near enough to help if it should be necessary. I dare say he thought his regiment capable of whipping any number of Indians (a common error) & wanted it all to himself. Anyhow he marched his regiment 75 miles in 36 hours, resting about 5 hours so for 31 hours his men were in the saddle with but one interval. They were then, about 8 A.M. of the 25th where they could see the smoke of a big Indian Camp on the Little Horn, and very soon after, Custer, becoming satisfied that he was discovered, determined to attack at once so as to give them no chance to leave. He ordered Captain Benteen with 4 companies to guard the pack train and proceed toward the bluffs[40] while he with 5 companies attacked from one end of the village & Reno with I believe, 3 companies was to charge down toward Custer from the other. Before making his final disposition, he sent a scout ahead to find out where the tepees (lodges) were the thickest, as there was where he would charge. The scout returned & it is said that when he reported told Custer with perfect terror, that there were lodges as thick as the grass & begged him not to fight so many. Custer merely said with a laugh that he was glad they were all there. Then giving his orders to Reno & Benteen, he left them.

Where he charged from was very bad ground, from the top of the bluffs to the river was a slope of about 2 miles [probably from where they first clearly saw the village], the village lying in the valley across the stream in plain sight the whole length of the slope. Custer and these men gave their yell and charged down for a ford. They did not strike it exactly—but had to move along a cut bank for some distance, under heavy fire from the timber opposite. Finally on reaching the ford they were met by an immense body of Indians fighting on foot. They crossed in the face of this terrible fire but were driven back, dismounted & put in one or two volleys, remounted & retreated alternately, until what was left of them reached the summit of the bluffs. At this point they were met by another large body of Indians who

_____

40. In reality, Capt. Benteen with three companies was ordered to scout the bluffs to the left (south and west) as the regiment proceeded to the valley. One company, Co. B, was assigned to guard the pack train.

had swept around behind them and here surrounded by about 2500 or more warriors they fought to the death.[41]

One Indian "Curley" says they began to fight before the sun was yet in the middle of the sky & when he got away it was nearly half behind the bluffs — about 8 o'clock. They must have fought with desperation & it is thought they must have killed right there more than the entire number of soldiers in the outfit.[42]

Indeed they must have been so thick & in such short range that it must have been almost impossible to shoot without hitting someone. There was not a white man escaped out of about 250 with Custer, some 20 or so cannot be accounted for except by the fear that they were carried off alive or dead. Among those whose bodies were not positively identified were Dr. Lord & Lt. Sturgis. Their under clothing found in the camp Sturgis with a bullet hole through the under shirt, show that they are gone. The dead were, when found, almost entirely stripped, slashed up and mutilated so as to be hardly recognized.

The officers were Gen. Custer — Capts. Keogh, Cooke, Smith, Yates & Custer — Boston Custer, Lts. Porter, Sturgis, Riley, Harrington, Crittenden & Calhoun, Dr. Lord — a friend of Gen. Custers, Mr. Reed & the Herald reporter Mr. Kellogg. I did not see any of these as they were buried where they fell & during the 2 or 3 days we were there I was too busy with the wounded from Reno's party.

While Custer was fighting, Reno with his 3 Companies went up the river & crossed in the timber & then charged from the valley toward the upper end of the village one (1) or two (2) miles away. As they galloped over the plain they heard several volleys from where Custer was, and soon after engaged themselves.[43] They were met by 1000 or 1800 warriors who began to pour in a fire through which these 3 Cos. (about 150) charged a mile or so. The Indians were mostly on foot, a great advantage, as Cavalry has to dismount to do any fighting. Reno was driven back, dismounted & fired. Charged a second time until met by a large body who had come from where Custer was fighting & driven back again this time making blindly for the river & by a provident accident making the water at a fordable place, the only place where they could have got over within a mile either way. opposite were bluffs several hundred feet high with a "cut bank,"

---

41. Paulding formed his description of the Custer fight from the speculation of the surviving officers of the 7th Cavalry and officers with Terry's column. He mentions this fact in a later letter (July 15).

42. According to published authoritative sources, this would put the number of Indian casualties way too high.

43. This statement is evidently in error, because Reno's command was undoubtedly engaged before Custer's battalion.

the river running close beneath. At this point there was a small shelf for a landing & from there they went up an almost perpendicular ascent to the top through loose sliding "bad land" earth.[44]

The Indians stood on the opposite bank firing at them as they toiled up here (protected however partially by ravines) and also some firing from their flanks on the same bank. They were not met by Indians on top, the idea probably not having occured to them of Reno's making for such a place. Benteen was also near this place with his 4 Cos. & pack train & that night they joined. They dug out small holes with their tin cups in the best place they could find and make barricades of their packs, cracker boxes & dead animals. Dr. de Wolf was shot going up the hill but it left one surgeon, an acting Assistant Surgeon from Bismark, a Dr. Porter, whom I knew very well at Lincoln. The mules were put in a circle with the "hospital" in the middle & every now and then a mule would drop into the ring, shot. They found it impossible to get water for 2 days. all day of the 26th they kept up a fight from different spots where the Indians had taken positions. The Indians charged their works but were repulsed & Benteen made a counter charge. This fight kept up all day of the 26th letting up about noon as they think from the Sioux running short of ammunition. A party of men undertook to crawl down a ravine hoping to reach water under the concealment by the bluffs on each side of the ravine, & the smoke from the burning timber on the opposite bank set fire to drive out some of our men who had taken refuge there. They got some water although some were killed and some badly shot in the effort owing to their having to run the gauntlet of 20 or 30 feet to the river & back into the ravine.[45] The Indians hauled off on the evening of the 26th & then they got water — all they wanted. We (Gen. Gibbons column) were lying quietly in camp about 8 miles off when the Indians left. Dr. Williams and myself were ordered ahead to Reno's position as soon as it was discovered & when we got there they did now know where Custer was. Varnum[46] (whom I thought was dead & who was with me last year on the White River) came up & shook hands. He said "Where is Custer? is he coming up with your column? ["] & when I told him he turned, broken down

---

44.   During the fight in the valley and retreat to the bluffs, Reno suffered heavy losses, amounting to one third of his command. Three officers, three civilians and scouts, and twenty-nine enlisted men were killed. In addition, seven enlisted men were wounded and nineteen were temporarily missing in the timber.

45.   During the attempts to get water for the wounded, one man was killed and six or seven wounded. Later, the nineteen men who participated in the operation were awarded the Medal of Honor.

46.   2nd Lt. Charles A. Varnum, Co. A, was in command of the detachment of scouts during the valley fight and was wounded in the leg, Hammer, *Biographies*, 45-46.

completely, crying like a baby. All the officers & men were when I got there, in spite of hardships & suffering, cheerful & apparently cool and nonchalent as though nothing much had happened & tho. The announcement of Custers fate fell on them like an unexpected shock they soon rallied. The fact is that now we are quietly lying in camp they appear to be just beginning to realize what it all means. For the next day or two we were busy enough caring for the wounded of whom there were 50 left. Lt. Hodgson died this morning.[47] Lt. MacIntosh[48] was killed in the 2nd charge and the total loss of this part of the regiment was then 41 killed in the charges & during the fights of the 25th & 26th: several of the wounded 2 or 3 have since died. The rest were sent down the river in the steamer "Far West" with my last letter of the 2nd. We had a hard job carrying off the wounded, marching during the late afternoon & nearly all night of the 28th carrying them in hand litters.[49] This was slow and exhausting, and next day (we had'nt marched over 6 miles the night before) Doane of the 2nd went to work and made mule litters from timber frames with throngs [sic] of raw hide cut from some of the wounded horses we found in the camp & among the timber & which we killed & skinned for the purpose. These were wound over the frames making a sort of bed in which blankets & such canvas & tents as we had were laid. They were suspended with the projecting ends lashed over pack saddles & a mule at each end, and proved as easy traveling as a boat would have been: also very rapid & the night of the 29th we marched clear to the mouth of the river. It was very dark and raining & our guide got lost for about 2 hours, but at last found the steamer and we got our wounded aboard just before the sun rose in the morning of the 30th. I was nearly dead with the fatigue of the past 3 days & nights — on top of our hard march up there from the 24th with packs & when all was fixed & the men attended to you bet I did'nt make much bones about going to sleep for 3 hours. The next day the steamer came down here and I followed with the command including Reno's 7 cos. all thats left of the regiment. The 7th lost 16 officers, more than half, and about 329 men killed & wounded. also more than half. Varnum was shot in the leg slightly but dont show it at all. I dont know the exact figures yet. In addition they lost

---

47.   Paulding is in error here. 2nd Lt. Benjamin Hodgson, Co. B, was killed while crossing the ford during the retreat to the bluffs on the afternoon of June 25, Hammer, *Biographies*, 60.

48.   1st Lt. Donald McIntosh, Co. G, 7th Cavalry, Hammer, *Biographies*, 137.

49.   Removing the wounded by hand litters proved to be an utter failure. The next day, Lt. Gustavus Doane, 2nd Cavalry, constructed mule litters and effectively organized men and mules to move the wounded to the *Far West*, Gray, *Centennial Campaign*, 279-80.

Army surgeons improvised litters like this one used during Crook's "Starvation March" for the soldiers wounded in the Sioux War battles.   (Stanley J. Morrow, photographer, National Archives, RG3, SC 85704)

the regimental colors[50] & 5 guidons, about 400 head of horses killed, mules killed, wounded and captured with all their equipment and the arms of all the men killed. What we know of Custer depends of course on the signs discovered, and the statement of "Curley" who is a good, brave and truthful young warrior of the Crow tribe.[51] He says they fought well and were not afraid to die. After the boat left the Little Horn and as we were marching over the high bluffs at its mouth, we could see the smoke from a big camp off on the base of the Big Horn Mountains where the Little Big Horn river emerges from its Canon 40 miles away, or over that.

---

50.   The 7th Cavalry regimental colors had been with the pack train, and were not lost in the fight.

51.   Paulding, as other early writers of the Little Big Horn fight, puts much faith in Curley's statements of the battle. Though it is true Curley was the first to bring news of Custer's defeat to the *Far West*, he could not speak English and no interpreter was aboard; probably not much reliable information was obtained from him, Stewart, *Custer's Luck*, 478-80.

The same day about noon there went up two big signal smokes — Their mode of calling together their warriors, and the next day the entire country was covered with a pall of heavy smoke nearly render- ing invisible the mountains which are usually clearly & beautifully defined in this pure atmosphere. Our interpretation & the interpreta- tion of such scouts as we had along, was that they were having another fight the first day — that they had set fire to the grass on the 2nd day in order to scatter under the smoke and escape and we only hope Crook has at last found them. he should have been there before this, and if he struck them, short of ammunition and suffering severely from the fight with Custer, in which they are believed to have lost much more than ourselves, he must have whipped them completely.[52] If he has *not* we are in for a long tedious campaign.

On returning here we found information in the papers of which we knew nothing before starting & *they* knew what we did not dream — that there were between 3000 & 4000 warriors in the band & also pretty definately their where abouts. It came too late for us. We are now waiting here for news from the East and from Crook, and for orders as to what is to be done. Some Crows came down from the upper Yellowstone today & with them one who says Crook had a fight with a band of Sioux over 2 weeks ago on Tongue river, whipping the Indians but losing 18 men & that he had told them (the Crows of whom there were 140 with him) that he was going to have one more big fight and then go home. Some of the Sioux had a fight with the Crows about 60 miles from here above on the Yellowstone at Pryors fork, the Crows beating and getting away with 6 scalps. One of these fellows who came in today was shot by a glancing ball on the knee cap but dont appear to care much. I have been writing so hurridly and disconnectedly that my little yarn must be hard to untangle, but then I suppose you will have heard so many stories that it may be of interest to know the truth or as much of it as an eye witness could discover no matter how mixed his account is from having to scribble away so fast in order to get through by the time the mail goes. The steamer "Josephine"[53] came up yesterday to take the place of the "Far West" gone down with the wounded and it was a great pleasure to find they had on hand clothing to replenish our rags at any price.[54] By a chance the ladies from

52. Carroll wrote in his diary on July 1, "A large smoke was seen at the foot of the Big Horn Mountains. Some are of the opinion that General Crook has struck the Sioux Camp," Carroll, "Diary," 235.

53. The *Josephine*, skippered by Capt. Mart Coulson, was chartered along with the *Far West* for exclusive service to the campaign. Both were operated by the Coulson Line, Gray, *Centennial Campaign*, 87.

54. The *Josephine* arrived at the Big Horn River mouth on July 6, with a load of supplies and mail for the expedition.

Ft. Lincoln who were to have come up on the "Josephine" this trip
put off the excursion until next other wise Mrs. Custer, Yates,
Calhoun, Porter, Smith & Moylan would have been here a day or two
after we got back & found out the horrible news. I believe all of the
ladies of the Cavalry living at Ft. Lincoln excepting Mrs. Moylan have
lost their husbands in the fight.[55] I understood that Col. Reno has
made a report of the affair in which he reflects strongly on us[56] for
having gone into Camp on the evening of the 26th in the face of
the enemy & without attempting to satisfy ourselves as to the
character of a large body of men who crossed his front, or something
to that effect, referring to the Indians Roe's co. saw while scouting
or flanking the column on the march up to which I referred in my
last letter. . . . My last few letters have been sent June 27th from Little
Big Horn, July 2nd & the present from here. They all go together
& take the place of a diary more than anything else and as I haven't
been able to keep up my journal you might keep them if you care
to as a sort of memoranda to look over in future & I hope more
peaceful years. Love to all—The sisters & yourself.

Devotedly Your Son
Holmes Offley Paulding

Camp Yellowstone near Ft. Pease
July 15th 1876

My dear Mother

Your letter of the 29th has within the past few minutes reached
me after an unusually rapid trip due to the fact that an idea has at
last penetrated the official cranium & lighted up things so as to effect
a change in our mail facilities much for the better i.e. that instead
of keeping up our line of communication with Ellis by means of
Couriers (Cavalry men who as a general thing are about as well fitted to travel through a hostile country as pulling infants & go moon-
ing around at the mercy of any Indians who happens to catch sight
& takes the trouble to lay for them behind the first convenient ridge).
who with relays at odd intervals must travel at night & travel hard
to make 50 miles a day. They now use small boats which cost very
little compared with the wear and tear on horse flesh. These boats

55.   Elizabeth Custer later recalled a total of twenty-six women at Fort Lincoln
lost their husbands in the Little Big Horn battle. Elizabeth Custer, *Boots and Saddles*
(1885; reprinted, University of Oklahoma Press, 1968), 222.

56.   In Paulding's letter of July 8, as later copied by his sister, "Col. Gibbon who
was in command of our column" is substituted for "us" as found in this version. See
Holmes O. Paulding, ed. by Dean Hudnutt, "New Light on the Little Big Horn," *Field
Artillery Journal*, 26 (July-Aug. 1936), 343-60.

are started on the river within 25 miles of Ellis and traveling by daylight alone make nearly 100 miles a day, floating down the current.

You mention having sent a letter June 19th. It must have been mislaid or lost enroute. I am very glad to get a longer and more cheering letter than usual. *I* can only do all I can to keep you posted up to as late a date as possible & so try to avail myself of every chance to write, apropos of this. I do hope the scratchy scrawl I sent you from that horrible field on the Little Big Horn reached you soon after the telegraphic news of Custer's fight. Altho rather busy at the time I remembered that you would get the news & of course imagine my precious corporosity as among those of so many of my friends whom (some at least) I must have mentioned in my letters of last year. Indeed that might have proved the melancholy case but for circumstances, chief of them being the rashness, if nothing worse of Custer who pushed ahead his command, not withstanding unmistakable directions that he was to await our co-operation, & that we could not be near that spot before the 27th. He wanted it to be "Custers Victory" not Terry's nor Gibbons so on striking the trail drove ahead making *78 miles* in a continuous march with but 2 short halts necessarily made on account of the darkness, both amounting in all to 7 hours. Besides this we were kept out of a fight which we should have had and very easily could on the afternoon of the 26th, too late to save Custer but in time to avenge him, as we must have whipped after a more or less hard fight, the Indians being out of ammunition and running away when we stopped within 4 or 5 miles & in plain sight of them. Well my dear there's very little use grumbling. You must only remember in my history of this affair although I have inserted doubtless many of my own opinions which reflect rather muchly on prominent & ranking officials, still the facts are indisputable & all bound to come out, if anything ever does come out of this whole thing.

Since our arrival here at the mouth of the Big Horn, we have done nothing except to lie in camp and await such further orders & instructions from higher powers as they might send, thinking, naturally, that this might effect a change in the programme.[57] I am getting so accustomed to bumming around that a return to civilized modes of life would be a strange change. As you may imagine, our present way of living is slightly different to anything to which one has been brought up, and with all the little inconveniences there are so many pleasant features as to almost compensate. While we are with

---

57. This sentence is finished in the *Field Artillery Journal* version as follows: ". . . & that we should perhaps pass from under the disposition of an old poppycock into that of the younger but slightly more capable General Sheridan," Hudnutt, ed., "New Light," 358.

our train and in Camp Roe & myself live together and get along very
comfortable indeed. He is a 2nd Lieut, but commands a company
(F 2nd Cav) and as there are no other officers of this company present, has a very nice wall tent to himself. I also have a wall tent, so
Roe and I live together in one and use the other as a kitchen and
dining room. Our cook is an Alsatian by the name of Keyser & is
a regular first rate old french cuisinier (when he has anything in the
way of grub worthy of his steel) At present and for some time past
we havent had any meat except for bacon and ham because our beef
cattle ran away & I havent been able to leave camp for some time
lately to get any game. Game is scarce near camp and one has to go
10 or 15 miles away for any. It is'nt safe to go hunting without a large
escort so the only opportunity we have had are when one or two companies go off on scout. Last week Roes company crossed the
Yellowstone on the steamer and we improved the time running a
buffalo which we got just before dark. Low of the 20[58] (Ft. Snelling)
Ser'gt Anderson & I got the brute and butchered it but the men had
to pack the meat on their saddles and during a 15 mile gallop and
trot that night, they lost most of it.[59] The boats up the Yellowstone
(Josephine & Far West) brought us a fresh supply of canned things
on which we principally live—and though its rather expensive I think
the expense in that line justifiable. anyhow we wont get scurvy. I am
only afraid the disease may break out in part of our command which
has been out for over 4 months with very hard work & no variety
of diet. The instructions we were awaiting came down this morning
and knocked our hopes that we would go home & refit for a winter
campaign; Our force which started out from Montana 4 Cos. of the
2nd Cav. & 6 of the 7th Inf. was you know reinforced after Custers
fight by the remainder of the 7th Cav. parts of the 7 Cos. badly cut
up but over 200 men. Then on the "Josephine" there was a co. of the
17th under Captain Sanger, on the "Far West" Bakers Co. of the 6th
Inf.[60] Low with his battery of 3 Gattlings joined us at the Rosebud
and we now hear that 12 cos of Infantry from the Depts. of the Lakes
& the Platte are enroute to join us. Crook is also ordered to report

58.   Lt. William H. Low, 20th Infantry, commanded a detachment with the Gatling gun battery.
59.   Carroll's diary has this entry for Sunday, July 9, "Lt. Roe and company, with
Dr. Paulding and self, went up Tullock's Fork some twelve miles and sent the couriers
on their [way] at 8:15 P.M. We got across at 10 o'clock after a hard ride. Killed a buffalo," Carroll, "Diary," 235.
60.   Capt. Louis H. Sander commanded Co. G, 17th Infantry, that served as guards
for Terry's supply depots on the Yellowstone. Capt. Stephen Baker's Co. B of the 6th
Infantry was attached to Terry's headquarters and served as boat guards aboard the
Far West.

to Gen Terry who is now in command of the whole outfit. From this you see that instead of the 10 cos with which we have been roaming about for 3 months and over, not above 400 men, our force is increased to at least 30 cos besides Gattling battery & Crook's outfit & our force from 400 to nearly or quite 1500 Crook must have as many more (1500) and with this force if kept together we can cope with anything we meet. All are delighted that Terry is now in command. We will wait here until our column concentrates and then follow instructions to "push things" I suppose. I doubt however, if we find anything to push before winter. I think the large body of Indians which got together to give Custer a fight has divided all up into small bands and war parties and that they have cached their lodges in the inaccessible fastnesses of the Big Horn Mountains. A great number have also, no doubt gone back to their agencies for fresh supplies of clothing, food & ammunition, as no very large body can keep together and support themselves in this country. If we would only just *quit* issuing munitions of war, take possession of the agencies & burn the confounded holes, take the families left by the warriors & remove them to a safe place as hostages, and hang every white man found selling arms and ammunition, it would settle the question in a month or two without blood shed very effectually. I dare say we shall be kept hunting around for little parties until winter & then go in for a time at least, and perhaps afterward go on a winter campaign which will finish things up . . . . This sort of thing is liable to either toughen one tremendously or knock him up. It has had the effect of toughening me so that I never felt better in my life . . . .

Affec. Your Son—
Holmes Offley Paulding

Paulding's service continued in Montana at Fort Ellis and the Cantonment on Tongue River until December 3, 1877, when he went on a four-month leave. From May 1878 to May 1879, he was again stationed at Fort Lincoln and also at Fort Bennett, Dakota Territory, which guarded the Cheyenne River Agency. During this period, he also spent considerable time on field service, often in unfavorable conditions. In June 1879, he returned to Washington, and shortly afterward was assigned to Fort McHenry, Baltimore, where he attained the rank of Captain and Assistant Surgeon on November 10, 1879. Reassigned to the Department of the Platte, Paulding took assignment at Fort Laramie from November 1881, to February 1883. After a short leave, Paulding arrived at Fort Sidney, Nebraska, on April 5, to serve as post surgeon.

Although Holmes Paulding then was only thirty years of age, his health had already begun to fail. Hard field service in Dakota and Montana, indications of heart problems, and exposure to cold and wet, while attending to his duties at Sidney, took their toll. On April 21, 1883, suffering from an attack of acute rheumatism, he was confined to the post hospital, where he experienced a considerable rise in temperature, and delirium. Three days later, the surgeon from Fort D. A. Russell, near Cheyenne, Wyoming, arrived to attend to him. Although the pain gradually diminished during the next several days, Paulding suddenly died on May 1, after what was described as "Syncope or entire failure of the heart to act."[61] His wife was with him at the time; his two children were with his wife's mother at Alexandria, Virginia. On May 3, Paulding's body was shipped to Washington for burial. His obituary in the *Army & Navy Gazette* remembered Dr. Paulding as "an able, accomplished, modest, faithful, hard-working officer, whose death involves a public loss."[62]

ABOUT THE PAULDING LETTERS

The letters presented here are copies of seven letters Paulding wrote to his mother between April 21 and July 15, 1876, found in the Bradley Tyler Johnson Papers, located in the Manuscripts Department of the William R. Perkins Library at Duke University, Durham, North Carolina. The last two letters, dated July 7 and 15, have been published from copies of the originals made by Paulding's sister.[63] However, the first five letters have never before appeared in print.

Undoubtedly the Duke series of letters are copies made at a later date, because one letter will end on the same page as another starts. In addition, they are all copied on the same stationery and in the same hand. There exists reasonable possibility that Paulding made this copy for himself for sentimental reasons, realizing the historical significance of the 1876 campaign. He did advise his mother to keep the letters as "sort of a memoranda to look over in future & I hope more peaceful years." A comparison of the handwriting with that of Paulding's diary suggests they were done by the same person. At some point Bradley T. Johnson, a Baltimore lawyer and politician, acquired the copy. Johnson, a former brigadier general in the Confederate army, was evidently interested in Civil War and American military history and could have obtained this copy of the letters because of their historical value. Because he was from Baltimore, Johnson could have been

---

61.   Report of Assistant Surgeon William J. Wakeman, May 2, 1883, found in Paulding's A.C.P. File, RG 94, NA.

62.   *Army & Navy Gazette,* May 1883.

63.   Holmes O. Paulding, ed. by Dean Hudnutt, "New Light on the Little Big Horn," *Field Artillery Journal,* 26 (July-Aug. 1936), 343-60.

acquainted with Paulding, or his family in Washington, and procured the copy from them.

The letters are presented as the original copies, with no change to spelling or punctuation. For reasons left but to conjecture, there are several differences in phrasing between these letters and the aforementioned copies made by Paulding's sister. The variations are cited in footnotes. —T.R.B.

Bear Black (Black Bear) rides down a fleeing white man, striking him with his rifle and counting coup on him. (National Museum of the American Indian, Smithsonian Institution)

The early pages of the duty roster, including these two, list the names of the men in Company G, Seventh Cavalry. The symbols and letters indicate the daily duty each man performed during May and June, 1876. (National Museum of the American Indian, Smithsonian Institution)

High Bull's Victory Roster

by Father Peter J. Powell

There were sure signs of trouble ahead. It was late November, 1876, five months almost to the day after the Cheyenne and Lakota Sioux victory at the Little Big Horn. Most of the *Ohmesëhese*, the Northern Cheyennes, were camped in one great village in the Big Horn Mountains. Cheyenne scouts, the "wolves," had already spotted soldiers moving along the country near the Powder River, with Indian scouts riding along to guide them. These were the forces of General Ranald Mackenzie, bent on the swift, punitive destruction of the Northern Cheyennes.

After the wolf scouts returned to camp, the chiefs quickly gathered in their great double lodge at the center of the village. There they listened to the scouts' report. The four Old Man Chiefs were all present, sitting at their respective places in the sacred circle: Little Wolf, Morning Star (Dull Knife), Old Bear, and Black Moccasin. The Keepers of the two Great Mysteries, the Sacred Arrows and the Sacred Buffalo Hat, were also present. So were many of the other Chiefs of the Council of the Forty-four, the men who governed The People, as the Cheyennes call themselves.

Of the Chiefs, the most venerated was Black Hairy Dog, keeper of Maahótse, the Sacred Arrows. He was the holiest man of all, the one who sat in the place of Sweet Medicine, the Prophet who first brought the Sacred Arrows and the tribal code of laws to the People. To this day, older Cheyennes say that the Arrow Keeper is the man who owns the People, the one who holds them in his right hand. Thus, whenever Black Hairy Dog's voice rose in council, the other Chiefs listened with respect.

After the wolves made their report of soldiers along the Powder, it was Black Hairy Dog who spoke first. The People should break camp at once, he said. Then they should move out along the foot

*Father Peter J. Powell, "High Bull's Victory Roster," *Montana The Magazine of Western History,* 25 (Winter 1975), 14-21.

of the Big Horn Mountains until they reached Crazy Horse's Oglala camp, where the two tribes would be strong enough to hold off any soldier attack.

Seated behind the Council Chiefs were the chiefs of the Northern Cheyenne warrior societies: the Kit Foxes, the Elks, and the Crazy Dogs. Normally, in the presence of the Council of the Forty-four, these warriors sat quietly and listened. Then, once the Council Chiefs came to one mind, it was the warrior society chiefs who carried out their instructions. This time, however, Last Bull, head chief of the Kit Fox society, was on his feet at once.

"No!" he exclaimed. "We will stay here and fight!"

And, from the sacred circle where the Council Chiefs were sitting, no voice was raised against this arrogance.

Afterwards, the Chiefs instructed the wolves to continue their watch over the movements of the soldiers. Then, four nights later, a scout rode in with the news that the soldiers were near. The Chiefs, again gathered in council, decided that the people should move up on the side of the mountain, where they could erect breastworks for protection.

When Last Bull heard this decision, he was on his feet again. A few days before, his Kit Foxes had tangled with a hunting party of Shoshones. They had beaten these enemies badly, riding away with thirty of their scalps. Now Last Bull was determined to flaunt this victory of his own society.

"No!" he exclaimed. "We will stay here. We will dance all night!"

And again not one of the Council Chiefs raised a voice against the Kit Fox chief.

There were other signs of danger. At sunrise that day, Box Elder, the oldest and most venerated holy man among the Northern Cheyennes, was offering the pipe at the beginning of a new day. He was almost eighty years old, and for many of these years he had been blind. Yet his supernatural power was as strong as ever. As always, he prayed with his face turned toward the Southeast, the holiest of the four sacred directions. And this time, he saw a vision of soldiers and enemy scouts moving toward him, riding in on him from the East. They were charging right into the village, killing the people. When the vision disappeared, Box Elder quickly called to his son, Medicine Top, and asked him to ride through the camp, warning the people that there was fighting ahead. When the Cheyennes heard the news, many of them saddled their horses, preparing to leave camp for the safety of the rimrocks rising north of the village.

Just as they were ready to move out, Last Bull came riding up, his quirt raised to strike anyone who dared disobey him. Wrapped Hair, the Kit Fox second chief, and some other Fox society warriors rode

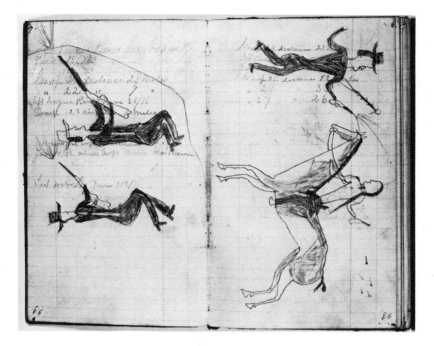

Yellow Nose, the brave one born a Ute, charges in on the soldiers. Two kneeling soldiers fire at him as he gallops in to strike a wounded trooper with his quirt and count coup on him. The soldier fires at Yellow Nose but cannot stop him. (National Museum of the American Indian, Smithsonian Institution)

with him. Pushing aside those who got in his way, Last Bull ordered his men to slash the saddle cinches of anyone who tried to leave.

"No one will leave! The people will dance the victory dance all night!" Last Bull shouted.

This time, the people themselves were afraid to disobey the arrogant chief of the Kit Foxes.

Later that evening, a great bonfire was built, and the dancing began. All night long it continued, the exultant voices of the Foxes filling the night air, while Shoshone scalps bobbed and danced from the tips of the peeled willow wands the women carried. Finally dawn arrived, and the celebration began to break up.

Just as the first weary dancers were starting toward their lodges, the sharp crack of rifle shots cut the still air. As the startled people looked up, they could see horsemen pulling up on the ridge above the village. These were the Shoshone soldier scouts, straining to charge right down into the camp to kill as many Cheyennes as they could find. As some of the dancers looked up the valley ahead of them, they could see their own horse-herders dashing back toward camp, crying out that soldiers were coming.

Women began to scream, trying to break away from the dance circle. Some of the younger girls who had been tied together for the scalp dancing, began to panic, tumbling each other into piles as they fought to break free from the leather strings that bound them. Finally someone cut the girls apart, and they scattered, too, racing off through the cold like fleeing prairie chickens. Some of the women headed for their lodges to rescue their children and a few precious belongings. Others dashed for the hills rising beyond the village.

The other mounted Indians came charging up the bed of the stream that wound through the center of the village. Some were dressed in war clothes, others wore the dark blue of soldier uniforms. These were the Lakota army scouts. Charging in behind then came the hard-riding soldiers of General Ranald Mackenzie.

Box Elder's vision had come true.[1]

Because of the swiftness of the attack, many Cheyennes had to flee their lodges half-naked. The fighting men rallied quickly and bravely, however, covering the flight of the women, children, and old people to the broken rimrocks above the valley. Even there, some of the soldier bullets reached them, spattering against the rocks like hailstones. Once beyond the rimrocks, the Cheyennes formed into smaller bands. Protected by the cover of the winter darkness, they straggled off through the snow and bitter cold.

Down in the village itself, the soldiers and their Indian scouts finally rounded up more than seven hundred horses. A few ponies managed to escape, and some of these were slaughtered by the hungry people, giving them the only food they were to eat for many hours. Darkness brought even more suffering, as thermometers in the soldier supply camp dropped to nearly thirty below zero.

In the mountains above them, the Cheyennes were suffering endlessly, the cold so terrible that eleven babies froze to death at their mothers' breasts. Occasionally a group of fleeing ones would pause long enough to kill another horse. Then some half-naked old person would hobble over to where the carcass lay. The horse's belly

---

1. Henry Little Coyote, Keeper of the Sacred Buffalo Hat, John Stands in Timber, and John Fire Wolf, to Father Powell, 1961-1962; Little Hawk to George Bird Grinnell, September 5, 1908, and Young Two Moon to George Bird Grinnell, September 20, 1908, George Bird Grinnell Papers, Braun Memorial Library, Southwest Museum, Los Angeles.

A full account of these events and the battle itself appears in Father Peter J. Powell, *People of the Sacred Mountain*, (2 vols., San Francisco: Harper and Row, 1979) 2:1009-33, 1052-71.

High Bull, owner of the victory roster, is chased by two Crows in a fight on Arrow Creek by the Cheyennes and Pryor Creek by the whites. (National Museum of the American Indian, Smithsonian Institution)

would be cut open, the old person thrusting hands and feet into the warmth of the entrails.

Finally the People struggled into Crazy Horse's camp on Box Elder Creek. The Oglalas shared what little they had — enough so that, for the first time in eleven days, no Cheyenne went to bed cold or hungry.

Meanwhile, destruction of the village continued, for Mackenzie's orders were to destroy it utterly. So terrible was the destruction that Northern Cheyenne art and material culture never recovered from it. Lodge poles were chopped to pieces and burned. Pawnee, Lakota, and Shoshone soldier scouts quickly moved in to claim their share of the captured horse herd. Saddles were smashed. Cheyenne bridles, many of them fashioned from hammered German silver, were destroyed. Bridle reins were cut, the metal bits broken. Soldiers smashed holes through kettles, pans, and canteens. Thousands of pounds of buffalo meat were tossed into the fires dotting the campground. Fine buffalo robes and other skins, most of them untanned, were either burned or carried off by the Indian soldier scouts.

More than two hundred tipis rose throughout the village. Most of these were fashioned from government canvas, although a number were made of tanned buffalo hide. Throughout the afternoon of

November 25, 1876, soldiers set fire to the lodges, destroying them one by one.

A few of the tipis, not more than half a dozen at the most, were great double lodges. These were the tipis of the Chiefs and the warrior societies. It was here, in the warrior society lodges, that the members gathered for council and relaxation. Here, too, some of the younger, unmarried men of each warrior society often stayed. The soldier attack had come so suddenly, however, that many warriors had been unable to return to their society lodges to dress in war clothing. As the troopers searched these tipis, they found their contents undisturbed. The peeled willow beds, covered with softly-tanned buffalo robes, remained standing. Around each lodge, extending above the floor to about the height of a man, ropes stretched from tipi pole to tipi pole. Vividly painted cylindrical parfleches hung from the ropes, their fringes deeply cut and flowing gracefully below them. Inside the parfleches rested the great eagle feather warbonnets of the chiefs and fighting men. Other painted parfleches, more trunk-like in shape, contained the war and ceremonial clothing of the men. Among these the soldiers found a number of sacred scalp shirts, richly quilled and beaded, painted, and fringed with locks of human hair.

The great double lodges contained linings formed from broad strips of white-tanned hide or canvas, almost as broad as a man is tall. Icy drafts flowed up from beneath the tipi covers in winter, the lodge linings serving to cut off the cold. More importantly, however, they served an artistic or heraldic function, for here a warrior artist could record his own brave deeds — or, in the military society lodges, the greatest deeds of the society members could be recorded. Here a warrior would be pictured cutting down a Pawnee, that most hated of Cheyenne enemies, with a sabre. Elsewhere, a chief of the Elk society would be shown striking a pompadoured Crow with one of his society's crooked lances. Or, on another section of such a lining, Cheyenne warriors would be pictured driving off a herd of horses, the animals branded US, marking them as captured soldier horses.

Some of the soldiers paused to examine these beautiful lodges with interest. Then they looted them, carrying off mementoes of their victory: a scalp shirt, a warbonnet in its painted parfleche case, a long-stemmed pipe, its red catlinite bowl inlaid with melted lead. Then the troopers held flaming torches against the tipi walls or painted linings, until the lodge cover caught fire.

As the soldiers moved on with the destruction, they uncovered reminders of the great Cheyenne-Lakota victory at the Little Big Horn. Horses branded US and 7C ran among the Cheyenne ponies. A Seventh Cavalry guidon was found covering a Cheyenne pillow. An officer's overcoat, two officer's blouses, and a rubber water-proof officer's cape were discovered in Cheyenne lodges. There was also a buckskin jacket, lined with taffeta, believed to have been the one worn by Captain Tom Custer. Saddles, canteens, nose bags, curry combs and brushes, shovels and axes—all marked with the letter of the Company to which they belonged, were re-captured. So was a silver watch, a gold pencil case, and pocket books containing currency and coin. Sharp Nose, one of the Arapaho soldier scouts, discovered forty-seven dollars in small bills in one wallet. Cheyenne tipis also revealed letters received from relatives of Custer's men, as well as letters the soldiers themselves had written, ready to be sent home. One letter was addressed to a young lady in the East. It was stamped, ready for mailing.

There were other relics of the allied tribal victory over Custer's men. Among them were the memorandum books kept by the First Sergeants of the Seventh Cavalry. The final entry in one book read, "Left Rosebud, June 25th."[2]

It was First Sergeant James H. Turpin, of Company L, Fifth Cavalry, who uncovered an especially important item, the black covered Guard Roster once owned by First Sergeant Brown of G Company, Seventh Cavalry. Penciled notations throughout it listed the troopers of that company, as well as their duties throughout the fateful months of May and June, 1876. Sergeant Brown's final entry read, "McEagan lost his carbine on the march while on duty with Pack Train, June 24/76."

Now, however, there were newer entries in the roster. Some of them obliterated the Sergeant's own writing, for at least three Cheyenne warrior artists had added their own roster of victories to this captured soldier ledger. These drawings were smaller examples of the vividly-painted battle scenes that covered the linings of the Cheyenne warrior society lodges. Here a mounted warrior charged across the roster book page, riding down a soldier, while another trooper lay bleeding on the ground behind the warrior's horse. Other pages depicted Cheyenne fighting men striking down various enemies, both Indian and white. A few drawings pictured warriors courting comely girls.

We can picture Sergeant Turpin leafing hurriedly through these pages, thrusting the roster into his pocket, and then moving on to carry out his part in the destruction. All night long the smashing, burning, and looting continued. Then the troopers mounted up, and, leaving a few Shoshone scouts behind, rode out of the valley.

Behind them lay the bodies of the Cheyennes who had died in the bitter fighting. Months later, when Little Wolf, Morning Star, and their

2.   John Gregory Bourke, diary, vol. 14, p. 1429f, Archives, Library of the United States Military Academy, West Point. See also, John G. Bourke, *Mackenzie's Last Fight With the Cheyennes* (New York: Governor's Island, 1890), 28.

A Cheyenne courting couple, wrapped in a blanket in the style of courting introduced to the tribe by the Lakota Sioux, is found on page seventy, which also lists several items of cavalry equipment. (National Museum of the American Indian, Smithsonian Institution)

people surrendered at Fort Robinson in Nebraska, they spoke of the killing of forty people in this fight. Because thirty of these had fallen into soldier hands, the fleeing Cheyennes carried the added sorrow of being unable to bury their dead. Crow Split Nose, chief of the Elk Scrapers, was the most prominent man to die. Shoshone soldier scouts scalped him and robbed his body, carrying off his sacred shield in triumph. The bodies of a number of younger warriors, not as renowned as the Elk chief, but no less brave in the fighting, lay sprawled on the frozen earth. Two young men, High Bull and Weasel Bear, were among them.

Soon after the last soldiers rode out of the valley, two or three Cheyennes slipped down from the hills. A day before this, two hundred lodges had risen proudly beside the stream, the mountains echoing with the singing of Kit Fox victory songs. Now the Cheyennes looked down on death and desolation. Nearly everything that fire could destroy lay in ashes, the falling snow throwing a white blanket over the smoldering rubble not yet consumed by flames. The day before, the mountain stream sparkled as it raced through the village; now its waters were choked with refuse. The nearly-naked bodies of two women lay beside the stream, sprawling stiffly across the frozen earth. The women's heads were nearly naked as well, for their scalps had been torn away by Pawnee soldier scouts.

Suddenly the canyon echoed with sounds again, this time cracking, high-pitched wails of Cheyenne grief.[3]

Twenty-two years would pass before the Cheyennes again saw the Guard Roster captured from Sergeant Brown at the Little Big Horn. Meanwhile, the ledger itself passed through a number of hands. From Sergeant Turpin the roster came into the possession of Colonel Homer W. Wheeler. He, in turn, placed it in the Museum of the Military Service Institution at Governor's Island, New York. A dealer who acquired it from there sold it to John Jay White, Jr., of New York City, a friend of the noted ethnologist-historian, George Bird Grinnell.

In the fall of 1898, Grinnell made one of his many visits to Northern Cheyenne country. Before leaving New York, he had borrowed the roster book from Mr. White, in the hope that some of the older Cheyennes would recognize it, and be able to identify the warriors whose victory drawings covered many of the pages.

When Grinnell arrived in the Tongue River country, he found two aging warriors, Old Bear and Bull Hump, Morning Star's son, still living there. Both had fought in the last battles with the soldiers, and Grinnell was anxious to record their recollections. Soon after his arrival at Lame Deer Agency, he headed for Old Bear's cabin, then located near the agency itself. As Grinnell approached it, he was carrying the roster in his pocket. As he began speaking to Old Bear through an interpreter, Grinnell slipped the roster out of his pocket, extending it toward Old Bear. Before the aging warrior had even touched it, he exclaimed in Cheyenne, "Why I know that book! I have seen it often. High Bull owned and kept it!" Then he explained that he and High Bull had been close brother-friends when they were young. High Bull had died in the fighting in the Big Horns, shot down by the attacking soldiers.

Bull Hump, Morning Star's son, was sitting close by as Old Bear recounted all this. Afterward, both warriors proceeded to identify most of the battle scenes and fighting men pictured in the roster book. Old Bear proudly pointed out two drawings of a fight with the Shoshones. These were his own drawings, and they showed his own bravery, he told Grinnell. Then he described how the Cheyennes

---

3. From an eyewitness account published in the New York *Herald*, December 24, 1876.

An unidentified warrior carrying a banner lance rides out against five white men. At least four are firing rifles at him.   (National Museum of the American Indian, Smithsonian Institution)

had tangled with some Shoshone Indians over on Powder River. Crazy Head had been hit during that fighting, and he fell to the earth bleeding. Old Bear saw him fall, and charged in to save his friend, the bullets flying like hail all around him. His sacred warbonnet had protected him that day, and he carried Crazy Head back to safety. Now both he and Crazy Head were still living, both of them still able to describe the battle pictured on the roster page.

The aging eyes of Old Bear and Bull Hump must have sparkled with new life as they re-lived those last days of Cheyenne freedom, days that all but ended with the burning of the great village in the Big Horns. Once the two old fighting men had identified the drawings, Grinnell again slipped the black-covered roster into his pocket. After his visit with the Northern Cheyennes ended, Grinnell carried the book back to New York. There, years later, presumably after Mr. White's death, Mrs. John Jay White, Jr. presented High

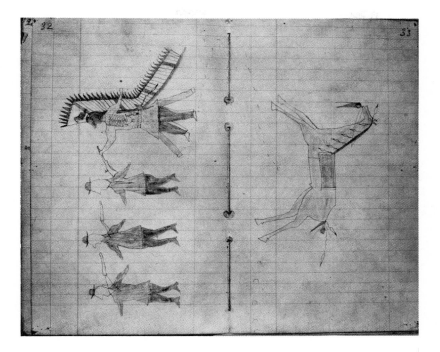

Crazy Wolf, also known as Mad Wolf, counts coup on three infantrymen while his horse looks on. (National Museum of the American Indian, Smithsonian Institution)

Bull's victory roster to the Museum of the American Indian, where it is today.[4]

There, far from the quiet mountain valley where High Bull fell before the soldier bullets, scenes of Cheyenne victories overlay the names of those who came to crush the People. In the muted colors of warrior drawings, we glimpse the faded colors of a Sun-scorched hill above the Little Big Horn, the hill up which the Cheyennes and Lakotas charged in that great wiping-out of Long Hair's men.

---

4. The High Bull Victory Roster is Number 10/8725 in the collections of The Museum of the American Indian, New York City; "Double Trophy Roster," Envelope 416, p. 2, and Bull Hump (Buffalo Hump) to George Bird Grinnell, October 18, 1898, Grinnell Papers, Southwest Museum.

All descriptions of Cheyenne drawings in the High Bull roster reproduced here are from Cheyenne informants to Grinnell.

Two color plates of pages from the High Bull roster appear in Powell, *People of the Sacred Mountain*, pp. 551, 993.

Author's Note

Research for this article was made possible by a John Simon Guggenheim Memorial Fellowship. Time for writing it was made possible by a grant from The American Council of Learned Societies. The author extends warm gratitude to both.

Special thanks also to the individuals and institutions who enabled the author to study the High Bull—Sergeant Brown roster and the manuscript material relating to it. Chief among these were the late Carl S. Dentzel, director, Ruth M. Christensen, librarian, and the staff of the Southwest Museum, Los Angeles, during the time of the author's research there. Warm gratitude also is extended to the late Ray A. Billington, formerly senior research associate, Henry E. Huntington Library, San Marino, California, and Mabel Crotty Billington, his most gracious wife. Special thanks also to Frederick Dockstader, former director, and Carmelo Guadagno, former staff photographer, of the Museum of the American Indian, New York City.

The Battle of Wolf Mountain

by Don Rickey, Jr.

The centennial summer of 1876 witnessed the completely unfore-seen, shocking defeat of the Seventh Cavalry in the Custer tragedy at the Little Big Horn on June 25, 1876. Telegraph wires hummed the message of disaster to Washington and to army headquarters at Chicago and St. Paul, and by early July several regiments had been ordered to the theater of hostilities in southeastern Montana. General Nelson A. Miles, 5th U. S. Infantry Regiment, which had served con-tinuously on the frontier since 1866, was among those ordered north against the Sioux and Cheyenne from its station at Ft. Leavenworth.

Companies of the 5th Infantry began construction of a log can-tonment on the Yellowstone River, at the mouth of Tongue River, in late August, 1876. From September to late December, Miles' 5th Infan-try and a few companies of the 22nd Infantry engaged in a series of small, arduous winter campaigns against the scattered bands of hostile Sioux and Cheyenne.

Crazy Horse, leader of the Oglala Sioux and allied Northern Cheyennes, eluded the troops until the beginning of 1877. On December 29, 1876, Miles marched up Tongue River from his can-tonment and by the evening of January 7, had pushed about 115 miles up river, to a point just southwest of present Birney, Montana, as the Cheyenne and Oglala warriors slowly withdrew further up the river. In the early morning of January 8th, Miles' soldiers were cook-ing breakfast in the snow, on a flat near Tongue River, when they beheld large numbers of warriors occupying bluff tops and ridges nearly surrounding them. Crazy Horse had chosen the place to make his stand and his braves outnumbered the troops by at least two to one. Seizing the initiative, Miles ordered his fur-clad Regular infantry forward against the warriors, driving them from their advan-tageous positions.

---

*Don Rickey, Jr., The Battle of Wolf Mountain," *Montana The Magazine of Western History*, 13 (Spring 1963), 44-54.

And scrambling upward
Through the snow and ice
Came doggedly, without a sign of fear,
The infantry of Miles. They didn't cheer,
They didn't hurry, and they didn't stop,
For all the rifle roaring at the top,
Until the gun-butt met the battle-ax.[1]

By noon, the Cheyenne and Oglala had lost heart, having been defeated at every point along the battle line, and having seen the prominent Cheyenne warrior Big Crow's "medicine" fail him as he fell.

Miles pursued the hostiles for several miles up the valley of Tongue River, as the Indians fled toward the Big Horn Mountains, abandoning much of their camp gear and their vital winter supplies of food and other equipment. The results of the battle came as a death blow to Cheyenne and Oglala hopes of remaining free of government control. Unable to move freely in the bitter Montana winter, the Indians now faced the fact that Government soldiers could campaign against them in all extremes of weather, and that there was no place where they could be safe in a snug winter camp. Surrender negotiations were begun soon after and Crazy Horse came in to give up early in the spring of 1877.

The winter of 1876–77 was extremely severe in Wyoming, Dakota, and Montana. Deep snows and sub-zero weather came early to the high plains and mountains of eastern Montana. Buffalo and other large game were scarce, and the Tongue River camps of the hostile Northern Cheyenne and Oglala Sioux contained little food for the winter.

Miles' soldiers had made many strikes against other bands, mainly those with Sitting Bull, north of the Yellowstone River. In every engagement the Indians had abandoned the field. Crazy Horse, the Oglala leader, and the headmen of his Cheyenne friends were considering peace negotiations by mid-December, as Miles' Indian scouts had spread the news that "Bearcoat" Miles would treat them favorably and justly if they came in to surrender.

The matter was much talked of around the camps, and it was decided that peace delegates should be sent to meet with Miles at his log cantonment at the mouth of Tongue River on the Yellowstone. The peace party arrived in the vicinity of the post just before noon, December 16. Captain Simon Snyder, an officer in the post, described what followed:

---

1.   John G. Neihardt, *Song of the Indian Wars* (New York: Macmillan Co., 1925), 214. No participant accounts of the fight mention any hand-to-hand fighting, and the author has slightly stretched his poetic license in his last line mention of gun-butt versus battle axe. Certainly, the poet has caught the essence of the conflict: disciplined, persevering Regular soldiers attacking twice their own number of enemies.

Colonel Nelson A. Miles and several Fifth Infantry officers posed in minus 40-degree temperatures at the Tongue River Cantonment on December 29, 1876, the day they marched after Crazy Horse. Left to right: Second Lieutenant Oscar F. Long; Major Henry R. Tilton, cantonment surgeon; Second Lieutenant James W. Pope; Miles; First Lieutenant Frank D. Baldwin; Second Lieutenant Charles E. Hargous; and Second Lieutenant Hobart K. Bailey. (Montana Historical Society Photograph Archives)

... [at] 11:15 a. m., rapid firing was heard in the direction of the Crow [scout] camp. The command was immediately turned out and deployed around the garrison, when it was discovered that five Sioux . . . had attempted to come in under a flag of truce, were discovered by the Crows after they had passed their [scout] camp, and all [*sic*] killed before they could reach the garrison. Genl. Miles was angry . . . and ordered Capt. Dickey to at once disarm the Crows, which being partly done, the Crows left in a body . . . Of the Indians killed, Bull Eagle, Tall Bull, Red Cloth and Red Horses have been recognized. All chiefs and head men.[2]

The fate of the peace negotiators was soon known in the Sioux and Cheyenne camps located up the valley of Tongue River, and all thoughts of early and peaceful surrender were abandoned. General

2. "Diary of Capt. Simon Snyder, 5th Infy, 1876," MS, Snyder-Ronayne Collection, Custer Battlefield National Monument, "Dec. 16 . . ."

Miles dispatched two of his Sioux scouts to find the hostile camp the day after the peace envoys were killed. However, the scouts either couldn't or wouldn't find Crazy Horse's camp, as they returned on December 21, with the peace gifts Miles had sent, reporting they had been unable to locate the hostile camp.[3]

On December 26, Sioux raiders ran off the post beef herd grazing near the cantonment. Miles was now convinced that only an immediate and determined campaign could compel the surrender of the Oglala Sioux and Northern Cheyenne.

Scouts informed Miles that the stolen cattle had been driven up the valley of Tongue River, toward the supposed location of the hostile winter camps. Miles at once ordered out Companies C and F, 22nd Infantry, and Company D, 5th Infantry, all under Captain Dickey's command, to pursue the raiders. Lieutenant Carter and Company K, 5th Infantry, followed Captain Dickey's command the next day, and Miles left the cantonment on December 29, with Companies A, C and E, 5th Infantry, and two cannon, to assume personal command of the expedition.[4] Miles' command numbered 436 infantry officers and men, and included a 12-pounder bronze Napoleon cannon, one 3-inch rifled Rodman gun, a few white scouts, and two Crow and one Bannock scouts, and several supply wagons. He intended to pursue the Sioux and Cheyenne through the ice and snow until they would be forced to fight or surrender, and he was prepared to remain out as long as need be, regardless of winter storms and sub-zero temperatures.[5]

The Infantry marched up Tongue River through drifted snow, and at times on a somewhat less strenuous route on the river ice. Mounted scouts ranged several miles ahead, and the artillery pieces and supply wagons brought up the rear. Miles' men skirmished with a few hostiles on January 1st and 3rd, and a soldier was killed while rounding up stray draft animals behind the column.

"A blinding snowstorm . . . [raged] early in the morning. . ." of January 6, and the troops passed through several recently abandoned Indian camp sites that afternoon.[6] The Sioux and Cheyenne were withdrawing up the valley as Miles advanced. The late afternoon of January 7 witnessed a hard fight between Miles' advance scouts and a large number of hostiles. Miles led a detachment of troops to their rescue, and the Sioux and Cheyenne withdrew.

---

3. Ibid., "Dec. 21. . ."

4. "Troop Operations, Tongue River Cantonment, Aug. 28, 1876-Oct. 1, 1877," Letters Sent, Fort Keogh, 1877, Record Group (RG) 98, National Archives, 55.

5. Miles's infantry marched eleven and one-half miles the day they departed, December 29, with the temperature at thirty degrees below zero. *Report of the Chief Engineers* [1877] (Washington, D.C.: Government Printing Office, 1878), 1693-94.

6. Ibid., January 6, 1877.

That same afternoon the scouts had captured a young Cheyenne warrior and seven women and children. Miles had the captives fed and given shelter, and learned that Crazy Horse and his Cheyenne allies were only a few miles further up the river.

The troops camped for the night in a grove of trees, near Tongue River, with many high, rugged ridges and hills on the left and right, and a cone or pyramid shaped butte immediately in front of them in the river valley. Miles and his scouts felt certain that the Sioux and Cheyenne would offer battle the next day. Snow fell during the night, while the temperature hovered near zero. By morning fresh snow, added to what was already on the ground, resulted in an accumulation of from one to three feet. A cheerless, grey dawn, with heavy leaden storm clouds moving in from the west, greeted the numbed soldiers as they lumbered out on to the valley bottom to build cooking fires on the morning of January 8, 1877.

Patches of snow were scraped bare, and coffee was quickly boiling while the soldiers broiled their frozen salt pork and munched hardtack crackers. As the troops ate their meager breakfast, the hills and ridges in front, to the right and left, and partly across the river behind them were quickly covered with more than twice their own number of Sioux and Cheyenne warriors.[7] A warrior's voice rang out across the valley taunting the soldiers, advising them to eat well, as it would be their last meal.

Miles immediately ordered his artillery placed on the bench facing the Indians ". . . to resist attack; or be held in reserve. . ."[8] His infantry companies were posted to battle formation, ready to repel an assault or begin an advance. Firing broke out at 7:00 a.m., with many warriors concentrating on the soldiers' right and others attempting a thrust to encircle the troops on the opposite side of the river.[9] E Company was moved to intercept the thrust to the right, and a detail of soldiers was sent to dig in on the commanding point across the river.

The warriors "fought entirely dismounted."[10] Launching a loosely maneuvered charge on the right, the Sioux and Cheyenne were forced back by E Company, and a detail of soldiers seized the top of the dominant high knoll now designated Battle Butte, removing

---

7. "Troop Operations, Tongue River Cantonment, Aug. 28, 1876-Oct. 1, 1877," MS, "January 8, '77. . ."

8. Luther S. Kelly (Milo M. Quaife, ed.) *Yellowstone Kelly* (New Haven, Conn.: Yale University Press, 1926), 172.

9. *Report of the Chief of Engineers,* 1694.

10. Col. N. A. Miles to Assist. Adjt. Gen'l., Department of Dakota, telegram, January 20, 1877, in *Annual Report of the Secretary of War,* 1877 (Washington, D.C.: Government Printing Office, 1878), 494.

Cheyenne warrior Wooden Leg depicted himself and two Sioux warriors carrying off the mortally wounded Big Crow in the Battle of Wolf Mountain (Marquis Collection, Custer Battlefield National Monument)

the threat to Miles' right.[11] Miles commanded from his position near the Napoleon gun, where he "... stood with a little switch in his hand directing operations."[12]

The "wagon gun" artillery crashed and reverberated through the valley, but did not seem to frighten the warriors, as they were now massing on ridges to the left of the troop positions.[13] Artillery had previously been greatly feared by the Indians, but the big guns apparently did not of themselves tip the scales of battle at Wolf Mountain, as Miles finally had to order his infantrymen to charge the Indian-held ridges to dislodge the warriors.

Two companies were ordered forward against the ridges where Indian riflemen lay " ... hidden behind rocks shooting toward the

11. Statement of battle participant H. C. Thompson, Sgt., Co. E, 5th Infy., 1877, in newspaper clipping by "Montana Lou" Grill, Montana Historical Society, Helena. Thompson went over the battle site with Grill in 1926, and also stated that the hostiles attempted to counterattack at this point, and came within fifty yards of the infantry line before breaking and falling back.

12. Kelly, *Yellowstone Kelly*, 173.

13. Mari Sandoz, *Crazy Horse, The Strange Man of the Oglalas* (New York: Alfred A. Knopf, 1942), 352.

soldiers."[14] Encumbered by heavy coats and foot gear, Miles' regular infantrymen began their charge, at a labored walk through snow two to three feet deep.

Just below the crest of Crow Butte, Big Crow, a leading Cheyenne warrior, danced and sang war songs proclaiming his invulnerability to white bullets. His feathered warbonnet tail swinging wildly as he moved, Big Crow was a striking figure in his red daubed war shirt and red blanket—shouting, gesturing, and occasionally stopping to fire a shot from his Springfield carbine.[15]

Companies A and D moved steadily ahead until they had almost reached the Indian positions. Bullets plowed little furrows in the snow, but most flew high, over the soldiers, because the Indians were not very good marksmen and they were shooting downhill. Stopping to concentrate their fire on the enemy, A and D companies fired away hundreds of cartridges. Fearing these men would run short of ammunition, Capt. Frank Baldwin grasped a heavy box of rifle cartridges, held it in front of him on his saddle, and raced to the skirmish line. Baldwin lost his grip on the ammunition box, and many shells spilled out on the snow. Though most of the cartridges were lost, Baldwin's arrival was very timely, as he ". . . hat in hand, and with a ringing shout, . . . newly inspired the weary men . . ."[16] Company C meanwhile had moved forward to support Companies A and D, and all three companies went up the glassy slopes toward the hostiles. A few men were wounded as the assault began, and one soldier was killed.

Deep snow and rugged terrain compelled the soldier line to break into uneven groups of struggling attackers. Two soldiers in advance of their comrades halted at a rock ledge, on the lower slopes of Crow Butte, and began firing at Big Crow. One of the soldiers was wounded by an Indian bullet, but between them they concentrated a carefully aimed fire on the red-clad warrior, and Big Crow fell mortally wounded.[17]

Capt. Frank Baldwin had only just joined the advance, swinging his hat to lead the men on. The ridge top ahead still spouted Indian bullets, but a few minutes later the hostiles abandoned their position and retreated, carrying the stricken Big Crow with them, as the

---

14. Thomas B. Marquis, *A Warrior Who Fought Custer* (Minneapolis: Midwest Co., 1931), 169.

15. The hostile Sioux and Cheyenne captured about 250 .45 calibre model 1873 Springfield carbines from Custer's men at the Little Big Horn. Wooden Leg's drawing text states that Big Crow used one of these carbines.

16. Maj. G. W. Baird, "General Miles' Indian Campaigns," in, *Century Magazine*, 20 (July 1891), 357. Sgt. Thompson recounted the same incident in Grill, "Crazy Horse's Last Stand," 3rd installment, in Miles City *Daily Star,* June 1926. Kelly, *Yellowstone Kelly*, 174.

17. Lou F. Grill, "Crazy Horse's Last Stand" 3rd installment, in Miles City *Daily Star*, June, 1926 (no other date). Marquis, *Warrior Who Fought Custer,* 170.

troops approached within 50 yards. Stumbling, slipping, and occasionally falling down, the soldiers ". . . took the ridge in storming fashion."[18] The last shots were fired about noon, as the continuing snow fall increased to near blizzard intensity.

During the engagement one soldier was killed and eight were wounded, one of whom died the next day.[19] All Indian casualties were carried away by their comrades. Wooden Leg stated that Big Crow was the only Cheyenne killed, and that two Sioux warriors were killed; which agrees with Red Sack's (Sioux) contemporary statement.[20] Red Sack further advised that three other warriors had been wounded, two of whom later died.[21] The engineer officer reported that many blood spots were seen on the snow in the abandoned Indian positions.[22]

Miles' men pursued the fleeing Sioux and Cheyenne for several miles up the valley of Tongue River, passing through the Indian camp where much of the hostiles' winter supplies and *materiel* were lost. The snow fall warmed to rain during the early evening of January 8, and Miles moved his camp site up on to the bench where his cannon had been during the action. Unable to pursue the hostiles, the tired soldiers retraced their route, down Tongue River, and arrived at the Cantonment (Ft. Keogh) January 18, after a total march of 242 miles.

Though casualties were light on both sides at Wolf Mountain; the hostile Oglala Sioux and Northern Cheyennes had suffered a severe blow in having their winter camp uprooted. "If a Crazy Horse camp could be struck, where would the people be safe?"[23] Some Cheyennes soon drifted into camp to surrender at Miles' post; others, remaining with Crazy Horse and his Oglalas, turned themselves in to the authorities in South Dakota.

Miles' victory at the Wolf Mountain Battle convinced Crazy Horse and his followers that further resistance was futile. Less than six months after the allied Sioux and Cheyenne had experienced their peak of triumph at the Little Big Horn, only a few scattered rem-

---

18. Kelly, *Yellowstone Kelly*, 173-74.

19. Capt. O. M. Smith, "The Twenty-Second Regiment of Infantry," in, T. F. Rodenbough and W. L. Haskins, eds., *The Army of the United States* (New York: Maynard, Merrill & Co., 1896), 687. Private Bernard McCann, Co. F, 22nd Infantry, was the man who died on January 9. He was posthumously awarded the Congressional Medal of Honor for bravery at Wolf Mountain. The three men that Miles reported killed included Pvt. McCann, one man killed during the assault, and the herder killed on January 3. Only one man was reported killed on January 8 in *Report of the Chief of Engineers*, 1695.

20. Marquis, *Warrior Who Fought Custer*, 171.

21. "Feb. 13, Cheyenne [Wyoming Territory] *Sun*," quoted in Missouri *Republican*, February 14, 1877.

22. *Report of the Chief of Engineers*, 1695.

23. Sandoz, *Crazy Horse*, 353.

nants remained dangerously at large. Sitting Bull and his followers fled to Canada, Crazy Horse and his cohorts were preparing to surrender, and with the capture of Lame Deer's Village of Miniconjou Sioux May 7, 1877, the powerful hostile bands of mid-1876 had been swept from eastern Montana, Wyoming, and Dakota. It was in September, 1877, that the 35-year-old Crazy Horse, fighting blindly to escape his captors at Camp Robinson, Nebraska, was killed by repeated stabs from a sentry's bayonet.

HARPER'S WEEKLY.

A JOURNAL OF CIVILIZATION

VOL. XXII.—No. 1147.]   NEW YORK, SATURDAY, DECEMBER 21, 1878.   [WITH A SUPPLEMENT. PRICE TEN CENTS.

Entered according to Act of Congress, in the Year 1878, by Harper & Brothers, in the Office of the Librarian of Congress, at Washington.

THE NEW INDIAN WAR.

NOW, NO SARCASTIC INNUENDOES, BUT LET US HAVE A SQUARE FIGHT.

PART THREE
Sioux War Sidelights

Within days of Custer's shocking defeat at the Little Bighorn, scout H. M. "Muggins" Taylor raced with dispatches to the telegrapher at Fort Ellis announcing the unthinkable tragedy. Taylor completed his initial mission on the afternoon of July 3 and immediately sought out and recounted his story for the editor of the Bozeman *Times*. The *Times* issued an "Extra" later that evening, which became the first printed word on the Custer disaster. In a few more hours details of the fight spread across Montana, then flashed across the nation.

The claim for this Custer battle news "scoop" is an interesting sidelight of the Sioux War story. In an essay appearing in *Montana* in 1976, Rex C. Myers gives credit to Montana's editors for breaking the news of the Custer fight. In addition, Myers explores the territory's straightforward acceptance of the "disaster." Custer's death was shocking, but Montana residents saw it matter-of-factly. In their view it represented the cost of opening their territory, and it was a price worth paying.

Paul L. Hedren follows with a 1983 *Montana* essay on the activities of a single infantry company deployed in a behind-the-scenes role during the Sioux War. These men did not campaign with Crook, Terry, or Gibbon. Rather, they were assigned a protection and patrol mission on the important Cheyenne-to-Black Hills road that proved as militarily significant as that performed by their comrades on the war front. The essay also offers the only available demographic study of 1876 infantrymen, becoming a useful companion to the far more numerous studies of Seventh Cavalry personnel.

Geography played a significant role in the conduct of the Great Sioux War, especially in shaping transportation routes used to support the army columns. Of the several modes of conveyance on the northern plains, steamboating on the Missouri River was a well-established enterprise by 1876. Although a less-well-known river, the Yellowstone also had been successfully navigated. In the Sioux War of 1876–1877, the army contracted with the Coulson Line for the services of the steamers *Far West* and *Josephine* to support Terry's and Gibbon's soldiers. In a 1985 *Montana* essay, William E. Lass explores the multifaceted story of steamboats on the Yellowstone during the heady days when soldiers and pioneers wrested the valley from the Indians.

Montana Editors
and the Custer Battle

by Rex C. Myers

General John Gibbon paused briefly on the bluffs overlooking the valley of the Little Big Horn late in the afternoon of Wednesday, June 28, 1876. As his men fashioned litters for the remnants of Major Marcus Reno's command and dug graves for the remains of Custer's, the General took out his personal notebook and penciled a note to inform his superiors and the world of what had transpired in the southern part of Montana Territory during the last three days.

"We will start down the river to-day for the steamboat with the wounded of Custer's command, . . ." the message began. "General Custer's command met with terrible disaster here on the 25th. Custer, with five companies, were so far as we can ascertain, completely annihilated except two of our Crow scouts. . . . Roughly stated the loss of Custer's command is about one-half, say 250 men." Between 1,800 and 2,500 warriors, according to Gibbon's estimate, had inflicted a resounding defeat upon the men of the Seventh Cavalry.

Beyond recounting the engagement's particulars, Gibbon had two more messages to convey. First, commanders at Fort Ellis, Fort Shaw, Camp Baker, and Washington, D.C., as well as his wife and friends, should know that the bulk of Gibbon's troop was "intact and in fine order." Second, Matthew Carroll, the expedition's freight master, asked that news of the battle be conveyed to Montana Surveyor General A. J. Smith in Helena, who would, in turn, pass it on to the Helena *Independent* for publication.

Finished, General Gibbon tore the pages from his notebook, summoned a scout—H. M. "Muggins" Taylor—and instructed him to carry them straight to Captain D. W. Benham at Fort Ellis, near Bozeman, M.T. It was the nearest telegraph station and here Captain Benham could send the necessary dispatches with all due haste.

---

*Rex C. Myers, "Montana Editors and the Custer Battle, *Montana The Magazine of Western History*, 26 (Spring 1976), 18-31.

E. S. Wilkinson, editor of the Bozeman Times, *published the nation's first report of the Custer fight in an "Extra" dated July 3.*   (Taylor Studio, Helena, Montana Historical Society Photograph Archives)

From these hastily penciled beginnings, the written word on Custer's battle swelled to astronomical proportions. Professional and non-professional historians have scrutinized and ballyhooed count-less facets of George Armstrong Custer, his last campaign, and the provocative legacy the two left behind. More than any other single incident, the Battle of the Little Big Horn brought, and continues to bring, attention to Montana. Yet scholars and buffs have almost universally ignored the reaction of Montana's Territorial residents to that engagement. By default, writers have assumed that word of Custer's defeat produced the same monumental reactions in Montana as it did in the eastern press.[1]

In the first published reports, according to Robert M. Utley's observations in *Custer and the Great Controversy,* one finds the inception and perpetuation of all the "errors, myths and legends that clutter the history of the Little Big Horn."[2] Utley tarried only briefly with the Montana press, however, as he attempted to unravel the question of who first published word of the Custer battle. He then deserted the Territory and moved eastward to the big urban dailies where fact, fancy, and legend absorbed the attention of large reading audiences. The Custer Mystique was a phenomenon that began that first week of July, 1876, and continued, almost unbroken and unbridled, for a century.

Brian W. Dippie, in a recent article entitled "The Southern Response to Custer's Last Stand [included in the present anthology — PLH]," examined the reaction of the press in the Reconstruction South. He concluded that the battle was "irrelevant." Of import were "the various uses to which it could be put" — primarily Democratic and political in nature.[3]

Whether the Southern press used Custer and the Battle of the Little Big Horn for its political implications, or whether the eastern papers capitalized on it for purposes of circulation and political chess, these utilizations served to perpetuate not only the memory of the battle but of Custer himself. Herein lay the genesis of a century of public attention and debate — a stark contrast to the public reaction in Montana.

Glorification of Custer and his defeat served no purpose in contemporary Montana. Concerns of Montanans were more pragmatic: the Battle of the Little Big Horn was one of a series of engagements

---

1. The significance or nature of Montana's reaction has received little attention despite its proximity to events. Edgar I. Stewart's work *Custer's Luck* (Norman, University of Oklahoma Press, 1959), includes seven Montana newspapers in the bibliography, but only three were contemporary to the actual events. Stewart omits the Bozeman *Times* and the Helena *Herald,* among others. Fred Dustin's famous Custer bibliography, originally published in 1939 (*The Custer Tragedy,* Ann Arbor, Mich.: Edwards Brothers), and later expanded in Col. W. A. Graham's *The Custer Myth* (New York: Bonanza Books, 1953), contains 631 separate citations, including the Bismarck *Tribune* of July 6, 1876. There is not a single Montana newspaper mentioned.

2. Robert M. Utley, *Custer and the Great Controversy* (Los Angeles: Westernlore Press, 1962). Utley's chapter 2, "The Press," adequately covers the reaction of the major eastern newspapers.

3. Brian W. Dippie. "The Southern Response to Custer's Last Stand," *Montana The Magazine of Western History,* 21 (Spring 1971), 18-31.

in the Indian wars. These wars and their potentialities were utmost in importance. The Custer battle was like a "flash in the pan" — a manifestation of something that territorial settlers knew was there all along.

Montana Territorial Governor Benjamin Franklin Potts had an ominous message to convey to new Secretary of War Alphonso Taft in a letter dated May 1, 1876: "It is now evident that the Yellowstone Valley will soon be the scene of bloodshed. The Sioux Indians are numerous and determined and great apprehension is felt for the safety of our eastern settlements. . . . I fear [General Gibbon's] force is not sufficient to meet the Sioux if they concentrate their entire strength . . . and attack his little band."[4]

Montanans had long been concerned with the "Indian Situation" and the Washington politics which produced it. Repeatedly, Governor Potts addressed letters to Commissioner of Indian Affairs J. Q. Smith suggesting that all arms and ammunition trade along the Missouri River be suspended. The material, he warned, was reaching hostile hands and would bear bitter fruit.

Early in 1876, motivated by the same desire to protect eastern Montana, Congressional Delegate Martin Maginnis had introduced legislation to authorize construction of a new military post on the Yellowstone River, and another on the Musselshell. Throughout the spring, his bill had remained in committee, its future dubious.

Meanwhile, in Montana, pragmatic Governor Potts realized action was needed soon. In the same letter of May 1, 1876, and again two weeks later, the Governor requested new, breech-loading rifles to help arm Territorial residents. He also offered to raise a 1000-man militia "to protect the Montana frontiers." Montana did not have a general militia law, so the Governor needed authorization from the War Department to call up volunteers. He got neither the rifles nor the authorization: "[T]his Department does not require the service of such a force . . . in the protection of settlements alleged to be threatened by Indians. . . ."

Rebuffed, the Governor had all available breech-loaders secured in armories at Helena or Virginia City. Attempts to alter Indian policy, to secure protective forts, and to arm and organize a militia had gone for naught. Governor Benjamin F. Potts and all Montana waited to see what transpired in the Yellowstone Valley during the summer of 1876.

Carrying General Gibbon's notes, which told the biggest news story of the year, "Muggins" Taylor left camp on June 28 and began a circuitous trip to Fort Ellis. On the evening of July 2, he arrived in the

---

4. Benjamin Franklin Potts to A. Taft, May 1, 1876, B. F. Potts Correspondence, Montana Historical Society (hereafter MHS).

small community of Stillwater, now Columbus, Montana. Too exhausted to continue, he rested that night in the general store of William H. Norton and Horace Countryman. Norton was a "correspondent" for the Helena *Herald*, a rival daily of the *Independent*. As he read Gibbon's words he realized he had a "scoop." He questioned Taylor further about Custer's defeat, wrote a story for the *Herald*, and dispatched his partner to hurry it to Montana's capital city.

Horace Countryman and "Muggins" Taylor left Stillwater early on the morning of July 3, arriving at Fort Ellis by mid-afternoon. Taylor delivered his dispatch to Captain Benham who, in turn, took it to the telegraph office for transmission as General Gibbon had instructed. For reasons still not known, the telegraph agent delayed transmission until after the Fourth of July.

His assignment completed, Taylor sought out E. S. Wilkinson, editor of the Bozeman *Times*, and recounted his story. Hurriedly, Wilkinson assembled a work crew and published a single sheet "Extra" which was ready for distribution by 7:00 o'clock that evening.

Taylor embellished the account a little, undoubtedly using some of his own observations on the battlefield. The total number killed, he said, was 315, while Indian forces included 2,500 to 4,000 warriors. The battleground looked like a "slaughter pen." The *Times* printed it all, with a concluding observation: "The situation now looks serious."[5]

Editor Wilkinson's "Extra" of July 3 became not only the first published word of the Custer battle, but the initial source of information for the rest of Montana's newspapers. By the morning of July 4, details about what had happened at the Little Big Horn began to spread throughout the Territory.

Very early on the Fourth, Horace Countryman resumed his trip to Helena. To Norton's July 2 account he added a copy of the *Times* "Extra." When he arrived in Helena late that afternoon, he found Helena *Herald* co-editor A. J. Fisk amid the Centennial celebrants and delivered his cargo.

Like Wilkinson, Fisk wasted no time putting out a special edition which hit the streets at 6:30 P.M. Under the headline "A TERRIBLE FIGHT," Fisk informed Helena residents that Custer and 315 soldiers were dead, and the Seventh Cavalry "Cut to Pieces." The columns carried two dispatches: the first W. H. Norton's; the second, a verbatim text of the Bozeman *Times* special issue. The enterprising Fisk also got the story on the Associated Press wire service later in the evening of July 4 and brief notes about the battle appeared in Salt Lake City and San Diego papers on July 6. For many years, Clement A.

---

5. No copy of the July 3, 1876, *Times* "Extra" is known to exist. The complete text of that issue appeared in the Helena *Herald* issue the next day, and in the next regular edition of the *Times*, published July 6.

Lounsberry of the Bismarck (D.T.) *Tribune* claimed his paper was the first to publish the news. While the fact that his issue of July 6 carried the most complete early account cannot be denied, Lounsberry was not the first editor to break the news, and many writers have garnered public attention with accounts — factual and otherwise — to prove the point.[6]

Word of the battle and Custer's death fell upon the Centennial festivities in Helena "with a gloom that could not be shaken off," according to the *Daily Herald* in its July 5 issue. The news reached Butte, Deer Lodge, and Virginia City about the time Countryman was seeking out Fisk in Helena. James Mills and Henry C. Kessler, publishers of both the Butte *Miner* and the Deer Lodge *New Northwest*, issued an "Extra" of their own on the evening of July 4 under the logotype of the latter paper. Such somber news quieted Independence Day celebrants in both communities. Residents lowered flags to half mast and the topic of conversation changed from gay celebration to somber reflection.[7]

Governor Potts received unofficial word of the battle from the *Herald* on July 4, and official confirmation by telegram from Captain Benham the next morning. He hurried to the telegraph office and sent out his own message to Commander of the Army W. T. Sherman. For statistics he relied on Gibbon's account rather than on Taylor's or Norton's, concluding with a note that Montanans were greatly excited at the news. He restated his offer to raise 1,000 volunteers.

By the time *Independent* editor Hugh McQuaid received official notification of the battle, the news was stale. McQuaid had not intended to publish his normal morning issue of the Helena *Independent* on July 5, because employees had taken the previous holiday. He could not let his competitor publish another paper (as the *Herald* would and did that evening) without attempting to get some public attention. Using the wordage of Potts' telegram, McQuaid issued his own "Extra" on July 5, telling Helena residents and all Montana that volunteers would soon be mustered in and the war continued by Montanans themselves.[8]

---

6. For varying accounts of who said what first, see Graham, Stewart, and Utley, cited above, and Hugh McQuaid's account in the Bozeman *Avant Courier,* June 6, 1902, p. 8; E. A. Brininstool, *A Trooper With Custer* (Columbus, Ohio: Hunter-Trader-Trapper Company, 1925), 158-65; Harrison Lane, "Custer Massacre: How the News First Reached the Outer World," Montana Heritage Series, No. 7 (Helena: Historical Society Press, n.d.), 16-22.

7. Butte *Miner,* July 6, 1876, p. 3; *New Northwest,* July 7, 1876, p. 2. Thomas Deyarmon, editor of the *Madisonian* in Virginia City declined to publish a special edition on July 4. First mention of the Custer battle appeared in the July 6 issue of that newspaper.

8. See McQuaid in the *Avant Courier* of 1902, cited above, and *New Northwest,* July 7, 1876, p. 2.

Helena's *Herald*, in its first regular issue after word reached the city, responded to the situation in more subdued terms. Expressing "heart-felt sorrow" over the death of Custer and his troops, the paper quickly placed the incident in a more pragmatic perspective. If there was solace to be taken, the editor observed, it would be in the fact that Congress was still in session, and might yet come to grips with the "Indian problem" in Montana.

As news of Little Big Horn spread across the Territory to find its way into the columns of its press, the pattern of reaction generally followed that of the Helena *Herald*. On July 6, the Butte *Miner*, Diamond City's *Rocky Mountain Husbandman,* and the Virginia City *Madisonian* carried their first accounts. The next day the Bozeman *Avant Courier* and Fort Benton *Record* carried their initial stories, and a week later, on July 12, the Territory's westernmost paper, the *Missoulian*, completed the chain of reports. With each, the first issue or two contained emotional reactions to Custer's death and the battle. Later, while emotions remained high, the point of concentration was not on Custer, but rather on practical issues: potential Indian threats, organization of a militia, adequate arms for defense.

In the remaining months of summer, other issues received increasing news and editorial space in Montana papers. The Butte *Miner* retained its mining emphasis, as did the *Rocky Mountain Husbandman* with agriculture, and the Fort Benton *Record* regarding Missouri River trade. National and local political contests, the question of railroad development for the Territory, a population exodus to the new Black Hills gold fields, and local floods all assumed places of note during July and August. The number of column inches devoted to Custer dissipated in direct proportion to the proximity of the first news reports. By early August references to the Little Big Horn were scattered; by September, non-existent.

Of the ten newspapers published in Montana during the summer of 1876, five were Democratic in politics, four Republican, one Grange/Independent.[9] Yet political persuasion was of little significance when it came to criticizing Indian policies. The Democratic press, led by the Bozeman *Times* and the Helena *Independent*, was more vitriolic in its criticism, accusing the Grant Administration of pursuing a "foolish" and "insane" course, skimping on frontier troops and retaining sufficient forces in the Reconstruction South to influence forthcoming national elections.

---

9.   Democratic papers included: Bozeman *Times*, Fort Benton *Record, Missoulian,* Helena *Independent*, and *Madisonian*. The Republican papers were the Bozeman *Avant Courier*, Butte *Miner*, *New Northwest*, and Diamond City's *Rocky Mountain Husbandman* was independent or pro-Grange.

Republican stalwarts, like the Fisk Brothers and Mills and Kessler, criticized the "Quaker Policy" of peace and advocated increasing troops on the frontier until the Sioux nation was "exterminated" or "extinct." Even R. N. Sutherlin of the *Rocky Mountain Husbandman,* who refrained from siding with either the Democrats or Republicans in the 1876 elections, was unhesitatingly critical of existing policies. Calling the course of the Indian Bureau a "total failure," Sutherlin contended that "Indians should be treated in a manner that would be creditable to our nation, not wheedled and dallied with for the sake of private speculation. . . ." No wonder there was a war on the frontier, he concluded; the Indian uprising was justified.[10]

The recurring question of Custer's culpability in the Little Big Horn battle surfaced briefly in mid-July, corresponding with the heated debate then taking place in the eastern press. Montana's newspapers, however, did not dwell on the issue, confining themselves to repeating a story circulating elsewhere, if they mentioned the subject at all. Where editorial comments did appear, they often tempered rumors with appeals to wait for further reports or the results of an official investigation.

The major concern of Montanans and the Montana press in the summer of 1876 was still the Indian threat. Most papers carried regular accounts of "The Indian War," or "The Indian Situation" in their pages. Although many editors counseled objectivity, apprehension was widespread. A Sun River rancher synthesized all the Territory's fears in an excited letter which the Helena *Herald* printed on July 10. The great fear, he said, was that "Gibbon's little command" would be "eaten up" before help arrived. Such a defeat, coming on the heels of the Custer battle, would spur formerly peaceful Indians to leave the reservations and join the Sioux. Then, if the Indians defeated both Gibbon and Crook, "good bye, John! and everybody else, for they are strong enough to clear the country to the Columbia River."[11]

Hugh McQuaid of the Helena *Independent* exhibited the most editorial apprehension among Montana editors. In obvious competition with the *Herald,* which had "scooped" him on the original news of the Little Big Horn, McQuaid sought to be the first with significant Indian news — accurate or not. On July 9, the *Independent* reported a Sioux raid on Fort Lincoln, Dakota Territory. The report was false. Three days later there appeared an account of a massacre near Fort Pierre, D.T. — equally false. On July 13 and again the following day, McQuaid took up the idea that northern tribes might join the Sioux, adding speculation that the Sioux might cross over into the Gallatin Valley and raid there.

10. *Rocky Mountain Husbandman,* August 3, 1876, p. 2, August 10, 1876, p. 2.

11. Helena *Herald,* July 10, 1876, p. 3.

Governor Potts and the more cautious *Herald* attempted to allay citizen fears. On July 14, Potts wrote to several agents of the northern tribes, asking them to tell Indians under their charge that the Sioux would be severely punished, and cautioning them against joining their more hostile brothers. The next day's *Herald* carried an editorial on "The Extent of our Danger" which concluded that there was no need for apprehension in established communities, and probably none in the Gallatin Valley.

On Saturday night, July 15, 1876, however, Governor Potts received two disturbing dispatches. Crow Indians were camped on the upper Yellowstone and had reported to the Indian Agent that they were out of ammunition. If the government did not resupply them, they would cross the river and leave southeastern Montana—including the Gallatin Valley—exposed to Sioux raids. The same evening a telegram arrived from Bozeman reporting signal fires in the surrounding mountains—reportedly a sign the Sioux were moving in that direction. Potts decided the best course of action was a visit to Bozeman and Fort Ellis. Arriving in the afternoon of July 17, he addressed a large crowd, counseling them to remain calm in the "seeming emergency." Then he met with Captain Benham to secure more ammunition to mollify the Crows. Unfortunately for Potts' efforts, about the time he was enjoying Bozeman's hospitality with a little food and drink, the Helena *Independent* received alarming telegrams from the Gallatin Valley.

At 8:15 P.M., J. C. Bennett telegraphed the *Independent*—more signal fires had been observed east of Bozeman the previous night. An Indian raid might be imminent. "Further particulars in a few hours," Bennett promised. Thirty-five minutes later he was back on the wire, reiterating what he had already said. Hugh McQuaid now faced a dilemma. He had to go to press shortly if the *Independent* was to be out at its accustomed early morning hour; but there was nothing to substantiate Bennett's reports. He wired Bozeman's S. W. Langhorn at 9 P.M. to ask if the Indian raid story was true. Langhorn responded immediately. He knew of no raids, but he would check into the matter.

McQuaid weighed the options—probably recalling the July 4 *Herald* "Extra"—and then acted. "INDIAN RAID—SIGNAL FIRES!!!—THE SAVAGES IN THE GALLATIN VALLEY!" screamed the headlines above the accounts of Bennett's telegrams in the July 18 issue of the Helena *Independent*. It was possible, the editor admitted elsewhere in an editorial, that the reports were "colored with an undue apprehension"; but, he assured his readers, the paper spared "no expense to get the truth . . . publishing all that we were able to learn."[12]

---

12.   Helena *Independent*, July 18, 1876, pp. 2, 3.

Helena photographers Bundy and Train probably took this view of the Herald *building on Broadway in the early 1870s. Main Street at the bottom of Broadway was built in Last Chance Gulch where gold was discovered in 1864.* (Montana Historical Society Photograph Archives)

Called to task by the *Herald* and the Bozeman *Avant Courier* for his unfounded alarm over what were probably charcoal or hunters' fires, McQuaid defended his actions with the retort that the reports at least made evident the fact that "such a thing is possible."[13]

Despite calming efforts, reports of more signal fire sightings kept the Gallatin Valley in a "state of apprehension" during the week of July 17. East Gallatin residents who felt the most threatened, met in

---

13. See the Helena *Herald* of July 18, 1876, p. 1, and the Bozeman *Avant Courier* of July 21, 1876, p. 2. For McQuaid's defense, see the Helena *Independent* of July 19, 1876, p. 2. See also the Fort Benton *Record*, July 21, 1876, p. 2, in defense of McQuaid, and the *New Northwest*, July 21, 1876, p. 2, advocating restraint and calm.

the Grange hall on Thursday, July 20, to discuss a course of action. Those in attendance agreed the threat appeared real, and at once formed several committees. One solicited subscriptions to pay for scouts. A second enrolled volunteers for a militia, if necessary. Another committee called on Captain Benham to see if he would support their actions. All East Gallatin residents agreed to meet again on Saturday to assess the results of their efforts.

Within the space of two days, however, the alarm dissipated. Benham assured local residents there was no cause for concern. Crow Indians were between the Sioux and the Gallatin Valley, but if residents felt threatened they were welcome to seek protection at Fort Ellis. There had been no more "signal fire" reports for several days and volunteer scouts scouring the countryside found no trace of alleged war parties. Reassured, East Gallatin residents voted to adjourn their organization subject to the chairman's recall. The group never reconvened, and with its dissolution went the height of excitement in Montana over the "Indian threat."

Despite an occasional return to the theme of a potential northern Indian uprising, emotions in Montana quickly cooled. By the first week in August, Governor Potts could write to Martin Maginnis with the assurance that "Northern Indians are all quiet and I think will remain so." J. V. Bogert, the *New Northwest's* correspondent in Bozeman, reported "not even a rumor" to enliven his dispatch. At the same time, Helena's *Herald* felt secure enough to offer mild support for the military's apparent inaction since the Custer battle—it was not a good time to fight Indians, anyway. The *Rocky Mountain Husbandman* even braved an observation that war on her frontiers would be good for the Territory's agriculture and livestock businesses. Perhaps it would also bring attention to Montana.

From July 5, when documentation of Custer's defeat convinced Governor Potts that volunteers were essential for defense, until well into August, the call for militia became the most apparent manifestation of the threat on Montana's frontier. Save the *Rocky Mountain Husbandman,* every newspaper in Montana called for the organization of either territorial or community militia.

Butte was the first community to offer troops to Governor Potts on July 6, the day after the Governor made his proposal to General Sherman. Four days later, Potts wired assurances to the Butte *Miner* that should he receive authorization, Butte's forces would be the first enrolled. That same day he notified Delegate Maginnis of his offer, and emplored, "Will you please see Sherman about Montana."[14]

---

14. Potts to Martin Maginnis, July 10, 1876, Martin Maginnis Papers, MHS.

Neither War Department nor Congressional approval was, however, forthcoming. On July 12, Potts received a telegram from General Sherman, dated the 8th. The War Department did not feel the need was sufficient to justify calling up volunteers, although the General was certain Montana militiamen would handle themselves well. Unless he received authorization from Congress or the President, Sherman said that Montanans would be free to look after their own mines and ranches. He suggested that local militias might be organized, but it would be a purely territorial matter, and such groups would probably not be mustered into federal service.

While some Montana editors questioned the wisdom of the decision, and others engaged in a debate over the superiority of cavalry vis-a-vis foot troops in fighting Indians, the issue of volunteers for federal service was all but dead. The question of local or territorial militias continued to garner editorial space, nonetheless.

Governor Potts made one more attempt to get federal authorization to raise a militia. Through Martin Maginnis he had a bill introduced on July 25, authorizing the President to accept the service of Montana volunteers. From the start, Montana's press realized the proposal had little chance of passage. It eventually succumbed to an unfavorable committee report.

If the July 5 telegram to Sherman did not bear fruit in the form of a volunteer call-up, it did produce action on Maginnis' proposal to construct forts on the Yellowstone and Musselshell Rivers. On July 8, the same day he cabled Potts to reject his offer, Sherman notified Congress that two new posts would prove beneficial. In a flurry of Congressional activity, the measure came out of committee and found its way into law by the middle of July.

When Montanans realized militias were to be a local matter, petitions went to the Governor for modern, breech-loading arms. The Territory's store of arms in July consisted of sixty muzzle-loading muskets in Helena, and another 1,200 in Virginia City. There was also a twelve pounder mountain howitzer in Virginia City (but the carriage had rotted away since its last use) and an untold number of breechloading Springfields previously issued to citizens on a consignment basis.

Potts tried to have the breech-loaders collected, or even accounted for, only to discover farmers and ranchers had traded many of them to Indians for horses. Potts' only recourse was to call in the remaining "needle guns," authorize needed repairs on the mountain howitzer, and request 2,000 new breech-loaders from the War Department. He took these actions, all the while attempting to assure uneasy Montanans that the 1,260 muskets currently in the Territory's possession would be sufficient should a real emergency arise.

Word reached Montana in late July that the War Department would issue 500 new Springfields to Montana Territory. It was not 2,000 as Potts had requested, and even then, there were two restrictions. Potts had to sign for the weapons personally, to prevent a repeat of the traded-for-ponies debacle, and Potts had to guarantee payment of the $1,081.51 freight bill. The Governor gave his assurances in both instances and the arms were sent on their way—anticipated arrival date, about mid-October. News that the arms were on their way revived only scant interest in organizing local militia groups. Indeed, the Indian threat had so subsided that only two communities expressed interest. Virginia City succeeded in organizing a "Home Guard" in early August, but only ten men participated. Efforts were even more frustrating in Butte. Despite a vigorous campaign by *Miner* editors Mills and Kessler on the benefits of militia membership—it "improves muscular development, gives . . . a free, springing walk, and renders [members] easy and graceful in all their movements"—the militia did not jell. Butte residents met on August 27 in the school house to consider the matter, then voted to form a fire department instead—"such members of this company as desire to do so, can enroll themselves in the militia company." None did.

One more facet of the Indian excitement which enveloped Montana during the summer of 1876 manifested itself in positive results. Governor Potts renewed his long-standing pleas to curb Indian traders' traffic in arms and ammunition, and with the exception of the Fort Benton *Record*, Montana's press supported him. While not justifying the arms trade in general, the *Record* did rise to the defense of T. C. Power and Company of Fort Benton, noting that not all weapons in the possession of hostile Indians came from traders—a situation demonstrably correct from the Governor's experience with earlier "needle guns" and frontier farmers.

To the relief of most Montanans, Indian Commissioner J. Q. Smith closed the arms and ammunition trade on August 22, 1876. His action affected not only Montana, but the territories—states of Colorado, Utah, Wyoming, Idaho, Dakota, and Nebraska as well.

The centennial summer closed without further battles of major significance on Montana's plains. For the Territory's residents, the excitement had ended by mid-August. Much of what they had sought earlier came to pass: Easterners were now aware of the true nature of the Indian wars; the official arms traffic had ended and a shipment of modern arms—albeit a small one—was on the way.

By the end of July, the *Madisonian* could even report the Custer debacle in mock seriousness: "Finest watering place in the country! . . . Salubrious climate, mountain prospects, pleasant sites for picnic parties in mountain dells about the forks of the far-famed Little Big

Horn River. Water with medicinal properties much praised by Major Reno and party, late visitors; in short, every attraction of a first-class fashionable abode for the heated term. The closest attention paid all visitors; charges moderate, and always on horseback . . . An elegant summer resort—Recumbent Bison proprietor."

When Benjamin F. Potts addressed the Tenth Montana Legislature on January 8, 1877, he made reference to the excitement of the previous summer only in routine matters which constituted an insignificant portion of his speech. He asked members of the Legislature to take care of financial obligations incurred, particularly the freight bill for the rifles and suggested the Territory have a general militia law to facilitate local organization, should such be necessary at a future time.

In Council Joint Resolution #1, legislators allocated money for the freight bill on the 500 breech-loaders. The warrant went to Governor Potts, who had paid the bill out of his own pocket. House Bill #24 took care of the expenses of Francis C. Deimling—$58.75—for rebuilding the carriage on the mountain howitzer.

On the Governor's last suggestion, however, the Assembly members were not moved. They made provision for the care and keeping of the 500 rifles in the Territory's custody to prevent further abuses, and provided for their allocation to militia groups should any be formed. It was not a general militia law, *per se*, but it did provide a basic framework in which militias could operate.

On February 3, 1877, House Member Louis Rottwitt of Meagher County rose to introduce Joint Resolution #1 suggesting that the name of the Little Big Horn River be changed to "Custer's River," in commemoration of the "dauntless courage, the disciplined valor, and the heroic death of Col. George A. Custer, and his men. . . ." Under a suspension of the rules, the measure passed the third reading unanimously, cleared the upper chamber that same afternoon, and received the Governor's signature by nightfall.

Not to be outdone, A. H. Mitchell of Big Horn County introduced Council Bill #62 on the last day of the session, changing the name of Big Horn County to Custer County, in commemoration of the same traits and events. Like the preceding resolution, there was a suspension of the rules, unanimous consent, and the Governor's signature in less than twelve hours.[15]

---

15. Despite these legislative efforts, the Custer River designation did not survive. The Department of the Interior's General Land Office Map of Montana Territory in 1879, contains both Custer County and Custer River. George W. Cram's "Cram's Railroad and Township Map of Montana," published the same year by the Western Map Depot, has Custer County, but retains Little Big Horn River. General Land Office maps after 1879 all reverted to use of Little Big Horn River. Montana remained without

These were perfunctory social obligations at best. Neither measure merited editorial comment in a single Territorial newspaper. This lack of concern for, or interest in, the Custer battle was representative of the position newspapers had taken the previous summer. In their pages during the term of the 1877 Legislative Assembly were discussions of politics, railroad questions, and local issues. There were no discussions of events along the Little Big Horn or the commander of the Seventh Cavalry who died there.

George Armstrong Custer's last battle has generated a greater volume of historical — and non-historical — literature than any other single United States military engagement. Placed in an historical context of United States/Indian confrontation during the Nineteenth Century, however, it is a tragic but not highly significant event. Montana and its press placed the battle in that context. At a time when it was attracting major attention elsewhere in the nation, the region most affected by the outcome relegated the actual engagement — and Custer — to a place of relative insignificance.

Of primacy to Montanans were the results of the Indian war. If the battle was significant it was so only because it made it possible for them to obtain goals they had sought before the summer of 1876. Governor Potts finally secured the close of the Indian arms trade; Martin Maginnis saw his legislation to construct forts on the Yellowstone and Musselshell get hurried passage; the Territory secured more modern arms for home defense; the legislation regulating the use of those arms became the basis for militia organization the next summer when the "Indian problem" renewed itself as the Nez Perce plunged across Montana in search of sanctuary in Canada.

Montana was the site of those events which occupied the attention of the nation a century ago. Its people and its press, however, were not the promulgators or the perpetuators of the controversy and verbiage which swirled out of the Custer Battle to flood the nation in rhetoric. These were eastern in origin.

---

a Big Horn County until 1913 when the Legislature created one out of part of what had been Custer County. Big Horn County contains the site of the Custer Battlefield. The Custer County name change went into effect immediately. When the state printer set type for the legislative proceedings, he listed Mitchell as a delegate from Custer County. Whereas the county name change was a Territorial matter, changing the name of the Little Big Horn River was something different. For many people outside Montana, it was a name made all too familiar through the columns of the nation's press in preceding months. Map makers used both Custer River and Little Big Horn River for several years, then reverted to the original.

Rustic field camps such as this at Cow Island on the Missouri River protected all manner of shipment and settlement during the Great Sioux War. (F. Jay Haynes, photographer, Haynes Foundation Collection, Montana Historical Society Photograph Archives)

An Infantry Company in the Sioux Campaign, 1876

by Paul L. Hedren

The lackluster induction of one Charles Reilly, of Philadelphia, into the United States Army in 1876 was typical of many foot soldiers' experience. After receiving a physical examination by the recruiting officer, hearing a brief description of army life, and being read several of the Articles of War, Reilly and two other enlistees were ready to become Regulars. The three "raw fish" only stood silent when the lieutenant asked if they had further questions. And so the officer led them in repeating the Oath of Enlistment.

> I, _____, do solemnly swear that I will bear true allegiance to the United States of America, and that I will serve them honestly and faithfully against all their enemies or opposers whatsoever, and observe and obey the orders of the President of the United States, and the orders of the officers appointed over me, according to the rules and articles for the government of the armies of the United States.

Charles Reilly could little imagine that in a few hurried months he would be on the windswept plains of eastern Wyoming, on duty with a company of infantrymen in the Great Sioux War of 1876. Reilly's experience in Company H of the Twenty-third Infantry, that of the foot soldier generally, is not of the type that is widely told, having been eclipsed by tales of cavalry action, important battles, and famous personalities. Yet infantry contributions during the Indian wars, and particularly in the 1876 Campaign, were significant, for it was infantrymen who insured orderly communications, safe travel on western roads, trails, and rivers, prompt shipment of war materiel to troops nearer the front, and who performed the endless patrol and response that so often characterized the army routine.

*Paul L. Hedren, "An Infantry Company in the Sioux Campaign, 1876," *Montana The Magazine of Western History*, 33 (Winter 1983), 30-39.

While comprehensive treatment of the role of the U.S. infantry in the Sioux War of 1876 awaits the historian's approach, a look at Company H is offered as an introductory case study. Company H is singled out because, like many similar units in 1876, it was brought into the fray by chance after the dispiriting tone of the campaign had been established. These soldiers constituted part of the army's hurried mobilization to check an enemy which, on all fronts, was far testier than had been anticipated. Like many other units, "H" was not sent to the battle front, but was strategically deployed well behind the newspaper correspondents and the men wearing the generals' stars. Moreover, the record suggests that Company H, in terms of composition as well as duties and accomplishments, was typical of infantry on the Northern Plains in the nation's centennial year.

Company H was one of ten companies that, along with headquarters, comprised the Twenty-third Regiment of Infantry. The unit was organized in 1862 as the Second Battalion, Fourteenth Infantry. This battalion emerged from the Civil War to be redesignated as the Twenty-third and was subsequently posted to the far West. The enlisted men and their officers gained substantial experience as Indian fighters after the war. George Crook, for instance, who was the regiment's lieutenant colonel until 1873, doggedly chased the Paiute Indians across the Plateau country of Idaho, Oregon, and Washington from 1867 through 1868 when they were finally subjugated. Crook, promoted in a single leap to brigadier general, moved to Arizona in the early 1870s, where he directed a massive campaign against Apaches. Elements of his former regiment also took part in that fighting. Meanwhile, the regiment's colonel, Jefferson Columbus Davis, by virtue of his brevet rank of major general, was ordered in 1873 to replace General Edward R. S. Canby, who had been murdered by Modoc tribesmen in California. Davis subsequently organized the final capture and punishment of the Modoc people. By the outbreak of the Sioux War of 1876, the regiment had been distributed to posts in Nebraska and Wyoming Territory. Headquarters was established at Omaha Barracks, Nebraska, where Companies D and H, the latter commanded by Captain Richard Isaac Eskridge, also took station.[1]

---

1. Theodore F. Rodenbough and William F. Haskin, *The Army of the United States: Historical Sketches of Staff and Line* (New York: Argonaut Press, 1966), 692-94; Philip Reade, "Chronicle of the Twenty-third Regiment of Infantry, U.S.A.," *The Journal of the Military Service Institution,* 35 (November-December, 1904), 419-27. In 1876 the regiment was dispersed as follows: Headquarters: Omaha Barracks, Neb.; Staff and Band: Omaha Barracks; Company A: Fort Hartsuff, Neb.; Company B: North Platte, Neb; Company C: Sidney Barracks, Neb.; Company D: Omaha Barracks; Company E: Cheyenne Depot, Wyo.; Company F: Fort D. A. Russell, Wyo.; Company G: Fort McPherson, Neb.; Company H: Omaha Barracks and Sage Creek, Wyo.; Company I: Sidney Barracks; Company K: Fort Hartsuff, Neb. and Fort Reno, Wyo.

It is often suggested that the tone of an army company—its general well-being and functional integrity—was directly influenced by one or more of the company's commissioned officers. Certainly, it was common for the officers to insure that the company was properly clothed, fed, and trained. And the commissioned staff frequently took an interest in the personal lives of the men. The healthy respect and rapport usually were results of an officer's own experiences, particularly if, earlier in his career, he had served in the ranks. Company H's Captain Eskridge and First Lieutenant George McMannis Taylor both had served as privates during the Civil War. Eskridge had risen from that grade to captain of a Fourteenth Missouri Cavalry company by 1865. When he was honorably mustered out of the volunteers after the war he obtained a commission in the Regular establishment in 1866. By 1873 he again wore the straps of a captain.[2]

Taylor, Eskridge's principal subaltern, served from Ohio during the war. In 1866 he too obtained a Regular Army commission, and a year later was promoted to first lieutenant in the Twenty-third.[3] The junior officer of the company was Second Lieutenant Julius Hayden Pardee. Pardee hailed from New Mexico, and was an 1871 West Point graduate. Although his initial appointment had been to the Twenty-fifth Infantry, a black regiment, in August 1871 he transferred to the Twenty-third. By 1876 he was in his fifth year with the outfit; from an enlisted man's perspective he was no longer a shavetail.[4]

The character of an army company could be shaped by more than the influences of the commissioned staff, of course. Sometimes the peculiar blends of backgrounds, personalities, and nationalities helped mold the men into a cohesive, professional outfit. Data from the Army's *Registers of Enlistment* and *Muster Rolls* suggest that these factors, too, were important in the social chemistry of Company H.

A surprisingly large percentage of the enlisted men of the company, for instance, were veteran soldiers serving in a second or further enlistment. For the American army of this period, approximately 26 per cent were veterans; for Company H this figure was 47 per cent. Eleven men alone were in their third tour; two were in their sixth, which meant they could well have been in uniform since the late 1840s. Of considerable importance, the "back-bone" of any company, was the non-commissioned staff. Of the nine men wearing NCO chevrons in Company H, seven were veterans, including all of the

---

2. Francis B. Heitman, *Historical Register and Dictionary of the United States Army* (Urbana: University of Illinois Press, 1965), 408.

3. Heitman, *Historical Register,* 946.

4. Heitman, *Historical Register,* 768.

sergeants. Moreover, all but one of these sergeants were in their third or fourth enlistments.[5]

Another statistic furthers the notion that these men were not juveniles mesmerized by blue uniforms and brass buttons, which were certainly a lure for some army enlistees. In 1876 the age span in "H" stretched from twenty to fifty-two years. The average was twenty-nine, a few years higher than the comparable figure for the entire American army.[6]

Two other details about Company H are enlightening; in both, the company reflected the national composition of America. Of the enlisted men, about half—twenty-four of fifty-three—were foreign born. Ireland contributed the most, with eleven men. Germany tallied seven, while England, Prussia, and Sweden were also represented. Also, when a soldier was enlisted into the army, he was asked to report a previous occupation. While laborers and farmers were common descriptives, there was a surprising array of skilled trades and craftsmen in "H," as indeed there was in the American army. Many men listed their previous occupation as that of soldier. While this usually indicated prior enlistment in the U.S. Army, it could also mean service in a foreign army. Henry Newman, who had served in the German military prior to immigrating to the United States, was just such an example in Company H.[7]

Collectively, these figures showing veteran status, age, nationality, and trade or profession suggest much. On the whole the men of this company were in the army not because they were society's unskilled misfits on escape to the military, or because they had been lured by false notions of army life, but because they wanted to be soldiers. They were older, and surely reflected their regiment's proud reputation and *esprit de corps*. Of the fifty-odd enlisted men of Company H in 1876, the majority were professional to the core.

Through the end of May 1876, Company H performed, to use the simple army vernacular appearing on its own records, "extra, daily, and garrison duty at . . . [Omaha Barracks] . . . since last muster."[8] This deceptively simple statement barely hints at the exhausting, mundane duties common to life at a western army post. Scheduled

5. Robert M. Utley, *Frontier Regulars: The United States Army and the Indian, 1866-1891* (New York: Macmillan Publishing Co., 1973), 23. Registers of Enlistment in the U.S. Army, 1866-1877, Microcopy 233, Rolls 36-40, National Archives, Washington, D.C. (hereafter NA).

6. Utley, *Frontier Regulars,* 22-23; Don Rickey, Jr., *Forty Miles a Day on Beans and Hay, The Enlisted Soldier Fighting the Indian Wars* (Norman: University of Oklahoma Press, 1963), 17.

7. Rickey, *Forty Miles,* Chap. 2.

8. Twenty-third U.S. Infantry Muster Rolls, Company H, February, April, 1876, Record Group 94, NA.

in a soldier's day were drills, occasional target practice, and common housekeeping chores known in the army as fatigues. From an enlisted man's perspective, fatigues must have been an endless round of wood to cut, water to haul, garbage to collect, and buildings to paint. Then, too, rotations provided that each man endure turns at guard duty, the exhausting, twenty-four-hour-long routine of police and internal security. Enlisted compensation for these duties, beyond the essential amenities, started at thirteen dollars per month, before deductions. Soldiers naturally groused about their misfortunes in the "government work-house." And with certain jocularity they chanted how "a dollar a day was damn poor pay, but thirteen a month was less!"

It was surely with some delight, then, that the men of Company H received Special Order 94 from Omaha Barracks on May 27, 1876, directing them to Wyoming Territory for field service.[9] The company probably had debated the probabilities of such an order for months. At issue on the Northern Plains were the Black Hills of western Dakota. Although the land had been guaranteed as sacred to the Sioux Indians by the Fort Laramie Treaty of 1868, the confirmation of gold "from the grassroots down" in 1874 unleashed a tide of Hills-bound prospectors. At first the army tried to enforce the Sioux Treaty by ejecting civilian trespassers. But the political and economic climate in the United States demanded that the Black Hills be opened, and by early 1876 the army was ordered to change roles. Rather than protect the Hills from invasion, they were now to wage war on the Sioux and Northern Cheyenne in an attempt to forcibly resolve what was being called the "Indian problem."[10]

The men of Company H packed their garrison belongings overnight and on May 28 they were ready for the trip. Eight enlisted men from "H" remained at Omaha Barracks on detached service, and Captain Eskridge availed himself of leave. In his absence Lieutenant Taylor assumed command of the company. As Company H boarded a Union Pacific train in Omaha it was forty-six men strong, including two commissioned officers, Taylor and Pardee.

Their westward journey passed uneventfully. The nation's first, and as yet only, transcontinental railroad was already seven years old and its presence insured orderly and speedy east- and west-bound movement across the heart of the West. Company H detrained at Cheyenne, Wyoming, and marched overland to Fort Laramie, about eighty-five miles north, arriving there on June 5, 1876. If the officers and men of "H" had uncertainties about their role in the present campaign, such questions were answered by Special Order 119 issued

9. Muster Roll, June, 1876, NA.

10. The emotional issues underlying the Great Sioux War are discussed in Utley, *Frontier Regulars*, chapter 14.

COMPANY H, TWENTY-THIRD REGIMENT U.S. INFANTRY, 1876

Name	Rank	Where Born	Age	Occup.	No. of Enl'ts.[1]	Remarks
Richard I. Eskridge	Capt.					With leave since 6-5
George McM. Taylor	1 Lt.					
Julius H. Pardee	2 Lt.					D.S.[2] with Merritt 7-16
Thomas McClane	1 Sgt.	New York	28	Soldier	3	
John D. Morgan	Sgt.	New York	34	Soldier	4	
John Hennesey	Sgt.	Ireland	37	Soldier	3	D.S. at Omaha Bks. 6-1
Henry Devoe	Sgt.	New York	26	Soldier	3	Discharged 12-5 on S.C.D.[3]
William S. Philips	Sgt.	England	27	Soldier	2	
Sylvester T. Winn	Corp.	England	27	Farmer		Reenlisted 7-29
Ralph Clark	Corp.	New York	26	Salesman		
Taylor Crowl	Corp.	Penn.	29	Soldier	2	
Henry Newman	Corp.	Germany	32	Soldier		In charge of Co. mess
Lawrence Davis	Mus.	England	20	Errandboy		
Frank Lewis	Mus.	New York	26	Laborer		
Charles Reilly	Art.	Penn.	23	Carpenter		
John Rice	Art.	Germany	34	Carpenter	3	D.S. at Omaha Bks. 5-28
Barrett, John	Pvt.	Ireland	31	Soldier	3	
Blake, Elmer E.	Pvt.	Illinois	22	Carpenter		
Clark, William	Pvt.	Illinois	26	Laborer		Ex. duty as nurse
Cramer, Robert H.	Pvt.	Iowa	24	Farrier		D.S. at Omaha Bks. 5-28
Doyle, John	Pvt.	New Jersey	25	Hatter		
Feeney, Michael	Pvt.	New York	30	Tobacconist	2	
Fitzpatrick, John	Pvt.	New Jersey	26	Currier		
Fogelstrom, Andrew	Pvt.	Sweden	28	Miner		
Gillaney, Michael	Pvt.	Ireland	37	Soldier	3	
Glass, Joseph A.	Pvt.	Ohio	39	Porter	2	Discharged 12-11
Hardt, Henry	Pvt.	Germany	43	Soldier	5	
Healy, Daniel	Pvt.	Ireland	24	Tailor		
Heintz, Frederick	Pvt.	Germany	25	Brewer	2	Discharged 11-13
Keeley, George	Pvt.	Illinois	21	Laborer		
Kennedy, Michael	Pvt.	Ireland	29	Soldier	3	Cook

Name	Rank	Where Born	Age	Occup.	No. of Enl'ts.[1]	Remarks
Koerfer, William	Pvt.	Illinois	25	Farmer		
Leek, Lycurgus	Pvt.	Ohio	21	Laborer		
Lennon, Robert	Pvt.	Ireland	31	Soldier	3	
Lines, Monterey	Pvt.	Iowa	29	Tinsmith		
Malloy, John	Pvt.	Ireland	25	Tailor		Joined Co. 5-19
Matthias, William W.	Pvt.	Penn.	21	Clerk		D.S. at Omaha Bks. 5-28
Miller, Charles	Pvt.	Germany	31	Carpenter	2	D.S. at Omaha Bks. 5-28
Murray, Daniel	Pvt.	New York	27	Moulder		
McGuire, George	Pvt.	New York	26	Farmer		D.S. at Omaha Bks. 5-28
McLalley, James	Pvt.	Michigan	24	Hostler		D.S. at Omaha Bks. 5-28
Newland, Andrew	Pvt.	Ohio	37	Soldier	2	Cook. Discharged 9-23
Packard, Robert S.	Pvt.	Ireland	22	Printer		
Redmond, John	Pvt.	Ireland	29	Soldier	2	Deserted 10-17
Revis, Joseph	Pvt.	England	44	Soldier	3	Transferred to Co. D. Twenty-third Infantry 5-27. Rejoined "H" 12-1.
Smith, John	Pvt.	Michigan	36	Soldier	2	
Skinner, James F.	Pvt.	Ireland	31	Carpenter	3	
Walter, William A.	Pvt.	Prussia	36	Shoemaker		
Walters, John	Pvt.	Ohio	25	Soldier	2	
Watkins, Joseph W.	Pvt.	Penn.	26	Farmer		
Wehih, Ezekiel	Pvt.	Germany	52	Soldier	3	
Werner, Anton	Pvt.	Germany	32	Shoemaker		D.S. 5-28. Rejoined 8-1
White, Benjamin R.	Pvt.	Ireland	48	Soldier	6	Clerk
Wickham, Horace	Pvt.	Ohio	46	Soldier	6	Cook vice Newland
Williams, Thomas	Pvt.	New Jersey	•	•	•	
Wright, Silas P.	Pvt.	Penn.	25	Baker		

•Illegible on records

1. Number of Enlistments
2. Detached Service
3. Surgeon's Certificate of Disability

at Fort Laramie on June 6. They were to establish a temporary field camp on the Black Hills road about sixty-five miles north of the fort, at the head of Sage Creek near the Wyoming and Nebraska boundary.[11]

By placing company H on the Black Hills road about midway between Fort Laramie and the gold fields, army officials hoped to accomplish several objectives. Most significant was the theoretical protection which thereby would be offered to Hills-bound travelers. This road, the favorite of several routes leading to the Black Hills, was plagued by Indians, who crossed it in their migrations to and from the agencies, and to a lesser extent by road agents who preyed upon travelers. Additionally, the army expected that the mere presence of troops on the Indians' Powder River trail would curtail to some degree the trafficking of men and war materials to the hostiles in the Powder River country.

Company H marched northward from Fort Laramie on June 12 and arrived at the site of their new camp three days later. The location was well known since it had been used a year earlier by troops who were then patrolling the road to keep miners out. The camp site was a good one. Just to the south about three miles was the Pine Ridge, a heavily timbered escarpment stretching from Wyoming into Dakota. Sage Creek was immediately at hand, offering abundant fresh water. And the ground for several miles around was open, with excellent defensive qualities.

Taylor's immediate concern at Sage Creek was the erection of shelter for his command. They expected their stay to be an extended one, so the temporary facilities that soon appeared were as permanent as field conditions would allow. A series of wall tents sheltered the men and provided necessary cover for the guard and administrative functions. To protect these canvas quarters, they constructed a rectangular, log palisade, using timbers obtained at the Pine Ridge.[12] The finished cantonment was dubbed "Camp on Sage Creek," although reference to Hat Creek, a stream thirty miles east in Nebraska, appears in some records.

With shelter thus provided, Company H established a daily routine that comprised an interesting blend of both garrison and field duties. Three enlisted men, for instance, under the guidance of Corporal Newman, organized the company mess. These cooks were on daily duty, which meant that for them cooking became a routine, recurring responsibility, at no extra pay but in lieu of certain other fatigues.

---

11. Muster Roll, June, 1876, NA.

12. Charles King, *Campaigning with Crook* (New York: Harper and Brothers, 1890), 28; W. C. Brown and Charles King, *Map Showing Many Battlefields of the Indian Wars and The Trail of the Big Horn and Yellowstone Expedition of 1876* (Denver: Clason Map Company, 1930).

Fashioning a palatable meal for their comrades probably represented a real achievement, since the company was located far from commissary warehouses or a post trader's store. Still, Newman and his cooks must have pleased the men with their preparation of the army basics of pork, beef, beans, rice, bread, and coffee, because the same threesome held the duty all year; in some army companies the chore rotated among all the men. One other private, Benjamin R. White, was assigned to daily duty as company clerk. Then, as now, the army thrived on paperwork and White kept company books, maintained records, and transcribed what must have seemed endless messages to higher commands and to other troops in the field.

Besides these routine garrison-type duties, a principal responsibility in Taylor's hands was the maintenance of order on the Black Hills road. After the soldiers deployed in 1876, this was accomplished in a variety of ways. In the carrying of dispatches, either northward to another small army camp established in the southwestern Black Hills, or south to Fort Laramie, armed soldiers were noted and their presence appreciated by civilian travelers. Other soldiers routinely patrolled the road. Because of this strategic positioning of troops, entrepreneurs in Cheyenne soon established a stagecoach service between southern Wyoming and the growing gold towns. Infantrymen from Company H occasionally rode along in these coaches to offer an additional measure of protection against the threat of hostile Indians or road agents.

The men of "H" were not the only soldiers on patrol in eastern Wyoming and western Dakota and Nebraska. After late June, eight companies of the Fifth U. S. Cavalry were also maneuvering in the area under orders to block Indian traffic between the Red Cloud and Spotted Tail Agencies of Nebraska and the hostile camps in Montana. These troopers, commanded after July 1 by Colonel Wesley Merritt, experienced much of the same tedium as the men of the Twenty-third Infantry. But in mid-July came news that would involve them all.

Captain William Henry Jordan, Ninth U. S. Infantry, commanded the army garrison at Camp Robinson, Nebraska, located adjacent to the Red Cloud Agency and about fifty miles east of the Sage Creek camp. All season long he had watched Indian movements to and from the agency, and he was keenly aware that he was one of the first to observe traffic of unusual nature. The army hierarchy, of course, also knew of the warriors traveling between the agencies and the Powder River camps in southern Montana, and they appreciated the intelligence collected by Jordan. Thus, his frantic dispatch on July 11 announcing that some 800 Cheyennes were preparing to leave the Red Cloud Agency was not unexpected. Jordan's message set in motion a series of precisioned army movements to counter this flight. They brought about the first military success in 1876, a year marked, up to this point, by the defeats of Colonel Joseph J. Reynolds at the Powder River, General Crook at the Rosebud, and Lieutenant Colonel George Armstrong Custer at the Little Big Horn.

Jordan's message passed from Camp Robinson to Fort Laramie, was promptly transmitted eastward, and also reached Colonel Merritt's command. Merritt received the news as his soldiers were marching toward Fort Laramie. He reacted quickly by deploying a company of the Fifth along the road between Camp Robinson and Fort Laramie, to keep that line of communications open. To head off the Cheyennes, Merritt's only logical recourse was to backtrack and place his regiment across their path. As one of his officers, Lieutenant Charles King, expressed it, ". . . to do this he must, relatively speaking, march over three sides of a square while they were traversing the fourth, *and must do it undiscovered.*"[13]

The Fifth's forced march was a gallant display of stamina and drive. In the course of thirty-one hours they covered eighty-five miles and easily slipped into a blocking position on the hostiles' trail. En route, Merritt's cavalry paused at Lieutenant Taylor's palisade on Sage Creek the morning of July 16 to refit and gather an additional escort for their supply train. The cavalry column had a number of army wagons following, and now, with the chance of a fight looming, Merritt bolstered the single company of Ninth U.S. Infantrymen accompanying the wagons by drafting the services of all but one squad of Company H of the Twenty-third.[14]

Most likely the foot soldiers at Sage Creek reacted enthusiastically to the prospects of an Indian fight. They speedily turned out with rifles and full cartridge belts, rations in their haversacks, and filled canteens. Taylor personally commanded "H" as they climbed into Merritt's wagons. His subordinate, Lieutenant Pardee, had already departed Sage Creek when the Fifth Cavalry resumed its march a few hours earlier. This left First Sergeant Thomas McClane next in command.

While Company H jostled along in the slower wagons, the cavalrymen reached Warbonnet Creek, Nebraska, on the evening of July 16. The Cheyennes had not yet passed that location, so Merritt was confident that his plan would work. As dawn broke on July 17, the Fifth Cavalrymen spotted the movements of an advance party from the Cheyenne camp. These warriors proceeded slowly down a coulee

---

13.   King, *Campaigning with Crook*, 26-27.

14.   Paul L. Hedren, *First Scalp for Custer: The Skirmish at Warbonnet Creek, Nebraska, July 17, 1876* (Glendale, Calif.: Arthur H. Clark Company, 1980), 60; Muster Roll, August, 1876, NA; *Wyoming, A Guide to Historic Sites* (Cheyenne: Wyoming Recreation Commission, 1976), 182.

toward Warbonnet Creek, and along the way made movements and gestures that at first puzzled the military men. Merritt and his officers were not mystified for long though, because they soon could see their own wagon train on the western horizon. The Cheyennes, unaware that seven companies of the Fifth Cavalry were poised at their front, saw, and reacted to , only the wagons. This impasse quickly ended when two cavalrymen carrying dispatches for Merritt rode forward past the supply wagons. As the riders drew close, the Indians saw an opportunity to head them off, thereby hastening the inevitable clash along Warbonnet Creek. The soldiers capitalized on the opportunity to charge these warriors; as they closed in, William F. "Buffalo Bill" Cody, the Fifth Cavalry's favorite scout, led a handful of troopers against the Cheyennes in a surprise attack. A sharp exchange of fire followed in which Cody killed a Cheyenne subchief named Yellow Hair. Almost simultaneously three companies of cavalrymen advanced into formation and charged the other warriors.[15]

The shooting was audible at the wagons, and with soldierly precision the men of Company H tumbled out and deployed as skirmishers to protect the supplies and animals. The soldiers, still several miles away, had a vantage point on high open ground, and could see the fight. Probably the infantrymen wished that they were closer to the action as they saw the Cheyenne warriors skedaddling southeastward toward the agencies, with the cavalrymen racing after them. As the action moved away, the doughboys again climbed into the wagons and drove up to Merritt's position. There the Fifth took on additional ammunition and rations. Merritt wanted to chase the Cheyennes back to the agencies, and he directed that the supply column follow as well as possible to Camp Robinson.[16]

For Company H, the brief morning interlude provided their sole moment of glory in the Great Sioux War. Although the unit's role was minor in the Fifth Cavalry's rush to cut off the Cheyennes, Merritt's action was later called the "one brilliant episode of the campaign,"[17] and that gave the doughboys of "H" something to talk about. "H" remained with the Fifth's supply train as it rolled through Camp Robinson and then turned southwestward to Fort Laramie. At Laramie the hardy infantrymen enjoyed a momentary respite at the trader's store before marching up the Black Hills trail to rejoin their comrades at Sage Creek. The official record credited the company for travelling 241 miles in this scout with Colonel Merritt.[18]

---

15. Hedren, *First Scalp*, 63-67.
16. Hedren, *First Scalp*, 68.
17. Charles King to the Army War College, February 18, 1929, U.S. Military History Institute, Carlisle Barracks, Pa.
18. Muster Roll, August, 1876, NA.

Although the skirmish at Warbonnet Creek prevented one sizeable body of Indians from joining their kinsmen in the hostile camps, other depredation continued along the Black Hills road. On August 2 hostiles attacked a Cheyenne-bound stage and chased it for twelve miles. Three of the four passengers were wounded in the melee, and eventually the coach was wrecked. The passengers luckily found cover in some brush and after dark safely made their way to the soldier camp. The next day a detail from Company H recovered the coach, but found that the Indians had cut up the harness, opened sacks of mail, and made off with the horses.[19] Among the mail lost in the raid was an official dispatch from Captain William S. Collier, commander of the Fourth Infantry company that was camped at the mouth of Red Canyon in the southern Black Hills. Collier's letter reported another lively Indian skirmish that had occurred near his camp on August 1. He subsequently learned that the mail was lost and forwarded a second report of the fight on August 6.[20]

Of a more routine nature were the personnel actions experienced by "H" while they were at Sage Creek. Second Lieutenant Pardee, who had been assigned as an acting aide-de-camp on Merritt's staff July 16, stayed with the cavalry column when they marched to meet General Crook.[21] This left Taylor as the sole commissioned officer with the command. During the summer five enlisted men were discharged at Sage Creek on expiration of their term of service. Corporal Sylvester T. Winn was the only one of the five to reenlist. One logically wonders: Did lure of the nearby goldfields attract the others? On October 17 Private John Redmond deserted his comrades and took with him $52.00 worth of ordnance stores. Redmond enjoyed three weeks at large before being apprehended near Fort Laramie on November 9 and confined in the post guardhouse. Redmond surrendered some of the stolen ordnance goods when he was captured, but in addition to the punishment meted out at his court-martial, he was penalized $20.00 for the remaining ordnance items, plus $30.00 paid to a citizen for his capture.[22]

In late summer the Cheyenne and Black Hills Stage Company formally established a stage station at Sage Creek adjacent to the military camp. Called "Hat Creek Ranch," the station shortly grew to include a hotel, post office, brewery, and bakery, besides butcher and blacksmith shops.[23] Taylor probably viewed the station as a mixed

---

19.   Agnes Wright Spring, *The Cheyenne and Black Hills Stage and Express Routes* (Lincoln: University of Nebraska Press, 1967), 157.

20.   Camp Mouth of Red Canyon, Letters Sent, August 6, 1876, Record Group 98, NA.

21.   Muster Roll, August, 1876, NA.

22.   Muster Roll, August, October, December, 1876, NA.

23.   Spring, *Cheyenne and Black Hills Stage*, 122.

blessing. The amenities offered by the bakery and butcher shops were surely offset by the availability of beer and liquor, libations which in the army's view were the most frequent source of disciplinary problems.[24]

As communities developed in the Black Hills, desires increased for telegraphic communications with the outside world. In the fall a telegraph line was constructed northward from Fort Laramie, paralleling the Black Hills road. Taylor's Company H protected the construction crews as they passed by his camp.[25] Shortly after the line was completed to Sage Creek, a telegraphic report of General Crook's September 9 victory over the Sioux in the Battle of Slim Buttes was relayed to Fort Laramie.[26] The fight was an important climax to the summer campaign, and a turning point in the long war to subjugate the Sioux and Northern Cheyenne.

Protecting the telegraph was the last assignment in Wyoming for Company H. On December 5 instructions arrived from the Department of the Platte ordering "H" to take station at Fort Gibson, Indian Territory. Replacing them came Company I, Fourteenth U.S. Infantry, from Camp Robinson. Company H marched from Camp on Hat Creek, as it was now designated, on December 13, 1876.[27] The men had been at the little stockade for over six and a half months.

From an individual soldier's perspective, duty at Sage Creek was probably best remembered by the tireless routine of guard mounts, daily fatigues, and regular patrols along the Black Hills road. In one brief episode, "H" joined Colonel Merritt's march to cut off hostile Cheyenne Indians, but the doughboys never fired a shot in that encounter. For that matter, there is no record of their shooting or being fired upon during the whole time they were in Wyoming.

In a broader sense the experience of Company H typified the way in which they and other foot soldiers protected communications and supply lines during the opening of the Black Hills and Northern Plains to white settlement. Each soldier of "H," therefore, contributed to the army's subjugation of the Sioux and Cheyenne in 1876, just as did the cavalry. Certainly this arduous and thankless job was completed with a spirit of professionalism, and with no loftier pretense than doing one's duty as a Regular.

---

24. Rickey, *Forty Miles*, 138.
25. Camp Mouth of Red Canyon, Letters Sent, September 23, July 4, 1876, NA.
26. Jerome A. Greene, *Slim Buttes, 1876: An Episode of the Great Sioux War* (Norman: University of Oklahoma Press, 1982), 107.
27. Fort Laramie Post Return, December, 1876, Record Group 98, NA.

In 1876 Grant Marsh captained the Far West *(shown here next to the* Nellie Peck *at the Bismarck levee in 1877) and immortalized the boat in an epic run to Fort Abraham Lincoln bearing wounded from the Seventh Cavalry. The speed of Marsh's journey on the Yellowstone and Missouri rivers has never been equaled.* (F. Jay Haynes, photographer, Haynes Foundation Collection, Montana Historical Society Photograph Archives)

Steamboats on the Yellowstone

by William E. Lass

"*Josephine*, June 7, 1875." When Captain Grant Marsh carved these words into the trunk of a large cottonwood tree, he marked the highest point ever reached on the Yellowstone River by a steamboat ascending from the river's mouth. The *Josephine* had surpassed any other attempt by about 250 miles, and Marsh quite likely believed that his feat would never be matched.[1]

Reaching what the press called "Grant Marsh's highest point" was the climax of the first thorough steamboat reconnaisance of the Yellowstone.[2] The impetus for the trip came from the U.S. Army, which wanted to protect the projected route of the Northern Pacific Railroad from potential attacks by hostile Sioux. Convinced of the need for new posts in the vicinity of the Tongue and Bighorn rivers, General Philip H. Sheridan, commander of the Military Division of the Missouri, arranged for the *Josephine*'s trip with Sanford B. Coulson, who headed the Missouri River Transportation Company. Coulson's company, based in Yankton, Dakota Territory, held the military transportation contract for the Upper Missouri, and his boats had been used on the lower Yellowstone. Sheridan and Coulson evidently selected the *Josephine* and Captain Marsh because he had been most successful in navigating the river. The *Josephine*'s success may have been because it was slightly smaller than most Missouri River steamboats, with a length of 180 feet, a maximum width of 31 feet, a hold 4 feet deep, and a capacity of 300 tons.[3]

*William E. Lass, "Steamboats on the Yellowstone," *Montana The Magazine of Western History,* 35 (Autumn 1985), 26-41.

1.   Joseph Mills Hanson, *The Conquest of the Missouri: Being the Story of the Life and Exploits of Captain Grant Marsh* (Chicago: A. C. McClurg & Company, 1909), 220. The point is in present-day Josephine Park in the eastern part of Billings.

2.   Bozeman *Avant Courier*, October 18, 1877.

3.   U. S. War Department, *Report of an Expedition up the Yellowstone River, Made in 1875, by James W. Forsyth, and F. D. Grant* . . . (Washington, D.C.: Government Printing Office, 1875), 1, 5; William E. Lass, *A History of Steamboating on the Upper Missouri River* (Lincoln: University of Nebraska Press, 1962), 108.

Lieutenant Colonel James W. Forsyth, assisted by Lieutenant Colonel F. D. Grant, headed Sheridan's reconnaissance party. Before entering the Yellowstone on May 26, Forsyth and Grant arranged for a military escort of 7 officers, 100 enlisted men, and 4 mounted scouts to join Marsh's crew of 43 men on the *Josephine*. The only other cargo was a month's subsistence for the group.

Until reaching Wolf Rapids just below the mouth of the Powder River, Forsyth observed that the Yellowstone, which averaged about three hundred yards wide, was easy to navigate despite some shoals. But Wolf Rapids was another matter. Forsyth reported that the rapids "are regarded as about the most difficult ones in the lower river," being relatively short, but quite steep, the water falling over rock ledges at a gradient of over ten feet per mile. Marsh steamed the *Josephine* back and forth across the rapids so that Forsyth could take depth measurements and examine the rapids "with great care." Buffalo Rapids, about twenty-six miles upriver and twelve miles below the mouth of the Tongue River, were nearly twice as long and almost as steep as Wolf Rapids, but Marsh navigated across them without difficulty.[4]

The Bighorn River was the only tributary of the Yellowstone that the party reconnoitered. Forsyth and Marsh were emboldened to push the *Josephine* up the stream after they observed that the river was about 150 yards wide and carried "an immense volume of water" into the Yellowstone.[5] The boat managed to ascend the Bighorn for twelve miles before Marsh turned it back because the river became shallower as it spread over a broad valley.

The character of the Yellowstone changed above the Bighorn. Its waters were clear and swifter; and in the Narrows, twenty-seven miles from the Bighorn, the river was only eighty-five yards wide. Battling an eight to nine miles per hour current, the *Josephine* made only one-sixth of a mile an hour. Forsyth reported that the boat appeared to be standing still even though it was under a full head of steam. For the first time on the trip, the crew had to resort to sparring and warping, time-consuming and frustrating procedures that became usual activities above the Narrows.[6]

---

4.   War Department, *Expedition up the Yellowstone*, 5-6, 7; Edward Maguire, "Annual Report of Lieutenant Edward Maguire, Corps of Engineers for the Fiscal Year through June 30, 1879," *House Exec. Doc.* 1, 46th Cong., 2d sess., August 12, 1879 (Serial 1905), 1102.

5.   War Department, *Expedition up the Yellowstone*, 8.

6.   Ibid., 8-9. Warping consisted of securing a line to a tree or a large log staked in a trench and then inching the boat forward by taking up the line with a steam-powered winch. In sparring, the same winch was used, but the line ran to the ends of two poles or spars that were fixed in the sand on opposite sites of the bow. As the line was tightened, the boat was lifted slightly and pulled forward. See Lass, *Steamboating on the Upper Missouri*, 12-13.

Marsh steamed the *Josephine* past Pompey's Pillar and through Hell Roaring Rapids before tying up for the night of June 6. The next morning, Forsyth, Marsh, and others explored the river above "for some miles" and found a powerful current broken into narrow chutes and channels by numerous islands. They decided to go no farther. Forsyth believed they could have advanced the *Josephine* somewhat, but "without any adequate reward for the labor expended." On June 7, Marsh carved his message on the cottonwood tree.[7]

News of the *Josephine's* accomplishment was widely circulated soon after the boat completed its quick, downstream trip to Bismarck, ushering in a new era for Yellowstone River steamboating that would last for nine years. The *Josephine's* trip demonstrated that at least one steamboat could be navigated nearly five hundred miles upstream from the river's mouth; and some optimists, overlooking the *Josephine's* lack of cargo, claimed that any boat could attain this distance. According to calculations made by Marsh, Forsyth, and Grant, the *Josephine's* highest point was 250 miles from the mouth of the Powder River and an estimated 485 miles from the mouth of the Yellowstone.[8] After experiencing the difficulties of navigation above the Bighorn, Forsyth and Grant entertained no illusions that steamboats could run above that point. On the map accompanying their report they noted that "practically Big Horn is at head of navigation on Yellowstone," an observation that proved to be generally accurate.

Before the *Josephine's* trip, there had been steamboats on the Yellowstone in only two other years, in 1864 and 1873. The first steamboats entered the Yellowstone in 1864 to supply Brigadier General Alfred Sully's expedition against the Sioux. Sully's orders were to establish new military posts on the Upper Missouri, including one on the Yellowstone, and to engage the Sioux for the purpose of safeguarding the Missouri River route to Montana. Sully pressed into service two small sternwheelers: the *Chippewa Falls*, captained by Abe Hutchinson of St. Paul, Minnesota, and the *Alone*, which was en route from St. Louis to Fort Benton. After Sully and his troops had established Fort Rice on the Missouri downstream from Bismarck, he ordered the steamboats upstream to a rendezvous site on the lower Yellowstone.[9]

It was August when the *Chippewa Falls* and the *Alone* arrived at the mouth of the Yellowstone River, and the captains were understandably cautious about steaming into unknown waters when stream

---

7. War Department, *Expedition up the Yellowstone*, 8.

8. Ibid., 11, 15; Bismarck *Tribune*, June 16, 1875.

9. U. S. War Department, *The War of the Rebellion: Official Records of the Union and Confederate Armies*, ser. 1, vol. 34, pt. 2, pp. 622, 624, 766-67, 806; vol. 41, pt. 1, p. 147; pt. 2, pp. 80-81 [*Rebellion Records*]; St. Paul *Pioneer*, November 15, 1864; Lass, *Steamboating on the Upper Missouri*, 29-30.

levels were dropping. Hutchinson reconnoitered the Yellowstone for forty or fifty miles and was satisfied that they could navigate the lower Yellowstone, so the *Chippewa* and the *Alone*, both loaded with about fifty tons of freight, steamed to a point a few miles below present-day Glendive. The captains had some anxious moments when they discovered that the troops had not yet arrived at the rendezvous. For two days, the boats steamed up and down the river, signaling with their whistles. On August 11, Sully's advance party, trekking through the Badlands and within about ten miles of the Yellowstone, heard the reverberating whistles.[10]

Sully, who had defeated the Sioux at the Battle of Killdeer Mountain in his overland march, hastened to the river and used the boats to ferry his 2,000-man expedition across the Yellowstone. The boats escorted the troops downstream and then ferried them across the Missouri two miles below the mouth of the Yellowstone. Because of the lateness of the season Sully did not attempt to establish a post on the Yellowstone River, and the army did not renew its interest in steamboating on the river until 1873.[11]

In 1873, steamboats were used on the Yellowstone to supply the Northern Pacific's surveyors, who carried their marking from the Heart River Crossing west of Bismarck to near the mouth of the Powder River. Because the army was required to provide an escort for the survey party, Sheridan decided to establish a supply depot for the troops on the Yellowstone. He arranged with Sanford Coulson to send the *Key West*, with Marsh as master, up the Yellowstone from Fort Buford. Major George A. Forsyth went along to gather intelligence about the lower Yellowstone and to choose a site for the supply depot near the mouth of the Powder River. In May 1873, Marsh and Forsyth reached Wolf Rapids, where low water and a rapid current forced them to turn back. Forsyth selected a depot site downstream near the mouth of Glendive Creek, where the Northern Pacific was likely to enter the Yellowstone Valley.[12]

The *Key West* carried supplies to the depot from Bismarck, Dakota Territory, at the time the terminus of the Northern Pacific. The *Key West* also ferried troops across the Yellowstone and forwarded supplies to them as they advanced up the valley. When David S. Stanley led the military escort out from Fort Rice, he had over fifteen hun-

---

10. Saint Paul *Pioneer*, November 15, 1864; "General Alfred Sully's Expedition of 1864, from the *Diary of Judge Nicholas Hilger*," *Contributions to the Historical Society of Montana*, (10 vols., Helena: State Publishing Company, 1896), 2:314, 320.

11. *Rebellion Records*, ser. 1, vol. 41, pt. 1, pp. 147-48, 158; "Sully's Expedition of 1864," p. 320.

12. P. H. Sheridan, "Report of Lieut. Gen. Sheridan," *Exec. Doc.* 1, 43rd Cong., 1st sess., October 27, 1873, (Serial 1597), 40-41.

dred officers and men, over three hundred civilian employees, nearly three hundred wagons and ambulances, and more than twenty-three hundred horses and mules. Transporting just the forage for the animals taxed both Coulson and the overland contractors.[13]

After the troops and surveyors had reached the Yellowstone Valley, Coulson transferred Marsh to the *Josephine*, which had just arrived from the Pittsburgh, Pennsylvania, area on its maiden trip. Marsh navigated the *Josephine* over Wolf Rapids with ease, and Stanley reported that the boat could have been taken many miles upstream, even "perhaps to the falls of the Yellowstone." Stanley's enthusiasm for the *Josephine* was undoubtedly a factor in her selection for the reconnaissance two years later.[14]

Although the *Josephine* reached a higher point than the *Key West* in 1873, fame eluded it. The *Key West's* role in a major expedition had been well publicized, while the *Josephine* steamed on the Yellowstone only part of the season and its mastery of Wolf Rapids occurred late in the summer.[15] The *Josephine's* reconnaissance in 1875, however, created immediate excitement.

While the army and the Northern Pacific were interested in opening the Yellowstone River Valley, Bozeman residents were more than enthusiastic, with the editor of the *Avant Courier* claiming that the route was vital to his town. Bozeman was the principal settlement in the Gallatin Valley, but it was somewhat remote from major supply routes. To the north, wagon routes connected the town to Helena and Fort Benton, the main Missouri River port in Montana Territory; and to the south, it depended on wagon transportation from the Union Pacific Railroad depot in Corinne, Utah. The *Avant Courier* editor believed that both Fort Benton and Corinne were back-door entries into eastern Montana and that the best route was by the "front door" up the Yellowstone River.[16]

Bozeman's boosters saw the *Josephine's* reconnaissance as an important step in liberating them from traditional supply routes. They hoped that the trip would be followed immediately by the establishment of an army post and perhaps a town near the Bighorn River.

13. Bismarck *Tribune*, July 11, July 13, 1873; *Personal Memoirs of Major-General D. S. Stanley, U.S.A.* (Cambridge, Massachusetts: Harvard University Press, 1917), 245, 248.

14. Hanson, *Conquest of the Missouri*, 183-84; Bismarck *Tribune*, August 6, 1873; David S. Stanley, *Report on the Yellowstone Expedition of 1873* (Washington, D.C.: Government Printing Office, 1874), 13.

15. See, for example, Bismarck *Tribune*, August 6, 1873. A *Tribune* correspondent erroneously reported that the *Key West* was "the first steamer that ever entered the Yellowstone."

16. Betty M. Madsen and Brigham D. Madsen, *North to Montana! Jehus, Bullwhackers, and Mule Skinners on the Montana Trail* (Salt Lake City: University of Utah Press, 1980), 171; Bozeman *Avant Courier*, November 5, 26, 1875.

To expedite matters, they organized a fleet of small boats to sail down the Yellowstone from Benson's Landing, about thirty miles east of Bozeman, hoping to meet the advancing steamboat and to locate a "thrifty town." The *Avant Courier* publicized the *Josephine's* expedition as "the turning point in the history of Eastern Montana of a most favorable and desirable character" and anticipated that the *Josephine* "or other steamboats, will make several trips to the mouth of the Big Horn during the season."[17]

The *Avant Courier* announced the completion of the *Josephine's* reconnaissance in bold headlines: "A SUCCESS! NAVIGATION OF THE YELLOWSTONE ARRIVAL OF THE STEAMER JOSEPHINE AT THE MOUTH OF CLARK'S FORK THE YELLOWSTONE NAVIGABLE TO THE CROW AGENCY." Not only did the editor err in claiming that the *Josephine* had reached the Clark's Fork River, but he compounded the error by adding that the boat had ascended that tributary for "a short distance." Readers were advised that the *Josephine* could have ascended as far as the mouth of the Stillwater River (near present-day Columbus), but the steamer was turned about because the army had contracted it for only a limited time. Within a week, the editor admitted erring about the highest point reached, but he still insisted that the Yellowstone was navigable high enough to be of great use to Bozeman. "What are our merchants and businessmen going to do about it?" he challenged. "Will they make an effort to utilize this great natural channel, or will they suffer it to flow on its peaceful course, uninterrupted by the demands of trade and commerce of our Territory, which require just such an auxiliary as the Yellowstone River offers to make business more prosperous."[18]

Bozeman's heady aspirations were boosted on June 17 when Fellows D. Pease led a well-armed party of about forty men to establish a town near the Bighorn. They were too late to rendezvous with the *Josephine*, but the expedition did reach the mouth of the Bighorn River, where it built Fort Pease. Fort Pease failed to attract any steamboats and was constantly harassed by the Sioux; the defenders finally abandoned it the following March.[19]

Despite the problems at Fort Pease, Bozeman's schemers still claimed that steamboat traffic on the Yellowstone was imminent. The *Avant Courier* regularly featured some positive aspect of Forsyth's report and lambasted the Fort Benton *Record*, which had the audacity

---

17. Bozeman *Avant Courier*, May 21, June 11, 1875.

18. Ibid., June 18, June 25, 1875.

19. Ibid., June 18, 1875; *An Illustrated History of the Yellowstone Valley* . . . (Spokane, Wash.: Western Historical Publishing Company, [1907?]), 263-65; Clyde McLemore, "Fort Pease: The First Attempted Settlement in the Yellowstone Valley," *The Montana Magazine of History*, 2 (January 1952), 21, 31.

to question the suitability of the Yellowstone for steamboat navigation. The *Courier* also eagerly seized on a rumor that Grant Marsh
was contemplating building a light draft steamboat expressly for the
Yellowstone trade. Marsh was hailed as the man of the hour, and local
businessmen were admonished to encourage him: "If material aid
is necessary to make the construction of the boat a certainty, it should
be freely given."[20]

No sooner had the rumors about the Marsh boat died out than
two Bozeman businessmen, Achilles Lamme and Nelson Story,
formed the Yellowstone Transportation Company to promote steamboats on the Yellowstone. Lamme and his son Edward left for the
East in early November to either purchase a steamboat or to have
one built, while Story began arranging for overland transportation
from the Yellowstone's head of navigation to Bozeman. The *Avant
Courier* heralded the steamboat-wagon train combination as a way of
providing inexpensive efficient transportation for Bozeman and
other Montana locations. The paper's editor prophesied: "The Landing of the first boat at the head of navigation on the Yellowstone next
season will be the dawn of a new era in Eastern Montana, bringing
with it general prosperity to our people, and making Bozeman the
most important town in the Territory."[21]

The company's steamboat, appropriately christened the *Yellowstone*,
was built at Jeffersonville, Indiana, and entered the Upper Missouri
in late May 1876. Lamme and Story intended to make one trip to
Fort Benton and then start the boat in the Yellowstone trade, but that
year the *Yellowstone* did not enter the stream after which it was
named.[22] The Sioux War of 1876 effectively delayed Bozeman's plans
to open a new route into Montana.

By the spring of 1876, government relations with the Sioux were
worse than they had been at any time since Red Cloud's War ten years
earlier. As gold-seekers streamed into the Black Hills, hundreds of
reservation Sioux sought refuge in the last important bison hunting
grounds, the area of the Powder and Bighorn rivers. As the army
prepared to move against them, steamboat support for the units advancing from the east was imperative.[23]

Three years before, new steamboat patterns had been developed
on the Upper Missouri. St. Louis had dominated the trade throughout most of the 1860s when Fort Benton and Montana's gold mines
were the principal destination on the Upper Missouri. In 1868, the

---

20. Bozeman *Avant Courier*, June 25, July 23, September 24, 1875.

21. Ibid., October 8, November 5, December 17, 1875.

22. Ibid., June 16, 1876; Bismarck *Tribune*, June 14, 1876.

23. Michael P. Malone and Richard B. Roeder, *Montana: A History of Two Centuries*
(Seattle: University of Washington Press, 1976), 97-98.

railroad linked Sioux City to Chicago, and the Iowa city had a short-lived reign until two new railheads were established in 1873: Yankton at the terminus of the Dakota Southern, a short track built to bypass Sioux City, and Bismarck, the Northern Pacific's end-of-track. Bismarck and Yankton controlled most Upper Missouri steamboating, with Bismarck having a distinct advantage for destinations upstream from that point.

During this period, the Missouri River Transportation Company, better known as the Coulson Packet Line, was the leading transportation firm on the Missouri. Sanford B. Coulson and associates had organized the company during the winter of 1872–1873, as the Dakota Southern Railroad was being completed to Yankton. They formed their "Old Reliable Line" to take advantage of Yankton's upstream location from Sioux City, and beginning in 1873 Yankton became the company's home.

The Coulson Line's main competition came from the Kountz Line, the Peck Line, and the Fort Benton Transportation Company. William J. Kountz, a Pennsylvanian, had been Coulson's employer for a time, and after the break their rivalry was bitterly personal. Coulson and his associates cultivated a gentlemanly image, but Kountz was an irascible character who spatted with other steamboatmen, army officers, and journalists, becoming one of the best-known individuals on the Upper Missouri. Campbell K. Peck, a former junior partner in the trading firm of Durfee & Peck, dominated the Peck Line, also known as the Northwest Transportation Company. Although the line was headquartered in Sioux City, it actively competed for freight originating at Bismarck and Yankton. The Fort Benton Transportation Company, or Power Line, was organized in 1875 by Thomas C. and John Power, primarily to supply their Fort Benton mercantile firm. All four companies usually operated six or more boats a season. There were also some independents who shared in the trade, including Walter A. Burleigh of Yankton, I. G. Baker and Company of Fort Benton, John H. Charles of Sioux City, and Amherst H. Wilder of St. Paul.

The big prize for the companies was the Upper Missouri military contract, which was let annually on a competitive bidding basis by the quartermaster general of the Department of Dakota in St. Paul. Because the successful bidder had the option of buying or chartering boats, a potentially uncertain situation, the army was not bound to deal exclusively with its contractor.[24]

When the army was planning its campaign against the Sioux in 1876, the Coulson Line received the steamboat transportation con-

---

24. See Lass, *Steamboating on the Upper Missouri*, 57-106.

tract for the river below Bismarck. Burleigh, who then owned only one boat, was given the contract for the area above Bismarck, including the Yellowstone River. The army's broad strategy was to subjugate the Sioux with armies advancing from Fort Ellis on the west, Fort Fetterman on the south, and Fort Abraham Lincoln on the east. Only General Alfred Terry's troops from Fort Abraham Lincoln depended on the steamboats for supplies.[25]

As Terry's army moved overland, quartermaster officers established a supply depot near the mouth of Glendive Creek. Even this stage of operations overtaxed Burleigh's resources, so the quartermaster officer at Bismarck chartered the Coulson Line's *Far West* and *Josephine* for use on the Yellowstone. Once Terry's expedition reached Glendive Creek, Captain Marsh used the *Far West* to shift the supply depot upstream near the mouth of the Powder River.[26]

The *Far West* then escorted the troops to the vicinity of the Bighorn River. Terry was determined to keep this supply vessel as close as possible to the field units, so he ordered Marsh to attempt to reach the juncture of the Bighorn and Little Bighorn rivers. Marsh was somewhat familiar with the lower twelve miles of the Bighorn, but there was no reliable information about the river beyond that point. Nevertheless, he steamed the *Far West* to the mouth of the Little Bighorn; and because the accompanying army officer was confused about their destination, he then took the boat about fifteen miles farther up the Bighorn.[27]

The *Far West* was waiting at the mouth of the Little Bighorn on June 27 when Marsh was informed that Custer's command had been annihilated two days earlier. After taking on some wounded men from other units and ferrying troops at the mouth of the Bighorn, Marsh was finally cleared to leave for Bismarck on July 3. Racing downstream, Marsh pushed the *Far West* approximately seven hundred miles to Bismarck in only fifty-four hours. This heroic effort helped make him the most famous steamboat captain in the history of Yellowstone River navigation.[28]

The Battle of the Little Bighorn hastened the army's decision to occupy the Yellowstone River Valley. Colonel Nelson A. Miles and most of the Fifth Infantry were ordered to build a cantonment near the mouth of the Tongue River to use as a base for further campaigns against the Sioux. By the time they arrived, the army had already decided to build a permanent post near the cantonment and a sec-

25. Ibid., 122; Malone and Roeder, *Montana*, 98-100.

26. Lass, *Steamboating on the Upper Missouri*, 122-123; Bozeman *Avant Courier*, June 9, 1876.

27. Bismarck *Tribune*, June 21, 1876; Hanson, *Conquest of the Missouri*, 268-74.

28. Bismarck *Tribune*, July 12, 1876; Hanson, *Conquest of the Missouri*, 306.

ond post at the mouth of the Little Bighorn. Emergency funds were
granted to construct the new posts, and in August the quartermaster officer at Bismarck frantically readied Coulson boats to
carry hundreds of carloads of building materials and supplies that
had been sent out on the Northern Pacific. By the time the supplies
were ready, however, the Yellowstone was too low to assure safe steamboat navigation, and the army postponed its fort-building until the
next season.[29]

Despite the delay, the Coulson Line was kept busy transporting
Miles's troops and their provisions, rushing immense quantities of
forage and supplies to the Tongue River Cantonment. All six Coulson
boats were used, and six others were chartered from rival lines, including the Yellowstone Transportation Company's *Yellowstone*.[30]

In 1877, the army was determined to quickly fortify the Yellowstone
Valley and solve the Sioux problem. But in a dismaying turn of events,
the transportation contract for the Missouri above Bismarck and the
Yellowstone was let to a company that had no experience on the
Missouri. At the bidding in St. Paul, Coulson was undercut by John
B. Davis, the agent for William F. Davidson, head of the Keokuk North-
ern Packet Line.[31] In utter disregard of the Bozeman-based company,
Davis, Davidson, his brother Peyton, and John H. Reaney, a St. Paulite
and veteran Mississippi River steamboat captain, named their new
venture the Yellowstone Transportation Company.

In order to be off the Yellowstone before late summer, the company intended to transport an estimated eight thousand tons of
freight from Bismarck in only two trips per boat. They spurned a
tender to lease boats from Charles and Wilder because they thought
the charge was too high and instead used some boats from the Keokuk
Northern Line and leased others in St. Louis. By May, Davis had
assembled an impressive fleet of fourteen steamboats, but none of
them was designed for the Upper Missouri.[32]

---

29.   *Personal Recollections of General Nelson A. Miles* . . . (Chicago: Werner Company,
1896), 212-18; Letters sent by Chief Quartermaster, Department of Dakota, July 24,
July 19, July 31, August 7, 1876, in Letter Register, March 20, 1873-August 19, 1879,
86, 88-90, 93, National Archives and Records Service, Washington, D.C.

30.   Bismarck *Tribune*, August 30, September 13, September 27, 1876.

31.   Coulson proposed to carry freight on the Missouri and Yellowstone at 19 ½
cents and 17 ½ cents per 100 pounds per 100 miles, respectively. Davis's bid was 15
cents for the Missouri and 57 cents for the Yellowstone. St. Paul and Minneapolis
Pioneer Press, March 17, 1877.

32.   John B. Davis to William F. Davidson, March 13, March 16, 1877, Statement
dated March 24, 1877, J. W. Reaney to Davidson, March 28, May 7, 1877, Davis to Peyton
S. Davidson, April 30, 1877, in William Fuson Davidson and Family Papers, Minnesota
Historical Society, St. Paul; St. Paul and Minneapolis *Pioneer Press*, April 11, April
18, April 20, April 26, May 23, 1877.

While the new Yellowstone Transportation Company's boats were straggling up the Missouri River to Bismarck, impatient quartermaster officers, under great pressure to demonstrate activity, chartered Coulson Line boats. In the meantime, the Davidson Company compounded its problems by experimenting with barges above Bismarck, some towed from St. Louis and others built at Bismarck. By carrying extra freight on the barges, the company hoped to minimize the number of round trips; but the barges seemed only to have slowed the steamboats. When the *Savanna* left Bismarck towing its barges, it was reported that it made less than three miles in three hours.[33]

Evidently, none of Davidson's boats even attempted to tow barges up the Yellowstone, but even without them they had great difficulty. In early June, two of the company's boats were aground at Wolf Rapids, and two others were detained assisting them.[34] The Coulson steamers, however, operated throughout the season and generally navigated Wolf Rapids without incident.

Yellowstone River steamboats had two principal destinations in 1877: Post No. 1, as Fort Keogh was first called, was being built at the mouth of the Tongue River; and Post No. 2, later named Fort Custer, was being established at the mouth of the Little Bighorn. Steamboats bound for the posts carried both freight and passengers, with the most common cargoes including provisions, building materials, and grain for animals. Other than troops, most of the passengers were laborers recruited in St. Paul and Minneapolis. During the spring of 1877, quartermaster officers had hired about two hundred carpenters, masons, and laborers to work on each post. The men were taken to Bismarck by rail before embarking on the Yellowstone Transportation Company boats. One of these boats reached the site of Fort Custer in June; and during the next several weeks four other Davidson boats, three Coulson boats, and the government's *General Sherman* landed at the post.[35]

These arrivals, however, did not prove that navigation up the Bighorn to the Little Bighorn was feasible. The Bighorn's shallow water and much consequent warping and sparring slowed the boats' progress. Normally, cargo had to be left along the riverbank to lighten the load. When General Sheridan and General William Tecumseh Sherman visited the forts in July, they were displeased to find caches

33. St. Paul and Minneapolis *Pioneer Press*, June 7, 1877.

34. Ibid., June 17, 1877.

35. Ibid., April 2, May 11, May 15, May 19, May 25, 1877; "Record of boats arrived at Fort Custer, Montana . . . ," handwritten manuscript in Northern Pacific Railway Company Records, Chief Engineer—Old Vault Files 10-B-1-2F, File no. 12-1, Minnesota Historical Society, St. Paul.

In 1875 the steamboat Josephine, *captained by Grant Marsh, charted an upstream navigation record on the Yellowstone River. A year later, this Coulson packet figured prominently in the Sioux War.* (Montana Historical Society Photograph Archives)

of cargo scattered along the Bighorn. The freight had to be forwarded by wagon, but much of it was difficult to reach and to safeguard. Therefore, the generals decided that Lieutenant Colonel Forsyth was right in 1875 when he reported that the mouth of the Bighorn was the practical head of navigation. Before leaving the area, they ordered the establishment of a depot on the south bank of the Yellowstone about two miles above the mouth of the Bighorn; and Terry's Landing became the usual rendezvous for steamboats and Fort Custer-bound wagons.[36]

The mouth of the Bighorn was the scene of much steamboating activity in 1877. Between June 27 and August 31, fourteen boats mak-

36.   U. S. War Department, *Reports of Inspection Made in the Summer of 1877 by Generals P. H. Sheridan and W. T. Sherman of Country North of the Union Pacific Railroad* (Washington, D.C.: Government Printing Office, 1878), 29-30; Richard Upton, ed., *Fort Custer on the Big Horn 1877-1898: Its History and Personalities as Told and Pictured by Its Contemporaries* (Glendale, Calif.: Arthur H. Clark, 1973), 36-38.

ing a total of twenty-six trips reached that point: the *Rosebud*, a Coulson Line boat, posted eight arrivals, including the last two; the *Big Horn*, another Coulson boat, arrived three times; two other Coulson boats, the *Peninah* and *Far West* arrived twice; and the *J. E. Rankin* arrived twice, the only Yellowstone Transportation Company boat to make more than one trip up the river.[37]

The Yellowstone Transportation Company retreated from the Yellowstone and the Upper Missouri in early August as soon as it had forwarded an estimated nine thousand tons of freight. Davis contended that the line had fulfilled its contractual obligations, but his pronouncement could not disguise the company's eagerness to return to the Mississippi. The company's barge experiment had not worked, and it lost one boat, the *Osceola*, near the mouth of the Powder River when a tornado tore off everything above the main deck and killed several crewmen.[38]

Between July 23, when the last Davidson boat reached the mouth of the Bighorn, and the end of August, Coulson steamers made thirteen landings there. Even without the annual military contract, the Coulson Line fared well in 1877, increasing its fleet to eleven boats and solidifying its reputation as the leading firm on the Upper Missouri and Yellowstone rivers. Some of the Coulson Line boats were reaping healthy profits: the *Big Horn* cleared over $14,000 on a trip from Pittsburgh to the Little Bighorn and return to Bismarck; the *Far West* had a net gain of $26,956.60 for seven trips, including one from Bismarck to Fort Keogh and two from Fort Buford to Keogh; the short Buford-to-Keogh trips realized an average profit of over $4,000.[39]

In 1876, some civilians took advantage of the army's presence in the Yellowstone Valley and established a settlement at the Tongue River Cantonment. The next year, however, Miles ordered their expulsion from Fort Keogh, so they moved downstream and established Miles City just outside the military reservation's eastern boundary. In June 1878, after the fort tract was reduced to the area west of the Tongue River, Miles City residents began shifting their town upstream about two and a half miles to get next to the fort, their main source of livelihood. "City" was a rather presumptuous term for a place of only about three hundred residents; but the ridiculousness was compounded when, for a time, the two parts of the community claimed the name of Miles City. Residents of "New Town" used the steamboat

37. Bozeman *Avant Courier*, October 18, 1877.

38. St. Paul and Minneapolis *Pioneer Press*, July 3, August 17, 1877; Mark D. Flower to William F. Davidson, June 30, 1877, Davidson Papers.

39. Bozeman *Avant Courier*, October 18, 1877; statements for 1877 of *Big Horn* and *Far West*, in Isaac P. Baker Papers, North Dakota Historical Society, Bismarck.

landing at "Old Town" until August 1881, when a new landing was developed near the mouth of the Tongue River.[40]

There was no settlement of note below Miles City. Other than the "few shacks" at the stage and mail station at Ferry Point, about seventy miles above Glendive Creek, there were only widely scattered ranches and woodyards. During the military crises of 1876 and 1877, there had been no woodyards on the Yellowstone, and steamboatmen had complained about delays caused by having to cut their own wood or to quarry lignite, which they used as an experimental fuel. The number of woodyards increased rapidly during 1878 and 1879, but by 1879 the surplus stockpiles at woodyards had severely depressed prices.[41]

As Miles City was being established, other small settlements developed near the mouth of the Bighorn. Junction City, on the north bank of the Yellowstone almost directly opposite the mouth of the Bighorn, was the base for wagon freighters who carried supplies from Terry's Landing to Fort Custer and the transfer point where the stage and wagon route that lay along the Yellowstone crossed the river.[42] Other small settlements and stage stations dotted the trail that followed the north side of the Yellowstone upstream from Junction City. The principal towns were Huntley, about fifty miles from Junction City, and Coulson, ten miles upstream—the highest point Grant Marsh had steamed to in 1875. Coulson had been settled by men from Bozeman who apparently hoped that it would be the regular head of navigation.

The approximately thirteen hundred white settlers in the valley by 1880 changed the nature of Yellowstone River steamboating. The military phase was replaced by shipping activity that combined military and private freight, which lasted from 1878 until 1881, when it was disrupted by the arrival of the Northern Pacific Railroad.

Despite the increasing importance of private freight, the contract for waterborne military freight was still the most important item for the steamboat lines. The Coulson Line received the Upper Missouri contract in 1878, but William J. Kountz was awarded a special contract for the Yellowstone trade, creating a rather unusual situation. Coulson boats were given all military freight originating at Yankton

40. *History of the Yellowstone Valley,* 343; Bozeman *Avant Courier,* November 15, 1877, October 3, December 5, 1878; Miles City *Yellowstone Journal,* August 20, 1881. On the social life of Miles City, see Mark H. Brown, *The Plainsmen of the Yellowstone: A History of the Yellowstone Basin* (New York: G. P. Putnam's Sons, 1961).

41. Bozeman *Avant Courier,* December 5, 1878; Miles City *Yellowstone Journal,* August 14, 1879.

42. Bozeman *Avant Courier,* December 5, 1878; [Frank W. Warner, comp.], *Montana Territory: History and Business Directory, 1879* . . . (Helena: Fisk Brothers Printers, [1879]), 109; Thomson P. McElrath, *The Yellowstone Valley* . . . (St. Paul: *Pioneer Press,* 1880), 47.

and Bismarck, but freight for Fort Keogh and Fort Custer was transferred to Kountz boats at Fort Buford, the entry to the Yellowstone. At one time during the season, Kountz had four steamboats on the Yellowstone.[43]

Kountz's career on the Yellowstone was short-lived. In 1879, Coulson received both the Missouri and Yellowstone contracts, which had been changed to reflect the quartermaster officer's belief that the Yellowstone was more difficult to navigate than the Missouri. Coulson was paid twelve cents per hundred pounds per hundred miles for all Missouri River cargo starting at Bismarck, but twenty-five cents when boats were navigating the Yellowstone. Passenger rates were also changed. On the Missouri, officers were transported for three cents a mile and enlisted men and government employees for a cent less, but on the Yellowstone the fare was a penny more in both categories. While the Yellowstone contract helped stave off the sharp decline of the Coulson Line, 1879 was its last big year. In 1880, its Yankton-based trade suffered from railroad extensions, and it lost the Yellowstone military contract to the Peck Line, which shipped exclusively from Bismarck.[44]

During the late 1870s, small concerns on both the Upper Missouri and the Yellowstone challenged the major steamboating companies. Amherst H. Wilder ran three boats out of Bismarck for Upper Missouri and Yellowstone destinations in 1878. Much to the delight of Bozeman's *Avant Courier*, the Lammes used the *Yellowstone* to transport private freight during that same season. Some cargo carried by the *Yellowstone* to Junction City was freighted to Bozeman, which proved that the Gallatin Valley could be served by the route it preferred. Nevertheless, Bozeman was becoming more dependent on wagon freighters coming north from the terminus of the Utah and Northern Railroad, which was being built toward Montana. The ballyhooing of the Yellowstone route was suddenly quieted when in early June 1879 the *Yellowstone* was wrecked on the rocky ledges of Buffalo Rapids. Bozeman's promoters were embarrassed because the 150-foot-long *Yellowstone* was considerably smaller than other steamboats on the river and had been advertised as being built specifically for use on the Yellowstone. The boat's cargo was saved and much of it freighted to Bozeman by wagon, but the *Yellowstone* was a total loss.[45]

---

43. Bismarck *Tribune*, September 4, 1878; Lass, *Steamboating on the Upper Missouri*, 119-20.

44. Lass, *Steamboating on the Upper Missouri*, 120-121.

45. Bismarck *Tribune*, September 4, 1878. By the fall of 1878, the Utah and Northern was completed from the Union Pacific to a point about thirty miles south of the Snake River. At that time, Oneida (near present-day Arimo, Idaho) was the starting point for Montana-bound wagon freighters. See Madsen and Madsen, *North to*

Two other one-boat lines entered the Yellowstone business in 1878. The *Eclipse*, which had just been built in the Pittsburgh area, became one of the most used boats on the Yellowstone, but its various owners seemed to have been jinxed financially until it was bought by Leighton & Jordan, post traders at Fort Buford. Joseph Leighton, the senior partner in the firm, was also the principal owner of the *F. Y. Batchelor*, another boat that was built at Pittsburgh in the spring of 1878. The *Batchelor*, named for Leighton's late father-in-law, became the best-known boat on the Yellowstone, and Grant Marsh commanded its maiden trip. After severing his long relationship with the Coulson Line, Marsh traveled to Pittsburgh to navigate the boat on the long trip from the forks of the Ohio to Fort Custer. Because of Marsh's fame and the *Batchelor*'s speed, the frontier press covered the trip. The Yellowstone Line, as Leighton called his one-steamboat business, was the third firm operating on the Yellowstone to use the name of the river in its corporate title.[46]

The government did some of its own steamboating on the Yellowstone and Upper Missouri. Quartermaster officers chartered privately owned boats at a daily rate of $350, an arrangement that steamboatmen seemed to favor over carrying freight on a standard contract. For several years, the federal government owned and operated its own boat, the *General Sherman,* which was put on the Yellowstone in the summer of 1877 and was used there and on the Bighorn for the next several years. It cost the government about $47,000 that year to construct the *Sherman* and the *J. Don Cameron* for the Upper Missouri and the Yellowstone trade. When the *Cameron* snagged and sank in the Missouri about forty miles below Sioux City, the government did not attempt to replace it and was content to operate only the *Sherman.*[47]

Yellowstone River steamboating followed a fairly standard pattern. The most common starting point was Bismarck, but there was some freighting from Yankton, Fort Buford, Sioux City, St. Louis, and even

---

Montana, 229; Bozeman *Avant Courier,* June 20, June 27, August 15, 1878, June 1, July 10, August 14, 1879; Frederick Way, Jr., comp., *Way's Packet Directory 1848-1983: Passenger Steamboats of the Mississippi River System Since the Advent of Photography in Mid-Continent America* (Athens: Ohio University Press, 1983), 483. The *Yellowstone*'s machinery was salvaged, but the hull was abandoned. Some years after the wreck, however, a man from Miles City retrieved oak timbers and planks from the hull, which he used to construct a lodging house in Miles City. See S[amuel] Gordon, *Recollections of Old Milestown* (Miles City: [Independent Printing Company], 1918), 9.

46. *Way's Packet Directory,* 140; Charles William Batchelor, *Incidents in My Life, with a Family Genealogy* (N. p.: Joseph Eichbaum & Company, 1887), 92-106; Hanson, *Conquest of the Missouri,* 388-95.

47. *Reports of Inspection . . . by Sheridan and Sherman,* 29; *Way's Packet Directory,* 183; St. Paul and Minneapolis *Pioneer Press,* May 20, 22, 1877.

Pittsburgh. The normal goal was to reach the mouth of the Bighorn River; but under favorable conditions boats would be taken above that point, either to Fort Custer or farther up the Yellowstone. From 1878 to 1882, the *Batchelor* reached Fort Custer nine times, a clear champion of that run. The only other steamboats to reach the fort during that period were the *Sherman* once, the *Helena* of the Power Line twice (but only by double-tripping from a point five miles below the fort), and the *General Terry* of the Peck Line. In 1878, one boat (probably the *Yellowstone*) reached Camp Bertie near Pompey's Pillar, and the next year Grant Marsh and the *Batchelor* delivered a fifty-ton cargo to Huntley, only ten miles below his highest point.[48]

In 1878, twenty steamboats arrrived at Miles City from downstream through July 12, by which time the navigation season was probably about three-fourths completed.[49] Despite the few arrivals, Miles City was a relatively active port; most boats also stopped there when returning from Junction City or Terry's Landing.[50] The number of boat arrivals and amount of freight carried to Yellowstone River destinations cannot be determined precisely. Newspapers sometimes reported freight amounts on individual boats but did not provide seasonal summaries. In 1878, army engineers concluded that they were "unable to obtain any reliable information from the citizens along the river of the amount and value of the freight carried up the Yellowstone . . . ." But for the 1880 season, engineers, using information from quartermaster officers, reported that private and government imports amounted to 6,000 tons, including over 1,000 tons of military freight shipped from Bismarck and about 240 tons from Yankton.[51]

Although imports always exceeded exports, the downriver trade was of some significance. Miles City was the base for bison hunters who slaughtered thousands of the animals in the area and stockpiled the hides in town until the first boat arrived. At one time, the

---

48. "Record of boats arrived at Fort Custer," in Northern Pacific Records; Bozeman *Avant Courier*, August 1, 1878; McElrath, *Yellowstone Valley*, 47-48.

49. Bozeman *Avant Courier*, August 1, 1878.

50. The editor of an 1879 business directory reported that for the entire 1878 season Miles City had fifty-four steamboat arrivals "from Bismarck and elsewhere." See Warner, *Montana Territory*, 110. With one essential difference, this number was reported later in Michael A. Leeson, ed., *History of Montana, 1739–1885* (Chicago: Warner, Beers & Company, 1885), 406. Warner did not state that the arrivals were all from downstream, but Leeson wrote: "The number of steamboat arrivals at Miles City, not including down river boats, in 1878, was fifty-four." The figure seems high. The twenty arrivals at Miles City through July 12 correlates generally with the notices of individual boat trips published in the Bozeman *Avant Courier* and the Bismarck *Tribune*, but the number of fifty-four for the entire season does not.

51. Maguire, "Annual Report," 1100; Maguire, "Improvement of Missouri River Above Mouth of Yellowstone — Improvement of Yellowstone River," *House Exec. Doc.* 1, 47th Cong., 1st sess., July 13, 1881 (Serial 2012), 1675.

Yellowstone Journal estimated that several boatloads were stacked on the levee and around the town. In 1881, 93,000 buffalo robes valued at $232,500, 263,000 pounds of hides worth nearly $100,000, and a quantity of wolf skins and furs were shipped out by steamboats. On one trip in 1880, the *Batchelor* brought about five thousand "bales and packages of furs and robes" from the Yellowstone Valley to Bismarck, a cargo reported to be "the largest single consignment ever made to this city."[52]

During the navigation season, travelers usually preferred steamboats to stagecoaches, which were less comfortable and often slower. Most passengers were army personnel, who were often transferred in groups to different river posts, and their fares were less than those of private citizens for cabin passage and about the same for deck passage. Applying the rates in Coulson's 1879 contract, officers paid about $24 and enlisted men paid about $17 to travel the 706 miles from Bismarck to Terry's Landing. Private cabin passengers who had the same accommodations as officers were charged $35, and private deck passengers who had accommodations like those of enlisted men were charged about half the cabin rate.[53]

The Yellowstone navigation season was typically short, with the first boat usually arriving in Miles City in late May and the last in mid August. Being without boat service for three-fourths of the year created problems; and while merchants tried to predict demand and order their goods accordingly, there were frequent miscalculations. Before the first boat arrived in 1881, for instance, a potato shortage drove prices up in Miles City and the town even ran out of beer.[54]

After the steamboat season, Yellowstone Valley inhabitants depended on stagecoaches and freight wagons. Stages ostensibly provided regular passenger and mail service to Fort Keogh and Miles City, which were termini for stage lines from Bismarck and Bozeman, but heavy snows caused long, aggravating delays. In December 1878, a military telegraph line connected Fort Keogh to the East, but the next year winter storms downed the line for a time, increasing the isolation of the long winter.

The Yellowstone was a natural highway, but to navigators, travelers, and businessmen it was a rather poor one, being even more difficult to navigate than the Upper Missouri. Normally, it took ten days for

---

52. Miles City *Yellowstone Journal*, January 24, 1880; Maguire, "Improvement of Missouri River Above Mouth of Yellowstone — Improvement of Yellowstone River," *House Exec. Doc.* 1, 47th Cong., 2d sess. July 8, 1882 (Serial 2093), 1746-47; Bismarck *Tribune*, June 18, 1880.

53. Lass, *Steamboating on the Upper Missouri*, 114, 121; McElrath, *Yellowstone Valley*, 128-131.

54. Miles City *Yellowstone Journal*, June 4, 1881.

a steamboat trip from Bismarck to Miles City; but in 1879, Captain John Todd with the Coulson Line's *Rosebud* made the trip in only five days and eighteen hours, reportedly "the quickest trip ever made by any boat."[55] Usually when steamboats stopped running because of low water, freight was stockpiled at Fort Buford. In the fall of 1878, it was estimated that as much as one million pounds of freight had to be shipped from the fort up the valley. This work was done by bullwhackers who kept their wagons on the trail until winter.[56]

Everyone concerned with Yellowstone River steamboating thought that army engineers should improve the stream. The *Avant Courier* called for improvement as early as 1875, and the army's experiences in 1876 and 1877 demonstrated the urgency of improving difficult passages. As part of the Rivers and Harbors Act of 1878, Congress appropriated $15,000 for Yellowstone River improvement; and in late 1878 and 1879, army engineers surveyed the river from Fort Keogh to its mouth, measuring the stream, gauging its volume, and taking thousands of depth soundings.[57] During 1879 and 1880, about two dozen men dynamited rock ledges to reduce the gradient and open a straight, deep channel through Buffalo, Baker's, and Wolf rapids. Steamboats were then able to pass through Buffalo Rapids without warping, but the engineer in charge reported that Baker's and Wolf rapids and some shoals needed further work.[58]

As on the Upper Missouri, improvement on the Yellowstone came late in its steamboat era. By the time any appreciable work was done, steamboats were on the eve of being replaced by railroads. After a long hiatus caused by the Panic of 1873 and the ensuing depression, construction on the Northern Pacific was resumed in 1879. During 1880, when it was generally believed that the line would reach the Yellowstone Valley the next season, even the *Avant Courier* abandoned its Yellowstone navigation plans and featured reports about the railroad.

During the spring and early summer of 1881, steamboating on the Yellowstone followed its customary pattern. Boats that had wintered at Bismarck were sent to the usual destinations, and five of them were used in one of the most memorable incidents in the history of Yellowstone River steamboating. Several thousand Sioux who had fled

55. Ibid., July 31, 1879.

56. Louis Pfaller, "The Fort Keogh to Bismarck Stage Route," *North Dakota History,* 21 (July 1954), 91-126; Miles City *Yellowstone Journal,* January 1, 1880; Bozeman *Avant Courier,* September 5, November 28, December 12, 26, 1878.

57. Bozeman *Avant Courier,* August 13, 1875; Maguire, "Annual Report," 1879, 1101; Maguire, "Improvement of Missouri River Above the Mouth of the Yellowstone — Improvement of Yellowstone River," *House Exec. Doc.* 1, 46th Cong., 3d sess., August 4, 1880 (Serial 1954), 1475.

58. Maguire, "Improvement of Missouri," 1674-75.

to Canada after the Battle of the Little Bighorn and had surrendered to U.S. military authorities in 1880 were put on temporary reservations at Fort Buford and Fort Keogh. Some Miles City residents wanted to keep the Sioux at Keogh to boost the local economy, but the government decided to place the Indians on the Standing Rock Indian Reservation south of Bismarck.[59]

Quartermaster officers coordinated the rendezvous of five steamboats at Fort Keogh to make the transfer. No single company could furnish enough boats to move the Indians in one trip, so the army used the Coulson Line's *Josephine*, the Peck Line's *General Terry*, the Power Line's *Helena*, the Yellowstone Line's *Eclipse*, and the government's *General Sherman*. At four o'clock in the morning on June 13, 1881, 1,712 Sioux were peaceably loaded despite some anticipated resistance, marking the passing of the Sioux era in the Yellowstone River Valley. Steamboating, which had been so vital in wresting the valley from the Sioux, would soon be gone as well.[60]

The last brief phase of Yellowstone River steamboating occurred in 1881 and 1882, when steamboats were used to link the various ends-of-track with upstream destinations. The impact of the Northern Pacific became evident soon after the line reached Glendive on July 5, 1881. Within a matter of weeks, Glendive boomed and became a bustling frontier town and mistress of the Yellowstone trade. Warehouses were hastily constructed on the levee, and Yellowstone-bound steamboats were ordered to the new port. Within fifteen days of the railroad's arrival, Glendive-based boats reportedly transported 4,000 tons of cargo, and by season's end the "Gate City" listed twenty-five upriver steamboat departures, mostly by the Yellowstone Line.[61]

As the military contractors for the Yellowstone route in 1881, Leighton & Jordan purchased the *Eclipse*, doubling the size of its line. After the Northern Pacific reached Glendive, the firm used the *Eclipse* and the *Batchelor* to transport both private and military freight to Miles City, Fort Keogh, and other points. Carrying relatively light cargoes, ranging from 90 to 160 tons, both boats steamed on the Yellowstone until early September, carrying flour, eggs, fruit, hardware, wagons, lumber, shingles, trunks, furniture, beer, and miscellaneous personal property.

In keeping with traditional practice, freight rates were increased as river levels dropped late in the season. Seasonally averaged rates for transporting hundredweights from Glendive to Miles City or Fort

59. Miles City *Yellowstone Journal*, September 11, October 9, 1880, June 4, 1881.
60. Ibid., June 18, 1881.
61. Glendive *Times*, May 4, 1882.

Keogh were as low as forty cents for beer and as high as two dollars for eggs and fruit. On one downstream trip, the *Batchelor* was loaded with 9,863 buffalo hides, for which shippers were charged thirty cents a piece, and a quantity of baled deer skins. Other exports were dried cattle hides, which were hauled at the buffalo hide rate, and sacks of wool, which were moved for $1.50 each.[62]

The short-haul steamboating that characterized the Glendive trade became more pronounced as the railroad advanced deeper into Montana. Track-layers reached Miles City in December 1881, and by the following May they were only sixty miles from Coulson, the acclaimed "head of navigation." Coulson held promise for a short time when railroad officials decided that it would become a division head-quarters, but the railroad located the facility in the new town of Billings, which was platted about two miles west of Coulson by the Minnesota and Montana Land Improvement Company.[63]

Billings was the major new market for Yellowstone River steamers in 1882. Rapid railroad construction prompted the Northern Pacific to enter steamboating, and the company purchased the *Batchelor* from Leighton & Jordan and moved one of its transfer boats from Bismarck to the mouth of the Bighorn.[64] During June and July, as track-laying crews approached Billings, the Northern Pacific, Leighton & Jordan, and the Peck Line all attempted to send lightly loaded boats to Coulson. None made it, but they could reach Huntley, ten miles downstream, where freight wagons carried their cargoes to Billings. Leighton & Jordan's *Eclipse*, captained by Thomas D. Mariner, was the most successful, making four trips in June and early July from the end of track to Huntley with cargoes averaging about one hundred and ten tons. Because of low water, the *Eclipse*, the *Batchelor*, and the *General Terry* were taken off this run over a month before the first locomotive reached Billings on August 22.[65]

62. *Batchelor* and *Eclipse* Freight Book, 1881-1885, in Baker Papers.

63. Billings *Weekly Post*, July 1, 1882; *Residence and Business Directory of Billings, Montana* ... (Minneapolis: Reynolds & Hammond Printers, 1883), 13-14; James Sanks Brisbin, *The Great Yellowstone Valley Described* (St. Louis: Commercial Printing Company, 1882), 72-74.

64. The Northern Pacific's two transfer boats were used to ferry railroad cars across the Missouri River at Bismarck. Each boat was specially constructed with railroad tracks running the 200-foot length of the deck so that six cars could be carried simultaneously. The first boat, known simply as *Northern Pacific Transfer No. 1*, began operating in August 1879; and the second boat, *Northern Pacific Transfer No. 2*, was first used in 1881. The Northern Pacific evidently used one of the boats near the mouth of the Bighorn to ferry trains across before a railroad bridge was constructed there. Bismarck *Tribune*, July 21, August 2, September 18, October 10, 1879, November 12, December 3, 10, 1880, November 12, 1881.

65. Billings *Herald*, June 8, June 15, July 6, August 24, 1882; *Weekly Post*, July 1, 22, August 12, 1882; Batchelor and Eclipse Freight Book, 1881-1885, in Baker Papers.

The completion of the Northern Pacific to Billings effectively ended commercial steamboating on the Yellowstone, but Northern Pacific officials still harbored fears of competition from continued boating. Before the opening of navigation in 1883, the company solidified its virtual monopoly of Yellowstone Valley transportation by making an agreement with the Benton and the Coulson lines. The steamboat companies agreed to keep their boats off the Yellowstone in 1883 in exchange for specified railroad freight rates from Minnesota points to Bismarck. The steamboat lines agreed not to carry freight bound for any Montana point on the Northern Pacific's line for the same period. With this agreement in hand, the Northern Pacific sold the *Batchelor* and removed its transfer boat from the Bighorn.[66]

Despite the seeming certainty of the Northern Pacific's dominance, Glendive's promoters believed that the "Gate City" could become the steamboat port for the Yellowstone downstream and the Missouri above the mouth of the river. The army's engineers also considered this vast area to be the last refuge for steamboating on the river. Reasoning that Glendive-based steamboats would create salutary competition with the Northern Pacific, during the summer of 1883 the engineers had a crew construct dikes to protect the Glendive boat landing and build dams to force the water into a main channel. Similar improvements were made over the next several years, but it became increasingly evident that there was no economic justification for the work. On July 20, 1887, the supervising engineer of the Yellowstone River area reported that there was no commerce on the river and that "there is no through or local trade demanding the use of steamers." Despite the pleas of a Glendive committee, army engineers did not attempt to improve the Yellowstone after 1886. After years of uncertainty about a possible resumption of the work, in 1899 the army removed the Yellowstone from its list of pending improvement projects.[67]

66. "Memorandum of Agreement made between T. C. Power, manager of the Benton Line of Steamers for the Benton Line and D. W. Maratta, Genl Supt. of Coulson Line of Steamers for the Coulson Line, and the Northern Pacific RR Co. for the transporation of freight during the season of navigation on the Missouri River for 1883, St. Paul, March 4, 1883," in Letter Press Book, October 13, 1882-June 14, 1883, 266, Baker Papers; Glendive *Times*, May 19, May 26, 1883.

67. Clinton B. Sears, "Improvement of Missouri River from Sioux City, Iowa, to Fort Benton, Montana, and of Yellowstone River, Montana and Dakota," *House Exec. Doc.* 1, 50th Cong. 1st sess., July 20, 1887 (Serial 2535), 1602; Glendive *Times*, May 12, 19, June 9, 23, July 7, August 4, 11, 1883; Charles F. Powell, "Improvement of Missouri River Above Sioux City, Iowa, and of Yellowstone River, Montana and North Dakota," *House Exec. Doc.* 1, 52d Cong., 1st sess., July 6, 1891 (Serial 2925), 2242; J. C. Sanford, "Improvement of Missouri River Above Sioux City, Iowa, and of Yellowstone River, Montana and North Dakota," *House Exec. Doc.* 2, 56th Cong., 1st sess., July 17, 1899 (Serial 3907), 2231.

Ironically, after the improvement projects were dropped, commerce on the river was briefly revived in the Glendive area. By 1906, wheat-raising farmers had settled in the lower Yellowstone Valley below Glendive; and because there was still no railroad to take their grain to market, two companies operated gasoline packets on the lower Yellowstone. The chief shipper was the Benton Packet Company of Bismarck, the successor of the Benton Transportation Company, which had been formed out of the old Fort Benton Transportation Company, or Power Line. Isaac Post Baker, who began his Upper Missouri career as the last superintendent of the Power Line, was the principal owner and manager of the company. Primarily operating gasoline packets after 1900, he stayed in steamboating long after everyone else on the Upper Missouri. Baker's Yellowstone business was discontinued in 1909 when a lockless irrigation dam was completed eighteen miles below Glendive. A Pierre, South Dakota, company ran two boats on the river below the dam in 1909 and 1910, but this lingering business was dashed when a branch railroad was completed from Glendive to the mouth of the Yellowstone.[68]

This last, brief flurry of commercial boating on the lower Yellowstone was nothing more than a shadow of the past; despite the hopes of Baker and others, Yellowstone boating had succumbed to the technology of a new age. The inevitability of the railroad's supremacy, however, does not diminish the importance of steamboating to the Yellowstone River Valley. Although the steamboat era was brief, it was vital at a time when soldiers and pioneers were opening the way for the occupation of the valley.

---

68. Lass, *Steamboating on the Upper Missouri,* 153, 161-64; "Yellowstone River, Mont. Letter from the Secretary of War . . .," *House Doc.* 83, June 30, 1911, 62d Cong., 1st sess., (Serial 6116), 4-5, 13, 17-18; John G. MacDonald, "History of Navigation on the Yellowstone River" (master's thesis, Montana State University, Missoula, 1950), 136-37; Gary Williams and Alan Newell, "Yellowstone River Navigability Study," August 12, 1974, 19-20, Montana Historical Society Library, Helena.

HARPER'S WEEKLY
JOURNAL OF CIVILIZATION

VOL. XX.—No. 1022.] NEW YORK, SATURDAY, JULY 29, 1876. [WITH A SUPPLEMENT. PRICE TEN CENTS.

Entered according to Act of Congress, in the Year 1876, by Harper & Brothers, in the Office of the Librarian of Congress, at Washington.

THE NEW ALLIANCE.

"We stand here for Retrenchment, and *Reducing the Army of the United States.*"

PART FOUR
Sioux War Aftermath

By mid-1877 the aggressive campaigning of Nelson Miles had forced most Sioux and Cheyenne Indians from the Yellowstone basin to their respective agencies in Nebraska or along the Missouri River. Sitting Bull led his followers to Canada, where they remained until 1881, the last holdouts of the Great Sioux War. White civilization, meanwhile, spilled into the region and transformed the northern plains from open grasslands that sustained roving Indian peoples and enormous buffalo herds to a landscape of fenced rangelands for cattle and sheep and scattered towns, rail junctions, and coal mining centers. The nation barely mourned the losses of 1876–1877 as it moved into the final decades of the nineteenth century.

In an essay appearing in *Montana* in 1971, Brian W. Dippie explores the manner in which the defeat of Custer in distant Montana Territory played across the Old South. Emerging slowly from Reconstruction, the South quickly and easily condemned President Ulysses S. Grant and his scandal-ridden administration for Custer's death. Still deeply torn by partisan politics, Southern leaders pointed to presidential scandals in the East and Indian "massacres" in the West to remind the nation that all was not yet right with the world.

In the wake of the army's early setbacks against the Sioux and Cheyennes, General Sheridan renewed his call for the establishment of a substantial military presence in the Yellowstone country. The notion was an old one, yet it took Custer's defeat at the Little Bighorn to bring it about. Robert M. Utley's essay, which appeared in *Montana* in 1985, recounts the army's travails in its campaign for "war houses" on the Yellowstone. Eventually, Fort Keogh rose at the confluence of the Yellowstone and Tongue rivers, while Fort Custer was established on a bluff overlooking the Little Bighorn and Bighorn rivers. General William T. Sherman inspected Fort Keogh in mid-July 1877 while the post was still under construction. With the new quarters and barracks rising about him, Sherman observed prophetically that "the Sioux Indians can never again regain this country."

In time the army and white settlers won far more than these two new military posts. Cantonment Reno, established late in 1876 near

Old Fort Reno in north-central Wyoming, was renamed Fort McKin-ney and reestablished nearer the Bighorn Mountains in 1878. Fort Niobrara was completed in 1880 in Nebraska to watch over the Brulé Sioux living on South Dakota's new Rosebud Reservation. Fort Meade, established in 1878 in the northern Black Hills, firmly planted a per-manent army garrison near the gold fields and underscored Custer's true mission in his expedition there in 1874. Montana also saw the creation of Fort Maginnis in 1880 at the center of the territory, and that of Fort Assinniboine in 1879, located nearer Sitting Bull's Cana-dian haunts. Each, ultimately, was a case of "too much, too late."

Meanwhile, several of the nation's newspapers called for the crea-tion of a national monument to Custer, and a full-blown fund-raising campaign soon commenced. Minnie Dubbs Millbrook provides an insightful look at this memorialization effort in a 1974 essay from *Montana*. The venture eventually involved Elizabeth Bacon Custer, the general's devoted widow who for fifty-seven years shaped and pro-tected her husband's memory religiously. Mrs. Custer was extremely well-connected politically and militarily, and she proved to be a force-ful figure in the drawing room. She later claimed never to have been consulted about the nation's first Custer monument, or to having approved of its sculptor, J. Wilson Mac Donald. And she hated Mac Donald's product when it was unveiled at West Point in 1879, calling it a "wretched statue" and "a great insult to Autie's memory." As testi-mony to her will, Mrs. Custer saw to the monument's removal. It was supposed to have been crated and stored, but today it is "lost." Mrs. Custer later approved of other efforts, including the heroic equestrian statue erected in Monroe, Michigan, the Custers' hometown.

Southern Response to Custer's Last Stand

by Brian W. Dippie

Reconciliation was to be the watchword of the United States in its Centennial year. Reconstruction was obviously in its twilight—only three Southern states remained "unredeemed"—and the patriotism aroused by the hundredth anniversary of American independence promised to alleviate sectional bitterness. But 1876 was also a presidential election year, and the dream of reconciliation fell victim to the actuality of partisan politics. The Democratic Party had emerged from limbo in 1874 to capture a majority in the House of Representatives. In 1876, for the first time in two decades, its prospects for winning the presidency were excellent in a country mired in depression and grown weary of federal mismanagement and scandal. Late in the afternoon of June 16, Rutherford B. Hayes won the Republican nomination in Cincinnati. Eleven days later in St. Louis, Samuel Jones Tilden received the Democratic nod. Thus, by the Fourth of July, 1876, the atmosphere was saturated with politics, and reconciliation had become one more gimmick in the politician's bag of tricks.

The Dallas *Daily Herald*, in a July 7 editorial titled "The War of Good Feeling," observed that the South, which for 15 years had "stood aloof, and declined to take part in the celebration of a day which seemed a mockery of her degradation and desolation," had gone all out for the Centennial Fourth.

"This more than anything else," the *Herald* averred, "shows that the return to a better feeling between the North and South has commenced, and that the spirit of harmony and fraternity which has long slept, is again awake in the hearts of the people. . . ."

The same issue of the *Herald* printed the first telegraphic reports of the disaster which befell George Armstrong Custer and five com-

*Brian W. Dippie, "Southern Response to Custer's Last Stand," *Montana The Magazine of Western History*, 21 (Spring 1971), 18-31.

panies of the Seventh Cavalry on the Little Big Horn River in Montana Territory on June 25 — as well as an editorial which found the Grant administration "directly responsible for this massacre": "If anything was necessary to convince the American people of the necessity for a change in the administration, this wholesale sacrifice of men upon the altar of administrative imbecility would."

The Dallas editor's remarks were symptomatic of the partisan climate of the times, in which, as Robert M. Utley writes, Custer's Last Stand "instantly became a pawn on the political chessboard."[1] A study of the Southern response to the disaster on the Little Big Horn is, then, an exercise in political, or, more precisely, Democratic, rhetoric and maneuvering. The event itself was irrelevant; all that mattered was the various uses to which it could be put. On the one hand, the Democratic Party's reform platform was negatively advanced by blaming the administration for the tragedy; on the other, the Republican platform, with its innuendo of continuing Southern white disloyalty to the Union, was positively countered by the South's willingness to defend the reputation of George Armstrong Custer, a fallen Northern general, and to avenge his death on the field of battle.

Aside from politics, the response to the Little Big Horn also provides an insight into the workings of the Southern mind in a significant year in its history, as it vacillated between sectionalism and nationalism.

The South, in accounting for the Custer disaster, turned automatically to the Grant administration. As a Carrollton, Alabama, weekly put it, the responsibility should be placed "just where it belongs, upon the duplicity, corruption and incompetency of President Grant and the Republican party."[2]

This was in keeping with the Democratic position everywhere. The guidelines had been laid down in the National Democratic Platform, in which nearly half of the planks began with the word "reform." Custer's defeat was just one more vivid example of the need for such reform — preferably by means of a Democratic victory in November.

A Dallas paper made the connection explicit for its readers: "The blood of Custar [Custer was often to serve as an illustration of Sherman's definition of military fame: "to be killed on the field of battle and have our names spelled wrong in the newspapers"] and his noble three hundred men cry, 'Reform! Reform'!"[3]

Specifically, according to the Charleston *Journal of Commerce*, "the tragic events" on the Little Big Horn were "hardly more than the logical results of the scandalous mismanagement of the army by our

---

1. Robert M. Utley, *Custer and the Great Controversy: The Origin and Development of a Legend* (Los Angeles: Westernlore Press, 1962), 39.

2. "An Indian War," Carrollton, Alabama, *West Alabamian*, July 26, 1876.

3. Dallas *Daily Herald*, July 8, 1876.

Lieutenant Colonel George Armstrong Custer, Seventh Cavalry, about March 1876.
(José M. Mora, photographer, Montana Historical Society Photograph
Archives)

military President and the infamous frauds, peculation and ineffi-
ciency which flourished in the Indian Bureau of the Interior Department. . . ."[4] Since they were to be the primary recipients of Democratic
criticism after Custer's Last Stand, the Indian Bureau, the Army and
President Grant deserve particular attention.

The Bureau of Indian Affairs, along with the Peace (or Quaker)
Policy which it administered, were time-honored targets for anti-
administration pens.[5] Following the Custer battle, an intensified barrage was to be expected. Though the Bureau and the policy were not
synonymous, they were often indiscriminately lumped together in
the press.

Typical was a sweeping indictment in the Atlanta *Constitution*, which
charged that the Indian "knows he has been robbed, swindled and
made to bear unutterable sufferings through the Quaker idiocy and
post-trader and contractor corruptions of the administration. Prom-
ises, treaties and laws have been broken in the interest of schemers
against him."[6]

When a differentiation was made, the Bureau was invariably casti-
gated for its venality, and the Peace Policy for its soft-hearted and
muddle-headed approach to a problem which demanded realistic
appraisal and action.

"Whenever a good system of general policy has been adopted," the
San Antonio *Express* observed, without suggesting that the Peace Policy
was an example, "there has been neither the wisdom nor the virtue
in the Government and its agents necessary to its successful execution."[7]

Keying on the notion that the whole Grant administration was
permeated with corruption, the Democratic press condemned Indian
management from its highest bureaucratic echelons on down to the
agents and traders in the field. Often mentioned was the illegal
disposition of Indian annuities. These were provided the agent by
the government for free distribution among his charges, but had a
habit of appearing in the post trader's stock, for sale across the counter

---

4. "The Indian Massacre," Charleston *Journal of Commerce*, July 7, 1876.

5. Grant's Indian policy, introduced in 1869, had two labels, often used interchangeably, though a distinction can be made: the Peace Policy referred to a pro-
gram of "conquest by kindness," whereby the Indians were to be concentrated on large
reservations and there instructed in the ways of civilization; the Quaker Policy referred
particularly to the practice of having the different religious denominations nominate
men to serve as Indian agents. The Sioux war of 1876 tended to discredit more the
humanitarian overtones than the long-range aims of Grant's policy. See Robert M.
Utley, "The Celebrated Peace Policy of General Grant," *North Dakota History*, 20 (July
1953), 121-42.

6. "The Indian War," Atlanta *Constitution*, July 7, 1876.

7. "Massacre of Custer and His Men—The Disasters of Our Indian Policy," San
Antonio *Express*, July 8, 1876.

to disgruntled Indians. Since agents and traders customarily received their positions through patronage, the link was quickly made.

"War with the Sioux," a Richmond paper contended, "is directly traceable to the Indian Bureau, and that Bureau is directly controlled by Mr. Grant and his personal friends."[8]

After the Custer fight, the Bureau's traditional corruptness came in for close scrutiny. In many quarters, its transfer back to the War Department (it had come under the newly-created Interior Department's jurisdiction in 1849) was urged as the only satisfactory plan. Before it could be purified, many argued, the Bureau would have to be purged.[9]

Equally volatile was the related issue of Indian armament. The frontier press waxed eloquent on the subject. An Austin, Texas, paper felt that the reason the government "did not furnish as good guns to the army as it did to the Indians" was "obvious": "It is much more profitable to sell the good guns to the Indians and give the inferior ones to the army."[10]

In short, the corruption of the Grant administration's Indian Bureau was heedless even of the lives of the frontier's citizenry. "The whole Indian policy of the administration," Little Rock's *Daily Arkansas Gazette* fumed, "for years has been shaped in the interest of rings, who have been enriched through their traffic with the Indians, which has extended even to supplying them with arms of the most approved style."[11]

In castigating Grant's Peace Policy, "that infernal combination of ignorant sentimentalism, arch hypocrisy and rascally corruption,"[12] the Southern press often took pains to distinguish their remarks from an attack on the Indians themselves. Indeed, "conquest by kindness" might even be acceptable in principle, but it had obviously not worked out in (Republican) practice.

"The Indian policy of General Grant's Administration," a Charleston editorialist wrote, "has been simply to pamper the Indians with the left hand while robbing them with the right."[13]

---

8. Richmond *State*; reprinted as "How the North Holds Grant Responsible for Custer's Defeat," Carrollton *West Alabamian*, August 2, 1876.

9. The transfer of the Indian Bureau from the Department of the Interior to the War Department had long been a pet Democratic project, and its advocates saw in the Little Big Horn an ideal opportunity to force the issue to a head. They had badly miscalculated the Congressional temper, however, and a bill to that end reintroduced in the House on August 3 failed. In the face of a major Indian war the transfer issue, instead of being reborn, was stillborn. For a general treatment of the subject see Donald J. D'Elia, "The Argument Over Civilian or Military Indian Control, 1865-1880," *The Historian*, 24 (February 1962), 207-25.

10. Austin, Texas, *Daily State Gazette*, July 29, 1876.

11. "The Indian Question," Little Rock *Daily Arkansas Gazette*, July 11, 1876.

12. Austin, Texas, *Weekly Democratic Statesman*, July 13, 1876.

13. "The Indian Massacre," Charleston *Journal of Commerce*, July 7, 1876.

This sentiment was common across the country and many Republican papers joined in questioning the wisdom of persevering with the Peace Policy. The time had come, it seemed, to face the fact that the Indians would have to be whipped and confined to reservations before they would be amenable to the gentler persuasions of civilization. The New Orleans *Republican* was typical of many disaffected party organs. "The latest news calls for a different line of action," it editorialized. "The death of Custer and his men calls for speedy vengeance. It is a mistaken policy for good men to pray with the Indians while bad men sell them guns . . . ."[14]

Having discredited the Peace Policy, several Southern papers proceeded to set themselves up as true friends of the Indian. Perhaps they sensed that the Republican Party's fumbling of the Indian question could be turned into a campaign issue of real magnitude, involving elements of racial prejudice that would offset charges of Southern brutality towards the Negro. (The latest Southern "outrage," the Hamburg Massacre, vied with the Custer Massacre for newspaper space throughout July, 1876, and the Democrats were anxious to play the story down.) Thus when Wendell Phillips assailed General Sherman for remarks which he interpreted to be an advocacy of Indian extermination, Southerners were intent observers.

A Charleston daily reprinted Phillips' letter in full,[15] while the Louisville *Courier-Journal*, commenting that Phillips himself "was once, if he is not at present, one of the most prominent advocates of the extermination of the white people of the Southern states," made this editorial point: "The Indian question has only recently agitated this unhealthy gentleman's mind, and the condition of the red brother certainly merits his sympathy. Mr. Phillips should vote for Tilden . . . in order to secure the overthrow of the Indian ring . . ."[16]

Here, then, was a chink in the armor of moral superiority which the North affected — a different racial question — and Wilmington, North Carolina's *Daily Journal* prodded at the vulnerability in a lengthy editorial, "Lo, the Poor Indian — How Is this Thus?" Can it be that the reason the Republican moralizers pay so little attention to the Indians, the *Journal* wondered, is "on account of their color, that they approximate too closely to the white and . . . that the talismanic key which will open all the floodgates of radical sympathy and radical affection must always be dyed in the wool? . . . The poor Indian happens not to be a negro, consequently he is neither a man nor a brother." The only logical reason for the Republicans' interest in the

14. "The Slaughter on the Plains," New Orleans *Republican*, July 7, 1876.

15. "The Indian Question," Charleston *Journal of Commerce*, July 22, 1876.

16. Louisville *Courier-Journal*; reprinted as "Wendell Phillips and the Indian Question," Little Rock *Daily Arkansas Gazette*, July 25, 1876.

Negro and indifference to the Indian was, simply, that "the one could be made a voter, the other could not."[17]

How much the South itself cared about the Indian was another matter. What was important, as Austin's *Weekly Democratic Statesman* intimated, was that the South's dislike of the black man was matched by the North's dislike of the red man — and, moreover, that each area was justified in its attitude. "Are there not immutable laws defining the nature and as well the necessary modes of life and relations of different races?" it asked, and answered: "There are inexorable decrees of Providence defining as immutable the relations of whites and blacks as of red and white men . . . ."

Common race was to be the bond between North and South, with each section respecting the rights of the other to handle its "racial problem" in its own way. "One or the other race must be supreme," the *Statesman* concluded, "and while Grant declares he will sustain the black power, even with Federal bayonets, we would know whether the white race of the North, properly or at least necessarily exterminating red men in the West . . . , will finally, when the question must be solved, pronounce with Grant against the white race and in favor of the Africanization of the Gulf States?"[18] For the *Stateman*, at least, a concern for the Indian was limited to his political utility.

The army was another focal point of attention in every discussion of responsibility for the Little Big Horn disaster. Here the Republicans had a strong upper hand, for the Democratic House on June 19 had passed an army appropriations bill reducing the peacetime establishment from 25,000 to 22,000 men. Too, the bill had allocated the army $3,750,570.94 less than for the previous year, and had lowered the salary scale for officers of all ranks.[19] Such an overt frontal assault on the army was bound to compromise the Democrats after the news of Custer's defeat reached the East on July 6. But that very day the Democratic defenses were laid.

Samuel S. "Sunset" Cox of New York, addressing the House on his ever-favorite topics of economy and reform, was interrupted by a Republican who wondered if he stood by remarks he had made at the Democratic convention to the effect that the Southern states needed "no Army until after November, and so far as the Indian wars were concerned, all we had to do was to turn the boys on our frontier loose and they would take care of the Indians."

Cox "clarified" this by saying that "we can very well afford until after the election to keep the Army from the throats of the Southern

---

17. Wilmington, North Carolina, *Daily Journal*, July 23, 1876.

18. "How the Races Jog Along with One Another," Austin, Texas, *Weekly Democratic Statesman*, August 31, 1876.

19. *Congressional Record*, 44th Cong., 1st sess., 4743, hereafter cited as *Cong. Record*.

people," and insisted that the Custer battle provided "another illustration that the insane policy of expending large sums of money for the Army is not the true policy of Indian retrenchment.

"You say that we have not troops enough and that this House cuts them off," he went on. "Where are the 25,000, not yet diminished by our legislation . . .? Three thousand of them and more are in the States of Mississippi and Louisiana, and in other Southern States. What are they doing there? There is no revolt there, no rebellion, no election yet."[20] And that, in a nutshell, was to be the South's position, volubly maintained throughout the Centennial summer of 1876 despite the figurative hands encircling her throat.

The July 7 issue of the Charleston *Journal of Commerce* noted on its front page that "already the disaster to Custer's command is being used as a potent argument against any reduction of the army"; then, on its editorial page, formulated a rebuttal: "The President cannot escape severe condemnation for suffering such a disaster to occur in the West while he is planning to control Southern elections by the bayonet."

This theme was reiterated everywhere in the South, with variations limited largely to the manner of presentation. Some took the factual approach, pointing out that there were only 3,200 soldiers in the theater of the Sioux war, while there were 3,500 men in Texas alone (though Texas, like most frontier states, wanted more, not less), and another 3,500 scattered throughout the other Southern states.[21]

A Brenham, Texas, weekly gave these particulars: "In a time of profound peace we have over one-half of the army stationed in the various Southern States, the largest numbers being in those States that are under Radical rule, South Carolina, Florida, Louisiana and Mississippi coming in for the lion's share."[22]

New Orleans' *Daily Picayune* preferred to agonize a little, constructing a defense of Democratic Congressional tactics that would not seem overly hostile to the military, since the *Picayune*, for one, felt that a full-scale war of extermination was in order, and that the army should be given support. "The duties required of it are onerous in the extreme, often dangerous, and sometimes for other reasons painful and disagreeable," an editorialist observed. Then, in one neat sentence that covered all angles, he toed the Southern line: "In the present embarrassed conditions of our finances . . . [the army] is, perhaps, as large as the country can well afford to have it; but certainly it is too small to spare a single man from the immediate scene of war."

---

20. Ibid., 4428-30.

21. Mobile *Register*; reprinted as "In a Nutshell," Wilmington *Daily Journal*, July 23, 1876.

22. "Troops in the South," Brenham, Texas, *Banner*, September 1, 1876.

If the point was too subtle, its elaboration was not: "It is, of course, uncertain what steps the Administration may see fit to take in this emergency. The general election is near at hand, and a large number of troops will be needed to overcome the Conservative majorities in the Southern States. Gen. Custer has been already sacrificed, and the Republican party would prefer to see the whole army murdered in detachments to risking the results of a fair election."[23]

The *Picayune's* conclusion suggests a third approach, in which logic was subordinated to indignant rhetoric. Believing Custer and his men to have been sacrificed to "a miserable, niggardly, partisan policy," the July 7 Dallas *Daily Herald* thundered: "If the troops now loafing and idling in the South, to influence the Presidential election in the interest of the Radical nominees, . . . had been where they belong, with Custar, [sic]" this massacre would not have "disgraced us in this Centennial year."

Two days later the *Herald* devoted a full editorial to this theme, concluding with a stirring call to its readers to unite "in one solid, unbroken column" to annihilate the Indians and, one supposes, the Republicans, figuratively speaking: "Texans to the rescue! Remember Custar's [sic] fate! Remember that the Republican administration gave him a less number of troops to fight the Indians . . . than to compel Louisiana and Mississippi to go for the infamous nominees of the Republican party!"[24]

The Southern line, in short, was to emphasize that the army was of sufficient strength to defeat the Sioux if the troops were correctly distributed. Once again, therefore, Grant was responsible for Custer's death. In his obsession with a Republican victory in November, he had neglected the army on the frontier in order that bayonets might preside over Southern ballot boxes. But Southern opinion in 1876 was hardly monolithic, and any general position was subject to variations. When, after much wrangling in committee, the Senate prevailed and an army appropriations bill was finally passed on July 19 with all of the House provisions relating to the "reduction, re-organization, and pay of the Army" struck down,[25] an audible sigh of relief escaped from the Victoria, Texas, *Advocate.*

The *Advocate* had followed the standard Democratic line in denouncing the folly of stationing troops in the South while Custer was "butchered on the plains," but it deviated enough later to admit that the House, in view of "the outbreak of the present Indian war,"

23. "The Death of Custer," New Orleans *Daily Picayune*, July 7, 1876.

24. "The Massacre of Custar's [sic] Command," Dallas *Daily Herald*, July 7, 1876; "Custar's [sic] Murder," ibid., July 9, 1876.

25. *Cong. Record*, 4721.

was wise in withdrawing from "its position on the military appropriation bill."[26]

Circumstances had changed, and the frontier's needs now took
precedence over party. The *Republican*, a weekly campaign tract
published in San Antonio from July through October, 1876, noted
in its first number another reason why Democratic efforts to reduce
the army should be discouraged. Even then, San Antonio was fatten-
ing on the military pork barrel, and Democratic reformer-econo-
mizers might conceivably shut the supply off at its source.

"We would have nothing to expect from a democratic administration but the annihilation of the army," the *Republican* warned. "Our
new military depot would become the play ground for rats, and desolation would mark the spot."[27]

It was an appeal attuned to the spirit of the New South — economic
self-interest over Democratic purity — and it presaged, in its assump-
tions, "the apostasy of the South" which effected the compromise of 1877.

The Little Big Horn raised another military consideration. The
disaster, it was argued, would never have occurred, even with an inade-
quate force on the frontier, had there not been incompetence in the
highest echelons of command.

By coincidence, the nation's top military men just happened to be
Ulysses S. Grant, Commander-in-Chief; William Tecumseh Sherman,
General of the Army; and Philip H. Sheridan, Lieutenant-General
and Commander of the Military Division of the Missouri. It was a
provocative trio of names, and many Southern editorialists echoed
"Sunset" Cox's taunting words to his Republican colleagues: "You ask
about the Army; why, a portion of it, its generals at least [Sherman
and Sheridan are meant], are rollicking now at the Centennial in
Philadelphia while Custer falls in the wilderness."[28]

The attacks on Sherman and Sheridan, however, were just needle
pricks compared to the broadsword blows which the South rained
upon President Grant. If Robert E. Lee, steeped in doomed nobility,
had become the symbol of the Lost Cause, then Grant, equated in
the Southern mind with defeat, repression, and humiliation, had
become the symbol of Radical Reconstruction. Thus Southern papers,
in attributing responsibility for Custer's Last Stand to Grant's administration and the Republican Party, often descended to the level of
personal vilification.

---

26. "Practical Demonstration," Victoria, Texas, *Advocate*, July 27, 1876; ibid., August
3, 1876.

27. San Antonio *Republican*, July 15, 1876.

28. *Cong. Record*, 4430. Cox was referring to the fact that both Sherman and
Sheridan, among other generals, were attending the Centennial Exposition at
Philadelphia when the news of the Little Big Horn broke.

Ulysses S. Grant, eighteenth President of the United States, 1869–1877. (Montana Historical Society Photograph Archives)

The Atlanta *Times*, avowing that "somebody is to blame for these disasters," mentioned "Grant's post traders," who supplied the Sioux with arms and ammunition, and "the officer in command, or the Secretary of War" for the expedition's faulty strategy, before settling on the Chief Magistrate himself, "mere soldier elevated by luck to a position beyond his capacity."[29]

The particular door which Custer's death opened to Grant's detractors had been set ajar earlier that year when Custer testified before a House committee investigating charges of malfeasance in the War Department, especially as they related to sales of post traderships.

Secretary of War W. W. Belknap, faced with impeachment proceedings, had resigned on March 2 when the scandal first broke, but the investigation and then his trial dragged on well into summer. The Democrats, with their eyes on the political main chance, introduced every possible witness who could cast aspersions upon the Administration's conduct, regardless of the legal validity of his testimony. Custer appeared before the committee on March 29 and April 4. His "hearsay" evidence, as he himself termed it,[30] snared not only Belknap, but also the President's brother, Orvil Grant—and thus, inevitably, Grant himself.

In his anger, President Grant first deprived Custer of command of the Dakota column, at that time outfitting at Fort Abraham Lincoln, Dakota Territory, preparatory to taking the field against the Sioux; then, on May 3, prohibited him from participating in the expedition. The Democratic press immediately rallied around Custer, and set up a clamor which abated only when Grant relented and allowed him to accompany the Dakota column in a secondary capacity.

When Custer fell at the Little Big Horn, it was natural that a link would be made with the Belknap affair and his disgrace at the hands of the President. And so, with occasional reports of the Belknap proceedings providing a melancholoy counterpoint (the trial was not decided until August 1, at which time Belknap was acquitted), Democratic journals everywhere unleashed their fury on the President. "Grant and Belknap are avenged," Augusta's *Weekly Chronicle & Sentinel* snapped, "and now the annoying witness has been effectually disposed of."[31]

In this climate of irrationality, fact was irrelevant, and Custer, who had begged Grant "to spare me the humiliation of seeing my regi-

---

29. Atlanta *Times*, July 7, 1876; "The Indian Campaign," ibid., July 8, 1876.

30. Custer to his wife Elizabeth, April 17, 1876, in Marguerite Merington, ed., *The Custer Story: The Life and Intimate Letters of George A. Custer and His Wife Elizabeth* (New York: Devin-Adair, 1950), 290.

31. Augusta *Weekly Chronicle & Sentinel*, July 12, 1876.

ment march to meet the enemy and I not share its dangers," was now pictured as having been sent West to his execution by a vengeful President.

"It was said at the time," a Montgomery paper remarked, "that he was put on the frontier as a punishment for his conduct in the Belknap matter. If it was desired to kill him off, the object has been attained."[32]

"Grant exiled Custar [sic]," the Dallas *Daily Herald* maintained, "and doubtless is glad that fear[less] soldier and unpurchaseable patriot is dead." Custer was simply "murdered in cold blood."[33]

"All the blood shed in the fight with the Indians in Montana is blood upon the skirts of the administration," the Atlanta *Times* charged. "It will never bleach out. The ghosts of the brave Custer and of his comrades will, and ought to, haunt the precincts of the White House and fill with horror the dreams of him who is master there."[34]

The assumption underlying all this was that "had the command of the expedition been intrusted" to Custer, "very likely . . . disastrous defeat might have been turned to victory."[35] Wilmington's *Daily Journal* was more adamant: "A gallant chieftain who had hitherto met with no defeat was stripped of his command and sent into the field as a subordinate, to execute a part, to carry out a detail, when he should have matured the plan and directed the whole. The result is known."[36]

Whether or not "the result" would have been otherwise was quite irrelevant. Grant had done it again. In a fit of pique, he had disgraced the proud young general, knowing full well, a correspondent in the Galveston *Daily News* asserted, that Custer "would court in battle an honorable *suicide*." "Grant gave the first stab, and knew when doing it that the Sioux would do the balance."[37]

As if it were not enough to be referred to in the press throughout the land as a murderer, the President had to endure the protracted sarcasm directed at his son, Frederick Dent Grant. Fred, a lieutenant in the Fourth Cavalry (the papers always said the Seventh), had the misfortune of being promoted to first lieutenant at the time the news of the Little Big Horn broke. The Democratic press set up a howl, nowhere with more glee than in the South. Fred Grant's unforgivable sin was, of course, that he failed to die with Custer.

---

32. Montgomery *Advertiser*; reprinted as "General Custer's Death," Carrollton *West Alabamian*, July 19, 1876.
33. Dallas *Daily Herald*, July 7, 9, 1876.
34. Atlanta *Times*, July 9, 1876.
35. "A Name Made Glorious," Albany, Georgia, *News*, July 20, 1876.
36. Wilmington *Daily Journal*, July 11, 1876.
37. "The Fall of Custer," Galveston *Daily News*, July 19, 1876.

"Absenteeism seems to be epidemic in the Grant family of late," a North Carolina paper commented. Fred was too busy playing with his baby to be fighting out West," so that when Custer and the others got killed Fred only got promotion. . . . And such is soldiering when a man happens to be President Grant's son!"[38]

For awhile, Fred Grant appeared well on his way to becoming the anti-hero to Custer's hero. "Lt. Fred Grant Safe," the Van Buren, Arkansas, *Press* headlined its contribution;[39] an Austin paper urged him to "abandon his feather-bed, bomb proof position at the White House and 'go West, young man, go West.' "[40] The *Constitution* took great joy in detailing young Grant's progress in that direction, noting that he "got as far as Chicago, on his way to exterminate the Sioux . . ." He was sent there "as soon as the Sioux war became serious . . . to be near the scene of action and protect the headquarters of Sheridan's department. His pa is no Brutus." The *Constitution* had already entertained its readers with a succession of puns on Sitting Bull's name, and it crowned its assault on Fred Grant with the suggestion that he be dubbed "Sitting Calf."[41]

The constant harassment and personal abuse would have riled a more even-tempered man than Ulysses S. Grant. It is not surprising, then, that when he at last delivered his assessment of the responsibility for the Little Big Horn disaster, it was intemperate and ungenerous. "I regard Custer's massacre as a sacrifice of troops brought on by Custer himself," he told a New York *Herald* reporter in early September, adding that the tragedy was "wholly unnecessary—wholly unnecessary."[42] Apparently the President had come to realize that praise of Custer equalled an implicit or explicit condemnation of himself and his administration. It was an equation which most Southerners had also mastered.

The more George Custer came under attack from the administration press, the more agreeable he became to Democrats everywhere. The South was no exception.

"It is noticeable," the *Daily Picayune* sanctimoniously launched an editorial, titled "Custer's Critics," "that the Administration papers are taking particular pains to blacken the memory of the gallant Custer by charging him with unsoldierlike conduct in the battle of Little Big Horn River."[43]

38. Wilmington *Daily Journal*, July 13, 1876.
39. Van Buren, Arkansas, *Press*, July 18, 1876.
40. Austin, Texas, *Daily State Gazette*, July 29, 1876.
41. Atlanta *Constitution*, July 26, 30, 1876. Since Fred Grant was aide-de-camp to Sheridan, Chicago headquarters was his rightful place.
42. New York *Herald*, September 2, 1876. Quoted in Utley, *Custer and the Great Controversy*, 44.
43. New Orleans *Daily Picayune*, July 18, 1876.

A Texas weekly coyly professed to find it "a little strange, that while Republican papers are filled with inuendo [sic] and sinister suggestions regarding Custer, the Democratic journals are the only presses that attempt to do justice to the dead hero."[44] The only thing "strange" about it was the bedfellows which politics traditionally make.

For Southerners wishing to combat Republican imputations of disloyalty, Custer, even with name incorrectly spelled, offered an ideal weapon. Brave, dashing and chivalrous, with a flair for the romantic, the Northern war hero had been greatly in sympathy with the South both before and after the Civil War. He was skeptical of Negro advancement, and an outspoken Democrat who more than once had been branded a Copperhead. Best of all, he was in Grant's manifest disfavor when he rode to his death. A more perfect tool for Democratic purposes could hardly have been fashioned, and Southern editorialists gave voice to their gratitude.

"To live in story is the fondest dream of the soldier," the Albany *News* affirmed. "A few years more or less of this life — what boots in comparison with enduring fame? The name of Custer is now enrolled with those to be remembered."[45]

A Richmond paper outdid all others. "The North alone shall not mourn this gallant soldier," it trumpeted. "He belongs to all the Saxon race; and when he carried his bold dragoons into the thickest of the last ambuscade, where his sun of life forever set, we behold in him the true spirit of that living chivalry which cannot die, but shall live forever to illustrate the pride, the glory, and the grandeur of our imperishable race."[46]

A note of uncertainty, however, sometimes crept into Southern accolades — a cautiousness which bespoke the unfamiliarity of the role. "A Veteran of the Army of the Tennessee" felt called upon to justify the "resolutions of regret and sympathy" for Custer's death adopted at a reunion of Hood's Brigade held in Bryan, Texas, on July 12. He thrice termed Custer "knightly," and concluded: "The resolutions express the feelings of all true Southern soldiers, who to-day would gather about the bier of the knightly Custer and drop the tear of sympathy for the misfortunes of a former foeman . . ."[47]

"Custer was a gallant officer," Charleston's *News and Courier* ventured to say, "and, now that by-gones, are by-gones, we deplore, as Americans, the loss of the brave soldiers who rode to death with him, under the 'old Flag'."[48]

---

44.   Burnet, Texas, *Bulletin*, July 28, 1876.
45.   Albany, Georgia, *News*, July 20, 1876.
46.   Richmond *Whig*; reprinted as "Virginia's Tribute to Custer," Dallas *Daily Herald*, July 16, 1876.
47.   "The Late Gen. Custer," Galveston *Daily News*, July 16, 1876.
48.   "The Defeat and Death of Custer," Charleston *News and Courier*, July 7, 1876.

This tone of guarded praise was best captured in Wilmington's *Daily Journal*. This paper discreetly waited several days, playing down the Little Big Horn news. When the drift of things became certain — the Democratic Party had taken Custer under its protective wing — it cranked out an editorial sprinkled with all of the prescribed epithets. But the strain inherent in this "just tribute" to a Yankee hero was evident.

"We care not now that the man won his first laurels fighting the armies of the South," the editorialist remarked, then proceeded to show just how much he really did care: "We remember not now that for four years he warred against us in bloody battle. We remember no longer in bitterness for him, the bloody fields that come back to us strewn with the dead bodies of friends and kinsmen, dear comrades all, though many of them fell before Custer and his command; for in the contemplation of the sublime courage and superb heroism . . . every feeling disappears save one of reverent admiration."[49] The praise which followed was more than tempered by this uneasy prologue.

Yet the overwhelming sentiment in the South, ostensibly in keeping with the Centennial spirit of reconciliation and reunion, favored Custer. If it could be argued that words were cheap, the rebuttal was ready: throughout the former Confederacy men were volunteering for service against the Sioux. Each offer was carefully identified in the papers as another example of Southern patriotism, and as further proof of the falseness of Republican "bloody shirt" campaign oratory.

Under the heading "Avenging Custar [*sic*]," the *Constitution* on July 9 printed a telegram sent to the Secretary of War the day before volunteering "by unanimous vote" the services of Atlanta's Cleburne Rifles "to avenge the death of Custer."[50]

"Noted ex-Confederate General" Joe O. Shelby's telegraphic request to President Grant that he be allowed to raise a 1,000-man company in Missouri received wide coverage, and the Fort Smith, Arkansas, *Herald* observed that "thousands of rebel officers and rebel soldiers are ready to respond to any call for such a purpose."[51]

Perhaps they were. Volunteer companies across the country were proffering their services, but the army had already decided to hold out for an increase in the enlistment of regulars instead. This, however, never dampened the enthusiasm of the volunteers.

A letter from Atlanta informed readers of the New York *Herald* that word of Custer's death had fired "the old-time spirit of the south."

49. Wilmington *Daily Journal*, July 11, 1876.

50. "Avenging Custar [*sic*]," Atlanta *Constitution*, July 9, 1876.

51. Fort Smith, Arkansas, *Western Independent*, August 2, 1876; Fort Smith, Arkansas, *Herald*, July 15, 1876.

A gentleman had told the writer that he could immediately raise 2,000 men who would "fight as hard as they fought for the 'stars and bars.' They would win patents of loyalty in the lava beds, or they would stay there with Custer."

"It is," the correspondent felt, "very gratifying to witness the patriotism evinced at even this temporary disaster to our national flag."[52]

In a similar vein was a letter addressed to Kentucky Representative Thomas L. Jones, dated July 9 at Louisville. "As this is the Centennial year of American Independence," it began, "I desire to let the world see that we who were once soldiers of the 'Lost Cause' are not deficient in patriotism. Will you be kind enough to intimate to the President, that I offer him the services of a full regiment, composed exclusively of ex-Confederates, to avenge Custer's death."[53]

In turn, Casey Young, Congressman from Tennessee, notified the Secretary of War that he had received telegrams from two units consisting of ex-Confederates, the Irish Volunteers and the Chickasaw Guards, as well as from the Jackson Guards and a Negro company, all "tendering their services in war against the hostile Sioux."[54]

Texas came through in characteristic style, her papers clamoring for the opportunity to turn the Sioux into "good" Indians. "Ten thousand Texans could be raised to go for the Indians who massacred Custar [*sic*]," one paper boasted. "Killing a mess of Indians is the only recreation our frontier rangers want."[55]

"Give Texas a fair show at the exultant Sioux," the Galveston *Daily News* promised, "and there will be consternation and mourning in their wigwams before many moons have passed."[56]

"Give our Texas boys a chance," an Austin daily echoed. "Texas deserves the honor of attempting to wipe out the Sioux, for she had a bloody fight with the Indian savage and has accomplished wonders in her own defence."[57] Of specific proposals, however, there was none.

A number of concerns were involved in all of this volunteer activity. Certainly there was a genuine desire on the part of many Southerners to demonstrate their loyalty to the Union in the Centennial year, and offering to fight the Indians was an approved avenue towards reconciliation. Without compromising the South's stance, or in any way endangering the sanctity of the Lost Cause, it presented an ideal outlet for patriotism. Indeed, it played off the Lost Cause tradition,

52. New York *Herald*; reprinted as "Southern Loyalty," Fort Smith, Arkansas, *Herald*, July 29, 1876.

53. "The War in the West," Charleston *Journal of Commerce*, July 17, 1876.

54. Ibid.

55. Dallas *Daily Herald*, July 8, 1876.

56. "If Trained Indian Fighters Are Called For," Galveston *Daily News*, July 8, 1876.

57. Austin, Texas *Daily State Gazette*, July 14, 1876.

which held that no other soldiers were equal to those who had fought for states' rights. Obviously, a company of ex-Confederates would be more than a match for any Indians.

But perhaps a Charleston paper best summarized the complex of emotions which led so many Southerners to volunteer their services: "Judging from the impression made upon some old 'Rebels' in Charleston by the news of our defeat in the Indian country, it would take only the shortest sort of brush with any troublesome neighbor to arouse in the South the ardent patriotism that, in years gone by, sent the South to the front in Mexico. This is our country. We have the right to abuse it if we choose; but we make common cause against the common enemy, whether he be redskin or white."[58] The logic, if not unassailable, was understandable. It was an American's prerogative to criticize his country if he saw fit—and Southerners were preeminently Americans.

Again, there was another side to the matter, and again it was Wilmington's *Daily Journal* which presented it. While most Southern papers took advantage of the volunteer activity as an opportunity for self-congratulation, the *Journal* adopted a belligerent stance, suggesting that the colored troops—the "sable warriors" so enthusiastically endorsed by Northerners as being alone in all the South "true to the flag"—prove themselves by following "that flag to the Black Hills and stirring up Sitting Bull."

"A number of white companies have volunteered," it petulantly remarked, "but then you know that's just like the white people of the South, always willing to help any one in any trouble even though they are slapped in the mouth all the time they are doing it, and though they get more kicks than coppers for their trouble."[59] For some Southerners, certainly, bygones were not yet bygones.

In the end, all the platitudes on the Glorious Fourth, patriotism and reconciliation in America's Centennial year finally could not conceal the fact that the South's viewpoint was a sectional one. National troubles were still read as Republican troubles—a weakness common to the Democracy, which often exhibited the irresponsibility of a party long out of power (just as the Republicans tended to the moral flabbiness of a party too long in power). A statesmanlike perspective would have to await victory at the polls. In the meantime, the South was not entirely uncomfortable in the role of observer-critic.

For one thing, it was a stance which permitted of emotional distance, and allowed readers of the Albany *News* to turn from an

---

58.   "The Defeat and Death of Custer," Charleston *News and Courier*, July 7, 1876.
59.   "The Colored Troops Fought Nobly," Wilmington *Daily Journal*, July 16, 1876. See also, "The Colored Troops," Atlanta *Times*, July 15, 1876; and "Sitting Bull and Doc Adams," Charleston *Journal of Commerce*, July 13, 1876.

account of "TERRIBLE BUTCHERY! . . . Seventeen Officers and Three Hundred and Fifteen Men Cold in Death" to this short item: "What glorious prospects ahead for the people of the South — the best crop year since the war; out of debt almost, and Tilden to be our next President. Would not this be glory enough for one year?"[60]

While scandals shook the American government in the East, and the Indians wiped out George Armstrong Custer in the West; while poets abhorred "this ruin and scathe" and searched "through the time's thick murk looking in vain for light, for hope," while the best minds of the generation deplored the falling away from national purpose which seemed to make a mockery of the Centenary of American Independence; down in the South, in 1876, it appeared to many that, if all was not yet right with the world, at least the year was at the spring and the day at the morn. Or, as a Texas commentator phrased it in an editorial on that state's rosy prospects, "brightly breaks the morning upon this land of promise."[61]

---

60. Albany, Georgia, *News*, July 13, 1876.
61. "How Brightly Breaks the Morning," Marshall, Texas, *Tri-Weekly Herald*, July 27, 1876.

Guard mounting at Fort Keogh, near the confluence of the Yellowstone and Tongue rivers, in 1882. (L. A. Huffman, photographer, Montana Historical Society Photograph Archives)

War Houses in the Sioux Country

by Robert M. Utley

On July 16, 1877, the broad valley where the Tongue River emptied into the Yellowstone provided the setting for a scene rich in meaning for the future of the northern plains. Here, on the south bank of the Yellowstone a short distance upriver from the collection of rude huts in which the Fifth Infantry Regiment had wintered, civilian laborers busily worked at constructing the fine new quarters and barracks of a permanent post. It would be named Fort Keogh, in honor of an officer killed a year earlier in Custer's bloody disaster on the Little Bighorn. A hundred miles to the southwest, another post rose from a flat bench above the junction of the Bighorn and Little Bighorn rivers. It was to be named Fort Custer, for the flamboyant commander who had led Keogh and more than two hundred of his comrades of the Seventh Cavalry to death and immortality.

On this bright July day in 1877 the steamer *Rosebud*, Captain Grant Marsh at the wheel, nosed into the bank at the Tongue River Cantonment and landed a distinguished military group. William Tecumseh Sherman, grizzled and acerbic head of the U.S. Army, had come to inspect the new forts in the Yellowstone country. Brigadier General Alfred H. Terry, commanding the Department of Dakota, and a bevy of staff officers filed down the gangplank behind Sherman. The post boasted no artillery to salute the four-star general, but the smartly uniformed Fifth Infantry band blared forth the honors and escorted the party to the cantonment.

Also a part of the group was the local commander, Colonel Nelson A. Miles, who had boarded the vessel at the mouth of Glendive Creek. More than any other officer, Miles had cleared the way for the new forts. This was a solid achievement, the result of ability, leadership,

*Robert M. Utley, "War Houses in the Sioux Country," *Montana The Magazine of Western History*, 35 (Autumn 1985), 18-25.

courage, energy, and above all persistence. Shamelessly vain and ambitious, the young colonel made certain the general in chief fully understood where the credit belonged. He deserved special recognition, Miles believed, not only because of his success but also because his wife Mary happened to be General (and Senator) Sherman's niece.[1]

Sherman and his party stayed for three days. Mary was at the post, so Sherman lodged with the Mileses while the rest returned to the *Rosebud* at night. They toured the old cantonment and the new fort and socialized with the garrison's officers at the quarters of the colonel and his lady. On the final day the regiment drew up in formation. Sherman pinned medals on the tunics of thirty soldiers in recognition of combat heroism. Then, behind its proud colonel, the band playing and banners flying, the Fifth Infantry passed in review before the commanding general. Only a week afterward, Miles again played host as Lieutenant General Philip H. Sheridan, commander of the Division of the Missouri, arrived with his staff to inspect Fort Keogh.[2]

In one sentence Sherman summed up the significance of these ceremonies: "The Sioux Indians," he said, "can never again regain this country." At last, with the establishment of Fort Keogh and Fort Custer, the Great Father's "war houses" had been planted in the very heart of the Teton Sioux domain. The generals, the bands, the flags, and the medals symbolized the culmination of almost fifteen years of striving for this goal. During this time, virtually all military activity in the lower Yellowstone Basin was either an effort to establish such posts or a costly demonstration of the need for them. Now the war houses had finally come, and, as Sherman had predicted, never did the Sioux regain the Yellowstone country.

The need for war houses on the Yellowstone, of course, was strictly a perception of the white people, not the Indians—an essential step if this country were to be taken from its Teton Sioux inhabitants. They had possessed it for nearly a century, ever since seizing it from the Crow. Two groups of Teton tribes overlapped and mingled along the Yellowstone. The Hunkpapa and Blackfeet Sioux tribes ranged north and east as far as the Missouri River. Oglala, Miniconjou, and Sans Arc Sioux, with their Northern Cheyenne and Arapaho allies, ranged southward in the valleys of the Powder, Tongue, Rosebud, and Bighorn and eastward to the Black Hills.

---

1.   Nelson A. Miles' boastful self-promotion may be traced in letters in the Sherman Papers at the Library of Congress and in Miles' letters reproduced in Virginia W. Johnson, *The Unregimented General: A Biography of Nelson A. Miles* (Boston: Houghton-Mifflin, 1962).

2.   Secretary of War, *Annual Report, House Exec. Doc.* 1, Part 2, Vol. 2, 45th Cong., 2d sess., 1877 (Serial 1794), 55-56, 542-45, 574-75; Johnson, *Unregimented General*, 178-81.

Not until the 1860s did an Indian threat to whites focus serious military attention on the Yellowstone Basin. Fur trappers had worked this country for more than half a century, and here and there they had even constructed short-lived trading posts. Army topographical engineers explored and crudely mapped the area in the 1850s. But it was not until gold was discovered in the mountains to the west in 1862–1864 that Indians confronted whites on the Yellowstone. Argonauts bound for the diggings went up the Missouri River by steamboat or, more ominously, sought overland routes. These travelers upset the Hunkpapa and Blackfeet Sioux. Other gold-seekers pioneered the route that became known as the Bozeman Trail, which angled northwest from the Platte, headed the Powder, Tongue, and Bighorn rivers, and struck the Yellowstone on its upper reaches. These whites disturbed the Oglala, Sans Arc, and Miniconjou Sioux.

Most Teton Sioux had remained haughtily aloof from relations with white officials. Some had signed the Fort Laramie Treaty of 1851 and another treaty, never ratified, imposed on them at Fort Pierre in 1857 by Brigadier General William S. Harney. A few, held in contempt by their tribesmen, accepted rations and supplies at Fort Pierre each year. But in 1862, even they broke diplomatic relations. The agent at Fort Pierre reported that the Teton Sioux declared they would tolerate no emigration, either by land or water. They said "they would not submit to it," he wrote, "as emigrants brought disease and pestilence into their country"; moreover, "the buffalo would not return to that section of the country where they had been pursued by white men."[3]

But the emigrants came anyway, and so did the army, which could not deal effectively with such insolent Sioux without a base in their country from which to operate. So, at least, reasoned Major General John Pope, the bombastic commander exiled to Minnesota after his defeat at Second Manassas. Pope had been assigned to clean up the wreckage of the bloody Sioux uprising of 1862, which spilled over into Dakota Territory as Santee Sioux fugitives fled from wrathful Minnesotans. Operating in Dakota in 1863 and 1864, Pope's subordinates, Brigadier General Henry H. Sibley and Brigadier General Alfred Sully, stirred up the Teton Sioux. One of Sully's assignments in the campaign of 1864, therefore, was to build a fort on the Yellowstone River from which to control the Teton Sioux.

Sully succeeded only partly, although he did extraordinarily well in his other missions. From newly constructed Fort Rice, on the Missouri River at the mouth of the Cannonball, he struck westward

3. Commissioner of Indian Affairs, *Annual Report*, 37th Cong., 3d sess., 1862, *House Exec. Doc.* 1, vol. 1 (Serial 1156), 196.

at the head of more than two thousand soldiers. Even though bur-
dened with a train of 123 wagons loaded with Montana-bound
goldseekers, he sought out and soundly defeated a large aggregation
of Teton Sioux at Killdeer Mountain. Then, harassed by Sioux war
parties, he marched across the parched, dusty Little Missouri
Badlands—"hell with the fires burned out," he called them—and
ultimately struck the Yellowstone. Here, to his great good fortune,
two supply steamers met the column.

But no other boats could be expected that season. As would happen often in future years, the river fell so swiftly that the vessels bearing materials for the new fort failed to reach their destination. Sully
compromised. Marching downstream to the Missouri, he laid out a
military reservation adjacent to the old fur-trading post of Fort Union,
established a supply depot, and left a garrison to man it. Although
the Yellowstone remained securely in the possession of the Teton
Sioux, Fort Rice and the incipient post at the mouth of the Yellowstone (which became Fort Buford in 1866) brought the military frontier to the very edges of the Indians' hunting range.[4]

Sully took the field again in 1865, but this year the fort-building
mission fell to Major General Patrick Edward Connor, a pugnacious
Irishman who had done well in Utah Territory and had been sent
to try his hand against the Sioux. From bases to the south, Connor
threw three strong columns into the Powder and Yellowstone country. They came close to disaster. The Indians simply kept out of the
way while Connor's logistical system broke down and left his striking arms to flounder about in rain, sleet, snow, and mud. Weather
killed nearly a thousand horses and mules; and as they fell, starving
soldiers stripped the flesh from the bones and devoured it raw.
Despite these reverses, Connor, like Sully, did succeed in placing a
fort on the edge of the Sioux country. On the upper Powder River,
his men built Fort Connor.[5]

Fort Connor was to prove less than durable. The following year,
renamed Fort Reno, it became the first of three forts built in the
Powder River country to guard the Bozeman Trail. Sioux anger focused

4. Official reports and correspondence relating to the Sully Expedition are in *The
War of the Rebellion: A Compilation of the Official Records of the Union and Confederate Armies*,
ser. 1, vol. 41, pt. 1, pp. 131-74, 795-96; pt. 2, pp. 38-39, 80-81, 228, 591, 616-17, 628,
675-79, 737, 767-68; pt. 3, pp. 219, 466-67, 626-28, 698-701. A good synthesis of the
evidence is Rev. Louis Pfaller, O. S. B., "The Sully Expedition of 1864 Featuring the
Killdeer Mountain and Badlands Battles," *North Dakota History*, 31 (January 1964), 1-54.

5. Reports and documents relating to the Connor operations are printed in LeRoy
R. Hafen and Ann W. Hafen, eds., *Powder River Campaigns and Sawyers Expedition of 1865*
(Glendale, Calif.: Arthur H. Clark, 1961). For a narrative account, see Fred B. Rogers,
*Soldiers of the Overland: Being Some Account of the Services of General Patrick Edward Connor
and His Volunteers of the Old West* (San Francisco: Grabhorn Press, 1938), chapters 18-24.

on the other two. In December 1866, Indians wiped out the eighty-man force of Captain William J. Fetterman near Fort Phil Kearny; and despite defeats at the Wagon Box and Hayfield Fights in the summer of 1867, they won the war. In the Fort Laramie Treaty of 1868, the United States surrendered to Red Cloud and his fighting men. The abandonment of Fort Reno, Fort Phil Kearny, and Fort C. F. Smith humiliated the army, but in truth the effort was no longer worth the cost: The rapid construction of the Union Pacific Railroad made the Montana mines much more accessible from points farther west.[6]

The Fort Laramie Treaty ended the war for the Bozeman Trail, but for the U.S. government it laid the groundwork for endless difficulties with the Teton Sioux in the very country where the generals had tried, and failed, to fix a permanent military presence. The treaty set aside all of present-day South Dakota west of the Missouri River as the Great Sioux Reservation, and the Indians were encouraged to settle there and draw rations at the six agencies established for their benefit (and management).   But the Teton Sioux had won the war, and concessions by the United States were in order. They took the form of "unceded Indian territory" west of the reservation. Here, Indians who did not want to live on the reservation could continue to follow the bison without disturbance from whites, who were excluded altogether. The treaty vaguely defined the unceded territory as north of the North Platte River and east of the Bighorn Mountains.[7] Whether it extended as far north as the Yellowstone might have been debated, although apparently it was not. In the minds of the Indians, there was no uncertainty; this was Sioux country, and had been ever since they wrested it from the Crow.

Although most of the Teton Sioux, perhaps twenty-five thousand, ultimately settled on the Great Sioux Reservation, the unceded territory afforded a refuge for the "hunting bands," or "northern Indians." These people wanted nothing to do with treaties, agencies, or white people, and so long as the bison ran they could maintain themselves comfortably in the valleys of the Yellowstone and its tributaries. These Indians looked for leadership to chiefs such as Black Moon, Gall, Crazy Horse, and, towering over all, Sitting Bull. This chieftain, enjoying commanding authority even beyond his own Hunkpapa tribe, had risen steadily in influence ever since the war

---

6. There is an extensive literature of the Red Cloud War. See especially James C. Olson, *Red Cloud and the Sioux Problem* (Lincoln: University of Nebraska Press, 1965), chapters 3 and 4. I have treated the subject and cited sources in Robert M. Utley, *Frontier Regulars: The United States Army and the Indian, 1866–1891* (New York: Macmillan, 1973), chapters 6 and 8.

7. For the text of the treaty see Charles J. Kappler, comp., *Indian Affairs: Laws and Treaties* (7 vols., Washington, D.C.: Government Printing Office, 1904-1941), 2: 998-1007.

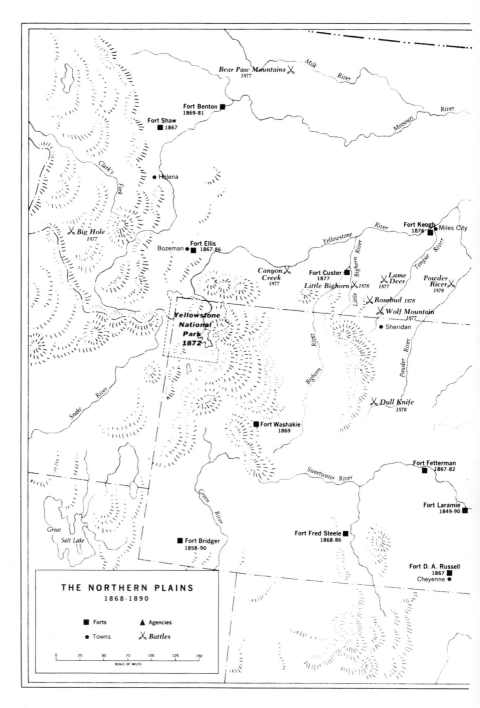

THE NORTHERN PLAINS
1868-1890

■ Forts   ▲ Agencies
● Towns   ✗ Battles

0   25   50   75   100   125   150
SCALE OF MILES

Courtesy of University of New Mexico Press

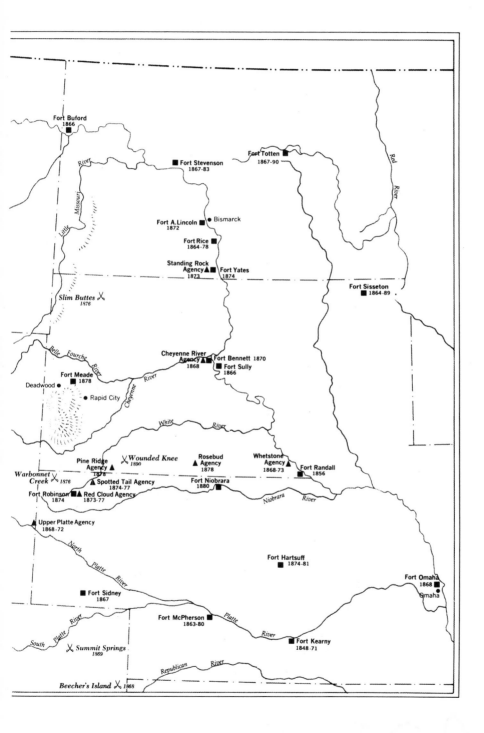

with General Sully. He stubbornly resisted all blandishments from white officials and all material attractions offered by the agencies.

The Indians of these hunting bands and the white people made constant trouble for each other. The groups in the unceded country offered haven for discontented agency Indians. Indeed, great numbers sampled the best of both worlds—the old free hunting life in the summer and the security and rations of the agencies in the winter. They created endless turmoil on the reservation, for they were unmanageable, dangerous to agency officials, and a bad influence on their brethren who remained there year-round. Off the reservation to the west, they and some of the hunting bands as well did not always stay within the unceded territory. Sometimes war parties raided along the Platte and among the Montana settlements at the head of the Missouri and Yellowstone rivers.

For their part, the whites did not take too seriously their promise to respect the lands guaranteed the Sioux in the Fort Laramie Treaty. As General Sherman observed in 1870, "I suppose we must concede to the Sioux the right to hunt from the Black Hills . . . to the Big Horn Mountains, but the ultimate title to the land is regarded as surrendered"[8] In fact, the authors of the treaty expected the bison to disappear swiftly and leave the Sioux no choice but to go to the reservation. This did not happen soon enough to forestall conflict arising from white pressure on the Sioux hunting grounds.

The first serious pressure came from the Northern Pacific Railroad, which expected to lay tracks up the Yellowstone Valley. "That Northern Pacific Road is going to give you a great deal of trouble," Sherman wrote to General Sheridan in September 1872, but the army ought to give every possible assistance, "as it will help to bring the Indian problem to a final solution."[9] Summer expeditions in 1871, 1872, and 1873 escorted railroad surveying parties into the Yellowstone country. In several armed clashes with the bluecoats, the Sioux made clear their attitude toward this invasion.

However disturbing these harbingers of an approaching railroad, the truly infuriating act of bad faith came in 1874, when the Custer expedition explored the Black Hills and discovered gold. The Black Hills were not in the unceded territory, but were part of the Great Sioux Reservation itself. The stampede to the diggings that inevitably followed stirred up the Sioux, agency and hunting groups alike, as no other provocation could.

---

8.   Sherman to Brig. Gen. C. C. Augur, June 9, 1870, Sherman Papers, vol. 89, pp. 168-69, Library of Congress.

9.   Sherman to Sheridan, September 26, 1872, Sherman-Sheridan Papers, Library of Congress. Sheridan's role as commander of the Division of the Missouri is ably set forth in Paul A. Hutton, *Phil Sheridan and His Army* (Lincoln: University of Nebraska Press, 1985).

So, early in the 1870s, the waning hope of war houses on the Yellowstone was reawakened in the minds of the generals. Already a blue cordon had tightened around the frontiers of the Sioux domain. Backing up Fort Rice and Fort Buford, Fort Stevenson (1867), Fort Lincoln (1872), Fort Yates (1874), and Fort Bennett (1870) sprouted along the line of the Missouri River in Dakota Territory. In western Montana Territory, where the Missouri curved around the far western reaches of Sioux country, the army established Fort Benton (1869), Fort Shaw (1867), and Fort Ellis (1867) to shield the Montana mining settlements. To the south, Fort Fetterman (1867), on the North Platte north of Fort Laramie, watched over the southern boundary of the unceded territory. Now, with the Sioux contesting the advance of the Northern Pacific, the generals once again wanted to leap into the midst of Sioux country.

Both Sherman and Sheridan urged Congress to appropriate $200,000 to build two permanent posts in the Yellowstone Basin. Explaining the need early in 1873, Sherman wrote: "This railroad is a national enterprise, and we are forced to protect the men during its survey and construction, through, probably, the most warlike nation of Indians on this continent, who will fight for every foot of the line. It is a matter of war requiring near two thousand troops, who in winter must be sheltered."[10]

That was the nub of it. If the troops were to fight a war of such magnitude, they must be sheltered in the winter. Connor's experience in 1865 had dramatized the perils that awaited strong columns trying to operate in this country without fixed bases. Most of their energies went into keeping themselves supplied, and even then they courted logistical collapse.

Sherman's justification turned out to be an accurate forecast of events to come. Each year for three years Congress debated the request without providing the money. Then, as the government made its final move against the unceded territory, the great Sioux War of 1876 broke over the northern plains. Like Connor before him, Sheridan launched three heavy columns into the Powder and Yellowstone country. The supply system—wagon trains provisioning Brigadier General George Crook from the south, steamboats supporting General Terry and Colonel John Gibbon on the Yellowstone—proved to be adequate during the summer months. The military reverses sustained by Crook on the Powder and Rosebud and by Custer on the Little Bighorn sprang from other than logistical failings. But after the Custer disaster, as the Indians scattered, the weather turned bad, and the columns swelled with reinforcements,

---

10. February 14, 1873, as read in House debates on the army appropriation act, *Congressional Globe*, 42d Cong., 3d sess., March 3, 1873, p. 2096.

A dress parade at Fort Custer about 1892. The post stood a scant dozen miles from the Little Bighorn battlefield, near the confluence of the Bighorn and Little Bighorn rivers. (Montana Historical Society Photograph Archives)

General Terry and General Crook came close to duplicating Connor's record. Crook's "Starvation March" was only the dramatic culmination of a logistical nightmare produced by supply lines that were too long and tenuous to support the scale of operations.[11]

Colonel Miles made up for the failures of Terry and Crook. The Indians called him "Bear's Coat" in tribute to the cold-weather gear he and his foot soldiers wore in their operations during the winter

11. The literature of these events is vast. I have treated them, and cited selected sources, in *Frontier Regulars*, chapters 14-15. A particularly cogent analysis of the role and movements of the hunting bands is John S. Gray, *Centennial Campaign: The Sioux War of 1876* (Fort Collins, Colo.: Old Army Press, 1976).

of 1876–1877. To the south, Crook and Colonel Ranald S. Mackenzie hounded the Indians, but it was the unrelenting pursuit of Miles, working out of the ramshackle cantonment at the mouth of Tongue River, that so demoralized them that they either gave up or fled north to the land of the Great Mother and her redcoats.

Miles's winter campaign validated the judgment of Sherman and Sheridan. They needed the permanent forts in the Yellowstone country. Even before "Bear's Coat" threw up the huts of the Tongue River Cantonment, the long-sought authorization had materialized. Scarcely two weeks after news of Custer's annihilation electrified the nation, Congress made haste to strengthen the army. One of the measures was to appropriate $200,000 for the new posts.[12]

The appropriation allowed the army to remain permanently on the Yellowstone. But for Fort Keogh and Fort Custer—and the tireless Miles—Chief Joseph and his Nez Perce could not have been cut off in their flight for Canada in 1877. But for these forts—and Miles—the Sioux refugees in Canada could not have been kept away from the Montana bison herds, their only hope of survival, and ultimately forced to surrender. By the time Sitting Bull handed over his rifle at Fort Buford in 1881, Sherman had persuaded Congress that Fort Keogh and Fort Custer were not enough, and he pointed proudly to Fort Maginnis and Fort Assinniboine while complaining that he needed still one more.

As he prepared to hand over his office to Sheridan and step into retirement, Sherman also took pride in the spread of settlement and the advance of railroads that such permanent military garrisons made possible. Even as the last spike went into the Northern Pacific tracks in 1883, stockmen and farmers overspread the Yellowstone and its tributary valleys. "Prosperous farms and cattle ranches exist where ten years ago no man could venture," the general wrote in 1880. "This is largely due to the soldier, but in equal, if not greater measure, to the adventurous pioneers themselves, and to that new and greatest of civilizers, the railroad."[13]

Truly, as Sherman prophesied in 1877, Fort Keogh and Fort Custer ensured that the Sioux would never regain the Yellowstone Basin.

---

12. 19 Stat. 95-96 (July 22, 1876).
13. Secretary of War, *Annual Report, House Exec. Doc.* 1, Part 2, Vol. 2, 46th Cong., 3d sess., 1880 (Serial 1952), 4, 54.

Custer is remembered in bronze. Indian memorials are mostly spiritual. L. A. Huffman titled this photograph poignantly but simply, "A Sioux Warrior's Grave." (Montana Historical Society Photograph Archives)

A Monument to Custer

by Minnie Dubbs Millbrook

Comrades, our children shall yet tell their story,
Custer's last charge on old Sitting Bull,
And ages shall swear that the cup of his glory
Needed but that death to render it full.

The writer of this quatrain, Frederick Whittaker, made the same prophecy more formally in the September, 1876, issue of *Galaxy Magazine*: "Whom the god love die young . . . [Custer] found the one thing needed to complete his character as an ideal hero of romance — a glorious and terrible death. . . . Requiescat in gloria."

Inventor of innumerable heroes in his widely read dime novels, Frederick Whittaker felt he knew the basic hero formula. Certainly George Armstrong Custer had all the attributes — youth, good looks, colorful and audacious personality, a brilliant and well-publicized fighting record in the Civil War and on the western plains. Finally he had been struck down on a flaming hill near the Little Big Horn River in the southern part of Montana Territory just as a prideful nation was celebrating its centennial summer.

The flaw in this otherwise heroic sequence was that the invincible commander had marched with more than two hundred men, not only "into the jaws of death," but into total defeat, leaving not one trooper alive on the battlefield. Indians had wiped out entire military detachments before, but never one so large or commanded by so renowned and experienced a leader. The wholesale death was shocking to the public mind, but the question remained about how glorious it was or indeed how strategic.

It is not the intention here to relate or re-argue the affair on the Little Big Horn. It has been done often enough; indeed, the prolonged, contentious debate has tended to obscure other details of the Custer story which add dimension and interest to the tragedy

---

*Minnie Dubbs Millbrook, "A Monument to Custer," *Montana The Magazine of Western History*, 24 (Spring 1974), 18-33.

that stirred the country so profoundly. Among these were the moves, taken very early, to raise monuments to the dashing commander, monuments designed to honor the shining knight and reaffirm the popular belief in the warrior epic. The image makers of 1876 may not have been as expert as the professionals of today, but they labored with diligence and dedication. And playing a counterpoint to all the efforts was the stubborn, critical presence of Elizabeth Bacon Custer, the widow who was to devote the remainder of her life—57 years— to preserving the heroic image of her fallen husband.

The New York *Herald*, a newspaper that always seemed to get there first with the most news about all the more spectacular happenings of the day, had a special regard for George Armstrong Custer. Its reporters had noted his brilliance in the Civil War, had kept an eye on him in the West, and finally a *Herald* representative had died with him. The newspaper defended Custer staunchly and vociferously, shouting down any intimation that the cavalry officer had been un- wise in his troop dispositions or had not precisely followed the orders of his superiors. Culprits aplenty were found to blame for the mas- sacre, ranging from President Ulysses S. Grant ("Behold your hands! They are red with the blood of Custer and his brave three hundred!") on down through the ranks to the subordinate officers of the Seventh Cavalry ("There is buried with the dead a terrible secret. Benteen, who won golden opinions . . . will have to explain why his battalion failed to appear . . . on the battlefield.")[1]

Encomiums were printed from the great and mighty as well as from old cavalrymen and youthful admirers. Although the calamity was not publicly known until July 6, 1876, and the story first appeared in the *Herald* of July 7, an editorial three days later suggested A NATIONAL MONUMENT TO THE BRAVE CUSTER.

> The *Herald* recommends that a national monument be erected to commemorate the heroism of General Custer and his kinsmen who fell with him. . . . Every contribution should be the free offer- ing of a generous and admiring citizen and the monument national in the sense of funds supplied by patriotic people in all parts of the country.

To start off the project, the newspaper announced it would pledge $1,000.00 and called for contributions from its readers.

In Monroe, Michigan, the residence of Custer's aged parents, his brother, Nevin, and many schoolmates, the idea of a monument also sprang quickly to mind. Four other men from Monroe, all of them personally close to the commander, had joined him in death at the

---

1. New York *Herald*, July 7, and September 21, 1876.

Little Big Horn. They were his brothers, Boston and Tom Custer, his brother-in-law, James Calhoun, and his nephew, Harry Armstrong Reed. It was no wonder that the first issue of the weekly Monroe *Commercial*, after the disaster, dated July 13, 1876, was printed with heavy black column rules. Besides a recital of the shocking details of the battle, the paper expressed the hope that a monument could be erected: "The fallen heroes deserve to be remembered in some more enduring form than speeches and newspaper articles. A monument is an outward memory; it is the concrete objective expression of admiration and reverence."

Although the Monroe group lagged behind the *Herald* in initiating solicitations, it seemed to have had a definite idea of the kind of monument it wanted and immediately approached Clark Mills, the country's most noted sculptor. The *Commercial* reported that Mills intended to represent Custer with his long hair and in his cavalry costume, brandishing his saber while charging the enemy.

Meanwhile, in New York, contributions were coming in. Judge Henry Hilton donated $1,000.00. Actor Lawrence Barrett, Custer's close friend, sent $250.00 and offered to give a benefit. Clara Louise Kellogg, the American prima donna, pledged $100.00. Miscellaneous gifts included 10 cents from a poor boy, and $2.00 from the waiters of the Union Hotel in Saratoga. One contributor enclosed a poem, which the *Herald* published on July 16:

> Here's to brave young Custer,
> Whose life we held so dear.
> He did what he could with the odds in front
> And a snake in the grass in the rear.

There were, however, some objections to the monument idea. A collection for Mrs. Custer was suggested as a more suitable alternative. "She is now reduced to beggary," an item quoted in the July 13 issue of the *Herald* said, ". . . Do you not think that if Custer himself could speak he would prefer bread for his widow to a stone for himself?" This was later refuted as nonsense, since Custer had been well insured for his time, and Mrs. Custer's father had been wealthy.

Even more directly opposed to the monument idea was General Samuel D. Sturgis, Colonel of the Seventh Cavalry, whose promising young son, Lt. James G. Sturgis, had died on that barren hill. His bitter comments were quoted in the New York *Times* in its issue of July 17:

> If a monument is to be erected to General Custer for God's sake let them hide it in some dark valley, or veil it, or put it anywhere the bleeding hearts of the widows, orphans, fathers and mothers of the

men so uselessly sacrificed to Custer's ambition, can never be wrung
at the sight of it.

The *Herald* retaliated quickly, publishing in some detail the mis-
adventures and defeats of Sturgis' own military career. He was pictured an old, worn-out officer cowering behind a desk while his brave
young subordinates went out to meet the danger and die.

Back in Monroe, the Custer Monument Association completed its
organization, naming General Philip H. Sheridan as president. He
lent the use of his "facsimile" signature, although he was too busy
to participate actively. Other prominent men were enlisted to head
auxiliaries in every state in the Union. John L. Bulkley of Monroe,
secretary of the association, became chief historian of the effort to
honor the town's hero. Bulkley had been a seatmate of Custer at the
Stebbins Academy and a groomsman at the Custer wedding early in
1864. Later he acquired the school desk at which he sat beside Custer
and kept some of the materials of the association in it. He remembered the appalling labors of his office; typewriters being then non-
existent, more than five thousand letters of appeal had been written
by hand.

On August 6, 1876, "one of the saddest parties ever brought to
Monroe" arrived from Fort Abraham Lincoln, near present-day
Bismarck, North Dakota, the post from which the dashing young commander had led his troops to battle four months before. Three ladies
who had so enjoyed the company of their officer husbands at the
post were in the party: Mrs. Custer, her sister-in-law, Mrs. James
Calhoun, and Mrs. George W. Yates, wife of the captain of Company
F who died on Custer Hill. The bereaved widows went into total retirement; later there was little recollection of their presence in Monroe
except when they appeared occasionally to walk by the river in a black-
clad line.

Although the newspapers had stated repeatedly that the widows
would make their permanent home in Monroe, Elizabeth Bacon
Custer had no intention of living out her life in her native town. The
wider, freer society of military life, together with the exciting inter-
ludes in Washington and New York, had convinced her that she could
never return to small town life. Undoubtedly the sentiments she had
expressed in a letter to her husband in July, 1873, were still valid in
August, 1876: "Monroe seems determined to spoil me. But I find it
hard to rise above depressing surroundings without your help. There
are not many joyous people here. The women are so fagged with
domestic cares, kitchen drudgery, leading a monotonous life, the men
without bright women to cheer them up. . . . No civil life for me except
as a visitor."

Yet fate had brought Elizabeth Custer face to face with civilian life. Although many historians portray her as a timid, retiring lady who could scarcely tie her own shoes without help, Mrs. Custer's course after her husband's death belies any such estimate. Decisively, she set out to affirm and amplify her general's fame. Of all the image makers, she turned out to be the most successful.

No one had consulted Mrs. Custer about the monuments for which both New York and Monroe were collecting funds, but it was her action that decided the matter. John Bulkley, who had planned so eagerly and proudly for the Monroe statue, recalled in a story printed in the Detroit *Post and Tribune* on September 1, 1879:

> . . . The statement was made in some newspapers that it was the expressed wish of Gen. Custer that whenever or wherever he should die his remains should be interred at West Point. This statement at once gave the impression that if his body was to rest at that place the monument should also be placed there. This was by no means a logical argument, but strong enough to kill the local interest in a great measure, which was the result, aided materially by the further announcement that Mrs. Custer preferred to have the monument at West Point or in New York. This, of course, ended the matter of having a monument at Monroe.

The monument association was caught with its letters written and on the verge of a general campaign. Monroe was set back on its heels. Nothing hurts like a beneficence scorned, and the schism opened between Elizabeth Custer and her home town never quite closed.

The *Herald* in New York continued its appeal. Subscription lists were opened in various clubs, at Delmonico's and in leading hotels. A ball was proposed at White Sulphur Springs; General Ramseur's brother sent a donation from Atlanta and August Belmont subscribed $100.00. Then for almost a year, beginning the last of August, 1876, the newspaper ceased to mention the monument or subscription drive.

Interest in Custer and the Battle of the Little Big Horn, however, persisted. The stubborn Hunkpapa Sioux medicine man, Sitting Bull, who in the eyes of the public had been Custer's chief opponent, had fled into Canada with his followers. Apparently he had many visitors there, for reports came back to the *Herald* of assorted interviews, which, confused and contradictory though they were, found space in the paper.

Sitting Bull said, in one interview published in the issue of November 16, 1877, that Custer had been the last to die: "He laughed having fired the last shot from his pistol." In another interview published on December 5, 1877, Sitting Bull declared that the

Americans were too tired to fight that hot day late in June: "Our powder was scarce, and we killed the soldiers with our war clubs."

Custer's widow apparently went to New York in September, 1876, presumably to collaborate with Frederick Whittaker in writing his *Complete Life of Gen. George A. Custer.* He freely acknowledged her help with the book, for it did indeed contain intimate stories of the hero's childhood that could only have been supplied by someone very close to the family.

More than that, the persuasive little lady had completely changed Whittaker's attitude toward the battle.

It is revealing to compare the ten-page biography, which Whittaker wrote for *Galaxy* magazine in September, 1876, with the 647-page book which emerged three months later. In the first account, Custer and his troops had simply been overwhelmed by superior numbers; in the second he had been left to die because his subordinate officers disobeyed orders to come to his support.

Furthermore, Whittaker set out on a crusade to not only secure public acceptance of this latter theory, but to punish the men who had let the gallant general down. Along with the New York *Herald*, Whittaker with Mrs. Custer would become one of the more potent makers of the Custer legend as well as the nemesis of Colonel Marcus A. Reno, the man they held most responsible for Custer's death.

Success in persuading and enlisting such a valuable aide as Frederick Whittaker encouraged Elizabeth Custer. She returned to Monroe, but in the spring of 1877 went back to New York to make her permanent home. She would not only tend the flame of her adored one's memory but would prune and shape it into ever more heroic form.

In July, 1877, Colonel Michael V. Sheridan journeyed to the Little Big Horn battlefield to bring back the bodies of the officers interred there the year before. On his return to Fort Abraham Lincoln, he telegraphed Mrs. Custer for further instruction. Hurriedly, she consulted General John H. Schofield, Commandant at West Point, and wrote Sheridan that she had arranged for the service to be delayed until October or November "as there will then be a full corps of cadets and officers at West Point and he [Schofield] can be better able to pay the honor he wishes to the heroic dead." In the interim, the "sacred dust" would be placed in a receiving vault at Poughkeepsie under the care of Mr. Philip Hamilton.[2]

The services held on October 10, 1877, were attended by thousands of people and even greater numbers lined the Hudson River to see

---

2. Elizabeth Custer to Michael Sheridan, July 18, 20, 27, 1877, Philip H. Sheridan Papers, Library of Congress.

the *Mary Powell*, draped in bunting, with flags at half mast, carry the remains from Poughkeepsie to West Point. All the river vessels meeting the funeral craft dipped their flags in respect.

Custer's casket was draped with the flag of Louis McHale Hamilton, who had died during his commander's attack on the Cheyenne encampment at the Washita River in Oklahoma on a bitterly cold November day in 1868, an action which had added immeasurably to Custer's fame as an Indian fighter but which at the same time had planted seeds of doubt in the minds of many, including some of his subordinates. The casket's only floral ornament was a major general's shoulder strap, two feet long and eight inches wide, the background woven of geraniums, the stars of tuberoses.

Mrs. Custer came to the chapel leaning on the arm of General Schofield, followed by the commander's aged father, Emanuel, and his sister, Margaret Calhoun, still in deep mourning for her husband. Dr. Forsythe, West Point chaplain, read part of the Episcopal burial service, and a choir of cadets chanted the 39th and 90th Psalms. Burial was in the beautiful little cemetery north of the post, and when the service was completed, a battalion of 300 cadets fired three volleys over the grave which "reverberated and died mournfully away."

Soon after the interment, the *Herald* once more took up the monument collection appeal, reporting that $4,051.20 had been subscribed and turned over to Banker August Belmont. Stimulated by this news, Actress Clara Morris gave a benefit performance of *Jane Eyre* at Wallack's Theater on Thursday afternoon, November 8, 1877. Since use of the theater, as well as the services of actors, orchestra and ushers were donated, a check for $1,798.50 was added to the fund. By December 13, Treasurer Belmont was holding about $6,000.00, and "we are informed that another thousand dollars is ready to be placed in the hands of the committee."[3] This was the money that had been collected by the monument association in Monroe and, without credit or mention as to its source, reluctantly turned over to the *Herald* fund.

Announcement was now made that designs for the West Point monument would be received. The small amount of money available ruled out an equestrian statue and perhaps made the commission less attractive to sculptors, for only two designs were submitted.

The model accepted was that of J. Wilson Mac Donald, a self-taught sculptor whose first piece had been a bust of Thomas Hart Benton, produced in St. Louis in 1854. Mac Donald had moved to New York and by 1877 had several statues to his credit, among them one of Fitz-Green Halleck in Central Park, New York City.

---

3. New York *Herald*, December 13, 1877; Detroit *Post & Tribune*, September 1, 1879.

A private showing of the Custer model was held for the press, a few invited guests, artists and connoisseurs on August 24, 1878, at the sculptor's studio in the Booth Theatre building.

A reporter for the New York *Times*, in the issue of August 25, remarked on two features of the figure: the closely cropped hair and the modelling of the left hand, "which is raised on guard." He thought many admirers would regret the absence of long hair, "one of the features of the romantic figure that the gallant cavalryman carved for himself in the popular imagination," and suggested the committee might have it changed. He reported that the committee also hoped Congress would support its project with money as well as sufficient bronze from discarded cannon to cast the figure.

Frederick Whittaker, meanwhile, was at last getting results in his campaign to rewrite the official record of the Battle of the Little Big Horn which was, in his view, "false and libelous to the memory of the late Lieut.-Gen. Custer." He had written many censorious and abusive letters that reached the public through some of the New York newspapers, but it was the one sent to the Hon. W. W. Corlett of Wyoming that brought action. When Corlett read the letter in Congress, Marcus Reno, unable to stand the prolonged accusation and calumny, asked for an official inquiry. The hearings were held in Chicago in January and February, 1879. Whittaker was present but, to the disappointment of both him and Mrs. Custer, Reno's conduct was not found worthy of censure.

This was a period of frustration for Elizabeth Custer. She had already played an important—if not the leading—role in protecting her husband's reputation. She had cooperated in providing a flattering biography. She had succeeded in having her hero laid to rest at West Point with reverent, dramatic and widely noted ceremonies. She had certainly been an ardent advocate of bringing Marcus Reno's shortcomings to public notice. But now she was not consulted about the design of her husband's statue. She wrote August Belmont asking who had selected the design. In his reply, Belmont named the committee that had approved the model and also stated that the monument was nearly completed and part of the funds had already been paid to Sculptor Mac Donald.[4]

In her capacity as secretary of the Decorative Art Society, a dispensary of art principles as well as of charity, Mrs. Custer must have heard a great deal about the more eminent artists and sculptors of the day. Mac Donald had not had any of the commissions that were just then beginning to ornament the squares of Washington, many of which

    4.   August Belmont to E. B. Custer, April 3, 1879, Elizabeth B. Custer Collection, Custer Battlefield National Monument, Microfilm Roll II, p. 1649 (hereafter CBNM).

cost from fifty to sixty thousand dollars. It was plain that her general was not receiving proper recognition.

In answer to her query, John Bulkley, the old Monroe friend, wrote Mrs. Custer on July 28, 1879. He had just received a nine-page letter from General Winfield S. Hancock, then in charge at West Point, who "entered very fully into a statement of what the committee . . . had done regarding the monument."

> He says that although the matter was fully stated in the press that designs were wanted—not an artist but LeClaire and McDonald [*sic*] presented any—and that the model of the latter (after a few changes suggested by the committee) was very satisfactory and very much admired by all who had seen it. The statue is completed, the stone for the pedestal on the ground, and everything in readiness to place the statue . . . The precise day had not been fixed. . . . I shall certainly try to be present.[5]

Although Elizabeth Custer was duly invited to the unveiling she chose not to be present. As the press inaccurately reported, she was at home in Monroe and would have to learn of the "honors paid to her hero husband only at second hand."

The monument was unveiled on August 30, 1879, the ceremonies attended by nearly 3,000 people. Many had come from New York on a special steamer chartered by the committee of the Custer fund. Among the names mentioned was that of John M. Bulkley of Monroe, Michigan. Some names were conspicuous by their absence; Clara Morris, who had given the benefit, was there, but not Custer's actor friend, Lawrence Barrett.

Algernon S. Sullivan, chairman of the statue committee, was introduced and made the presentation speech. "It is the good fortune of some soldiers," he said, "that with their death stroke they are swept along at once into the land of legend, and their names are enveloped in the purple mist of song." While the cadet band played *Garry Owen* and the light battery fired a salute of thirteen guns, the sculptor cut the cord and the statue was revealed. The *Herald* reporter described it under the headline, "*An Art Treasure!*"

> The bronze is a figure eight feet in height, and is an accurate likeness of the dead soldier. The dress is a colonel's uniform. The attitude is a spirited one, the left foot being advanced, and the motion of a charge on foot being forcibly expressed by the position. The sword is gripped firmly in the right hand and held well down, while the pistol is in the left hand which is held across the breast and forward. . . . The features

---

5. John Bulkley to Elizabeth Custer, E. B. Custer Collection, CBNM, Microfilm Roll II, p. 1646.

are set in the sternness of battle, and one looking at the statue can well imagine the moment of the gallant hero's struggle. . . .

The statue was accepted by General Schofield, and General Nathaniel P. Banks, greatest orator of the day, gave the main peroration. He began with an elaborate historical account of the Hessian states and people, paying high tribute to their soldierly qualities. Banks was under the impression, also favored at that time by Mrs. Custer, that General Custer was descended from a Hessian soldier who had remained in America after the War of the Revolution. Mrs. Custer would have taken great satisfaction in the whole speech as well as the other features of the day: the song written for the occasion, "Hail and Farewell," and the poem, "Custer's Last Charge," read by the eminent tragedian, John McCulloch.

The reporter from the Detroit *Free Press* also observed the statue favorably:

> The statue shone like gold in its newness. It is of heroic size and very striking in appearance. . . . The whole figure leans forward in the manner that gives the idea that every nerve and muscle is at their utmost tension. It represents Gen. Custer as he stood on foot dealing out pistol shots and saber blows to the last moment. The location is the finest in West Point. . . . It has been said that if Custer could have chosen a site for this monument, he could not have found a more historical or lovelier spot.

The reporter went on to relate some inside information he had picked up at the dedication:

> Strange as it may seem the officers at West Point, at least many of them, were rather lukewarm in their manner of celebrating the day. Several of them sneered at the statue and said it was a ridiculous one. That no solder ever held a sword and a pistol in that way and that Custer was a hero made by the newspapers and said that military men did not look on him as did the general public.

The cadets, however, had no reservations. When they arrived from New York after their long summer's parole and saw the shining statue as they came up the road from the landing, someone yelled, "Three cheers for Custer!" The cheering and whistling continued until the boys entered their quarters in spite of the officers who came out to quiet the bedlam.

John Bulkley wrote Mrs. Custer soon after he returned from West Point to assure her that he had not written the report in the *Free Press*, although it had been attributed to him. He had, however, sent

Elizabeth Bacon Custer hated the statue erected at West Point. She succeeded in getting it removed to storage in 1884. (United States Military Academy, West Point)

accounts to sixteen daily and weekly newspapers in the midwest containing "nothing that could in any way pain or displease you—or any friends
of the dear old fellow." He also felt that since an equestrian statue had
been impossible on account of the expense, the figure was "as satisfactory as any statue could be made—from one point of view especially,
the left front, the likeness is excellent and the attitude very fine. But
you will no doubt see it soon, and then you can give me your impression."

Bulkley also warned the little widow against Frederick Whittaker. He
had heard in New York that the man claimed to represent her and her
sentiments and was attempting to drag "the sacred memory of Armstrong
into public notice" to advance his own pecuniary interest.

Mrs. Custer did not see the statue soon. In fact, she refused to see
it at all. She wrote Vinnie Ream, a Washington sculptress, who had several
years before modeled a head of Custer from life:

> I do not dare trust myself to write but a line about the statue at West
> Point. I was never consulted and did not even know about it until it was
> done. The bitter disappointment I feel is such a cross to me to bear, it
> seems to me I cannot endure it. I shall not see the statue until I can do
> something to counteract the effect of such a face as Mr. McDonald [*sic*]
> has modeled. . . The face of the McDonald statue is said to be that of
> a man sixty years old. My friends are in despair about it and agree with
> me that it is better for me to remain away from West Point than see what
> would throw me into despair.[6]

Can an artist please everybody when he sets out to make a representation of a hero? If not, then who shall he please? Should he show his
subject in a familiar moment, attired in his distinctive habiliments so
that everyone may find him instantly recognizable? Or should he show
his hero in a supreme moment of crisis which immortalizes the event
as well as the man? The public saw Custer a long-haired youth, waving
his sword and galloping his horse into battle. But at the Little Big Horn
the general had no long curls, no sword and, at the end, no horse. He
wore a buckskin coat instead of an army blouse. Every artist of the several
dozen who have tried to paint Custer in his last battle have faced this
dilemma—how to make a definite identifiable picture of the cavalryman
on that day when he fought and died, stripped of all his trademarks.

Mac Donald had bowed to public opinion and given his Custer
long hair. No one complained of that unauthentic detail, although
most of the criticisms had touched on the inaccuracies of costume
and military posture. Mrs. Custer had a very definite idea of how
her husband should be dressed in a statuary representation. She was

---

6. Elizabeth Custer to Vinnie Ream, September 26, 1879, Vinnie Ream Hoxie
Papers, Library of Congress.

at this time arranging for a replica of Vinnie Ream's bust of the General. Hence she discussed in a letter what her husband should wear:

> I feel attached to his real western suit but since the frontiersmen have become show men and the sensational papers have spread broadcast the buckskin clothes I do not like to think of Autie as represented for all time in them. I have a sentiment and tender love for the style of dress that he adorned by his inimitable way of wearing them . . . The shoulder straps of a major genl, a blouse perhaps and open throat with a broad collar that Autie himself introduced when he first wore navy blue shirts. No one who knew Autie thinks of him dressed like Genl Wool or Genl Scott—buttoned up to the throat but for all that an undress uniform would be better I think than the buckskin . . .[7]

Some months later Vinnie Ream, now Mrs. Hoxie, wrote that Mac Donald and some of his backers were introducing a bill into Congress to have the West Point monument duplicated and erected in Washington. Mrs. Custer was indignant:

> I am so thankful to you for writing to me about this new effort of McDonald [*sic*]. If it had not been for you I should never have known about it—perhaps until too late as in the instance of the statue at West Point. My blood boils at the thought of that wretched statue being repeated. . . . I cannot think the statue else than a great insult to Autie's memory.

She gathered her forces to resist the duplication of the travesty at West Point. She wrote for help to Lawrence Barrett, her husband's "Choicest, dearest friend. Who then can I so fitly ask as the man my husband loved." Would he use all his influence in Washington? She went on again to describe the horrible statue:

> The face is that of a man of sixty. The dress is so non-military his brother officers shudder in looking at it. He is represented with a full dress coat the top boots that only belong to undress uniform. The whole costume is incongruous and incorrect. Then he is armed like a desperado in both hands—while some of General Custer's most brilliant charges were made without a firearm about him.

Vinnie Ream Hoxie had many friends among senators and congressmen whom she now alerted. Edward Whittaker, Custer's chief of staff in the Civil War, was at the head of the Washington Monu-

---

7.   Elizabeth Custer to Mrs. Hoxie, March 15, 1889, Vinnie Ream Hoxie Papers, Library of Congress. Although this letter is tentatively dated 1879 by the Library of Congress, it was probably written in 1880. See letter from Mrs. Custer to Lawrence Barrett on the same subject, April 6, 1880, also in the Hoxie Papers.

ment Committee and he denounced "the idea of representing General Custer in any other manner than mounted as commander of the Third Cavalry Division in April 1865."

Altogether the protesters prevailed. Mac Donald's bill, H.R. 4841, was reported unfavorably from the committee to which it was assigned. The Hon. Mr. Daggett cited a letter from Mrs. Custer disapproving the statue as well as a petition from certain citizens of Detroit, Michigan, and Rochester, New York, "against any measures being taken by Congress for the erection of a monument to General Custer on account of his alleged departure from the rules of organized warfare" presumably at the Battle of the Washita.[8] Elated at their victory, the plotters contemplated a bill of their own for erecting a proper monument in Washington, but the time seemed inappropriate.

The widow Custer set herself to get rid of the West Point monument once and for all. Historians have said she "cried it off its pedestal." Actually, the tears had to be applied in the right places — and persistently. General Sherman had helped her to get her pension raised. Now she wrote him again, in October, 1882:

> I had almost lost hope that anything would be done about removing the statue from West Point until last week. I met Secretary (Robert) Lincoln accidentally and was presented to him. He broached the subject himself and said that he had received my letter and that he knew from that, how deeply interested I was in the matter and that all agree that I was right about desiring the removal of the statue as every one pronounced it outrageous. He told me that he had made an effort in that direction but met with no sympathy from General Howard and had dropped the question on that account. Now that a new Commandant was appointed he would again bring up the subject and do what he could.
>
> I was amazed to find that the Secretary of War looked for assistance from the Commandant at West Point. I had an idea he would direct what he wished and the commandant would obey. It frightens me dear General Sherman, because of this vital matter to me rests so much in other hands, I have little hope. But what hope I now have rests in you the kindest and truest of friends to me, when I so need all that they can do to make my sad life endurable.
>
> I tell you frankly I do not believe that General Merritt will interest himself to aid the Secretary of War in hiding that statue unless you ask him to do it, dear General Sherman. A wife's love sharpens her eyes and quickens her instinct and years ago I knew (not from my husband) that General Merritt was his enemy. On the plains we entertained him and he seemed to have conquered his enmity and jealousy that was so bitter in the Army of the Potomac. But when he was placed

---

8. *Congressional Record*, 46th Congress, 2nd Session, 2629, 3264.

at the head of the Court of Inquiry that sat to investigate Col. Reno's conduct at Chicago—I saw all through the trial how General Merritt still felt towards his dead comrade. . . . I am afraid he will not care whether General Custer's memory is insulted by such an audacious and conspicuous representation as that surely is.

Mrs. Custer wanted the figure to be taken down and stored temporarily. She could then place on the pedestal a granite shaft and set it at the head of her husband's grave. It would not do just to move the monument further back to a more inconspicuous place because *still* she "would be compelled to get the figure out of the way in some manner," for she could not "live in peace and know that such a blot was before the people."[9]

Elizabeth Custer went to Europe, hoping that General Sherman would invoke his official influence and before her return the repulsive statue would have disappeared. But her hopes were blasted; the statue remained there. This matter of the statue had put the Secretary of War in something of a quandary. The money for the monument had been raised by public subscription from all parts of the nation; the design had been approved by prominent men of New York and the statue had been officially accepted for permanent exhibit at West Point. How could he announce that the figure was a travesty and must be hidden from sight? Sherman procrastinated.

But the persistent lady did not give up. She enlisted another supporter, the Hon. Leonard Swett of Chicago, Illinois, formerly a law partner of Robert Lincoln. Now her pleas for action to the Secretary of War went to Washington enclosed in letters from Mr. Swett. Lincoln's letter to Swett April 25, 1884, showed plainly the dilemma in which the Secretary was caught:

> This matter of what is to be done with the statue of Gen. Custer is not free of difficulty, but I have hopes of being able to accomplish something before I go out of office. . . . When I see Gen. Merritt this summer I am going to renew the subject with him. Possibly a gradual removal might be begun which would result in making it difficult to find the statue. If it had been put up by the government of course there would be no difficulty, but I understand that it was erected by the contributions of a number of prominent citizens, who presumably take great pride in it, and with whom it would be difficult to consult.

The hint was not lost on Mrs. Custer. The Secretary might hesitate to consult with the prominent citizens but the stubborn little widow

---

9. Elizabeth Custer to General William T. Sherman, Oct. 15, 1882, Sherman Papers, Library of Congress.

did not. She knew what she wanted and she could write a mighty persuasive letter. She asked, and received, permission from most of the large donors to move the statue.[10]

The *fait accompli* was apparently presented to Secretary Lincoln through another letter from his friend, Swett. The Secretary wrote on November 28, 1884:

> I do not think it practicable to comply with Mrs. Custer's request that the statue be removed to the battlefield of the Big Horn for two reasons; First the basis for its removal from its pedestal at West Point is that it is devoid of artistic merit and is offensive to the eye. Both of these reasons would be inconsistent with an order directing it to be set up in any public place. Secondly, in 1878, Congress made an appropriation of a number of bronze cannon to assist in the erection of the statue of Gen. Custer at West Point. No doubt these cannon went into this statue. It would be of doubtful propriety for me to order a statue thus made, the location of which was fixed in an act of Congress to be set up in a new position without congressional action.

Nevertheless the Secretary of War had decided what he could do to maintain the letter of the law and yet satisfy Mrs. Custer's persistent importunities:

> I have to advise you that after a careful consideration of all the circumstances connected with this matter and of Mrs. Custer's urgent application, I have directed General Merritt, Superintendent of the Military Academy, to cause the statue to be removed from its pedestal and to be securely boxed and stored at the Post.[11]

On December 12, 1884, General Merritt replied that the statue had been removed and asked permission to place the pedestal in the cemetery at the grave.

Although there seems to have been little notice in the public press of the removal of the monument, the *Army-Navy Register* in its issue of May 30, 1885, remarked on the changes at West Point:

> A change that was most likely to attract observation and remark is the removal of the General Custer Monument which stood out so boldly and prominently on the bluff south of the Headquarters' Building and

---

10.   None of these letters are in the E. B. Custer Collection at the Custer Battlefield National Monument. An unidentified newspaper clipping in the Monroe Historical Museum states that the Secretary told Mrs. Custer "the removal of the statue could be accomplished by obtaining the consent of those who had subscribed to the fund. This consent Mrs. Custer has obtained." Probably she consulted only the major donors.

11.   Letters from Lincoln to Swett are in the E. B. Custer Collection, CBNM, Roll II, pp. 1718-1820.

in front of the Cadets' Mess Hall. It was almost the first thing that would attract the attention of the visitor as he climbed the hill from the railroad depot or steamship dock and its attitude vividly brought to mind the terrible massacre the hero was a part of. . . . It will however, never be placed in position again as a memorial of the valiant deeds of General Custer, and the reason is that Mrs. Custer looked upon it as being very objectionable. . . . It is understood that it was unsightly to the skillful eye, because of the subject's pose, uniform and general character and so much so that the widow of the dead hero would never visit and look at it.

Sixty years later, John Byers, a plebe at West Point, became curious about the picture of the Custer monument he found in the 1879 and 1880 cadet class books. He had never before seen or heard anything about such a statue. What had happened to it? Aside from searching in the library, he began talking to the long-time employees at the Academy. In dusty files in the basement he found letters pertaining to the lost statue.

Byers published a lively account of his investigation in *The Pointer*, June 1, 1951. The gist: in 1885 the statue had been stored in the equipment shed to rest "for ages if not broken up again for the foundry furnace." It was still there in 1906. Mrs. Custer had finally placed the granite shaft on the old base of the monument in May, 1905.

Reminded, perhaps, of the banished statue and mellowed enough now to realize that a poor statue of her hero was better than none, Mrs. Custer wrote on June 20, 1906, to the West Point Superintendent, then Brigadier A. L. Mills, asking that before he left West Point, he order the head and shoulders to be cut from the statue that had been kept in retirement so many years. ". . . the bust is not so offensive as the whole figure and a place may be found for it at the Academy that my husband so dearly loved," Mrs. Custer wrote.

Mills replied on June 20 that the bust had been cut and as soon as an appropriate place was found it would be permanently placed. But the bust was never placed, and with all his burrowings into warehouses and storerooms, Cadet Byers failed to turn up the "dusty, long-haired, mustachioed bust of Garry Owen's wandering cavalryman."

It may be well to record here that in 1910 the State of Michigan erected an equestrian statue of General Custer in Monroe, Michigan. Mrs. Custer was consulted about every detail. As time passed, her memory had turned more and more to the Civil War days when Custer's reputation was still unflawed by criticism and controversy. This figure represents her General as she held his image in her devoted heart. He sits alert, taking a quick look at the battle situation just before he orders the charge. The General is meticulously turned out with the tie and collar he made famous, a graceful cape on his shoulder, his sabre hanging at his side and the broad hat he affected held inconspicuously in his right hand. The sculptor was Edward C. Potter, then and still recognized as one of the country's more able artists. Yet Mrs. Custer never saw her husband in such a pose nor did the Michigan Brigade remember him so. The image they treasured was that of a wild, flaxen-haired youth dressed in some crazy coat, yelling and brandishing his sword as he galloped headlong toward the enemy.

Shortly before her death in 1933 at the age of 92 Elizabeth Bacon Custer saw her husband honored with a third monument. This standing figure flanked by two horses' heads in bas-relief was erected by the State of Ohio near Custer's home in New Rumley, Ohio. In dress and accoutrements, Mrs. Custer is said to have judged this standing figure as "effeminate." If she attempted, in her last decade of life, to have this memorial removed also, there is no record of it. It stands today at the spot where her husband was born in 1839, unhurt by the patina of time but with the sword held downward in the right hand often missing—thanks, no doubt, to vandals.

And so it was that the Widow Custer never gave up in her efforts to project and preserve the public memory of George Armstrong Custer as she had idealized him—brave, tender, gallant, able, disciplined and commanding. She projects him so in her books about him and their life together, and in the one statue, the one in Monroe, Michigan, which she approved. But even her vision of the "ideal hero of romance" increasingly erodes with the probings of history and historians. One wonders if this is not, indeed, the fate of all the images fashioned by man. Time shreds the mask.

About the Authors

HARRY H. ANDERSON is executive director of the Milwaukee County Historical Society and a devoted scholar of the life and works of the soldier-novelist General Charles King. His writings include *German-American Pioneers in Wisconsin and Michigan* (1971), *Milwaukee: At the Gathering of the Waters* (1981), and an edited Charles King anthology titled *Indian Campaigns: Sketches of Cavalry Service in Arizona and on the Northern Plains* (1984).

ROBERT G. ATHEARN was for many years professor of history in the University of Colorado, Boulder, and book review editor for *Montana The Magazine of Western History*. Among his numerous works are *William Tecumseh Sherman and the Settlement of the West* (1956), *High Country Empire* (1960), *Forts of the Upper Missouri* (1967), and *Union Pacific Country* (1971).

MARK H. BROWN was a widely regarded western historian and collector who resided at the prosaic Trail's End, Alta, Iowa. Among many noteworthy works were two in collaboration with William R. Felton: *The Frontier Years* (1955), and *Before Barbed Wire* (1956). His popular *The Plainsmen of the Yellowstone* (1961) expanded greatly on the origins and saga of the Great Sioux War.

THOMAS R. BUECKER is the Nebraska State Historical Society's curator of the Fort Robinson Museum. His published works include articles on military topics for *Nebraska History, Annals of Wyoming,* and others. He is currently writing a history of Fort Robinson.

BRIAN W. DIPPIE is professor of history in the University of Victoria, British Columbia. He is the author of *Custer's Last Stand: The Anatomy of an American Myth* (1976), *The Vanishing American: White Attitudes and U.S. Indian Policy* (1983), *Looking at Russell* (1987), and *Catlin and His Contemporaries: The Politics of Patronage* (1990).

PAUL L. HEDREN is National Park Service superintendent at the Fort Union Trading Post National Historic Site, Williston, North Dakota. He collects the books, letters, and manuscripts of General Charles King and avidly researches the Sioux War. His most recent scholarly works include *Fort Laramie in 1876* (1988), and editorial additions to Don Russell's *Campaigning With King* (1991). He is presently writing a documentary history of George Crook's Bighorn and Yellowstone Expedition of 1876.

PAUL ANDREW HUTTON is an associate professor of history in the University of New Mexico, and executive secretary of the Western History Association. Among his numerous works on the Sioux War are *Garry Owen 1876*, ed. (1977), *Custer and His Times*, ed. (1981), *Phil Sheridan and His Army* (1985), and *Soldiers West*, ed. (1987).

WILLIAM E. LASS, an authority on Missouri River steamboating, is a professor of history in Mankato State University. His numerous books include *Frontier Photographer: Stanley J. Morrow's Dakota Years*, co-authored (1956), *A History of Steamboating on the Upper Missouri River* (1962), and *From the Missouri to the Great Salt Lake: An Account of Overland Freighting* (1972). Many of his recent writings have focused on Minnesota history.

MICHAEL P. MALONE is professor of history and vice president for academic affairs in Montana State University and former book review editor for *Montana The Magazine of Western History*. His essays with Richard Roeder exploring facets of "Montana in 1876," were published in *Montana as It Was: 1876* (1976).

MINNIE DUBBS MILLBROOK, was a Kansan, respected for her many scholarly investigations of George Armstrong Custer appearing in *Montana The Magazine of Western History, Kansas Historical Quarterly*, and other history journals.

REX C. MYERS is dean of arts and sciences and professor of history in South Dakota State University. A former research librarian for the Montana Historical Society, Myers has published numerous articles on Montana social history.

FATHER PETER J. POWELL, an Anglican priest, is an authority on the history and religion of the Northern Cheyenne Indians. His books include *Sweet Medicine*, 2 vols. (1969), *The Cheyennes, Ma'heo'o's People: A Critical Bibliography* (1980), and *People of the Sacred Mountain*, 2 vols. (1981). He is currently expanding his study of Northern Cheyenne ledger book art.

DON RICKEY, JR., a former National Park Service historian at the Custer Battlefield National Monument, is the author of many articles and books including *History of Custer Battlefield* (1967), and the.widely referenced *Forty Miles a Day on Beans and Hay* (1963).

RICHARD B. ROEDER, professor of history at Carroll College, Helena, has written on many Montana historical topics and is co-author of *Montana as It Was: 1876* (1976) with Michael P. Malone.

EDGAR I. STEWART was one of the mid-twentieth century's most accomplished Custer scholars. For *Montana The Magazine of Western History* he authored half a dozen articles exploring aspects of the Battle of the Little Bighorn and the Custer mystique. His books include *Custer's Luck* (1955), *The Field Diary of Lt. Edward Settle Godfrey*, ed. (1957), and *The March of the Montana Column*, ed. (1961).

ROBERT M. UTLEY is one of modern America's most active western historians. Among a dozen major works are *The Last Days of the Sioux Nation* (1963), *Frontier Regulars* (1973), *The Indian Frontier of the American West* (1984), and *Cavalier in Buckskin: George Armstrong Custer and the Western Military Frontier* (1988). He is presently writing a biography of the great Hunkpapa Sioux leader Sitting Bull.

Index